Sound Design Is the New Score

Sound Design Is the New Score

Theory, Aesthetics, and Erotics of the Integrated Soundtrack

DANIJELA KULEZIC-WILSON

OXFORD
UNIVERSITY PRESS

OXFORD
UNIVERSITY PRESS

Oxford University Press is a department of the University of Oxford. It furthers
the University's objective of excellence in research, scholarship, and education
by publishing worldwide. Oxford is a registered trade mark of Oxford University
Press in the UK and certain other countries.

Published in the United States of America by Oxford University Press
198 Madison Avenue, New York, NY 10016, United States of America.

Library of Congress Cataloging in Publication Control Number: 2019021204
ISBN 978–0–19–085532–1 (pbk.)
ISBN 978–0–19–085531–4 (hbk.)

Hardback printed by Bridgeport National Bindery, Inc., United States of America

Sound Design Is the New Score: Theory, Aesthetics, and Erotics of the Integrated Soundtrack.
Danijela Kulezic-Wilson, Oxford University Press (2020). © Oxford University Press.
DOI: 10.1093/oso/ 9780190855314.001.0001

Contents

Sound Design Is the New Score: Theory, Aesthetics, and Erotics of the Integrated Soundtrack. Danijela Kulezic-Wilson,
Oxford University Press (2020). © Oxford University Press.
DOI: 10.1093/oso/ 9780190855314.001.0001

Acknowledgements

I would first like to thank Senior Editor Norm Hirschy and Series Editor Daniel Goldmark for their support of this project and for steering the book in the right direction with their invaluable advice. I would also like to thank the anonymous reviewers for their helpful input but most of all Randolph Jordan for his insightful, constructive, and inspiring comments and suggestions.

This book was born out of passion for film and its soundscapes, and admiration for artists who have courage and vision to challenge conventions and explore new paths in audiovisual filmmaking. I was lucky that some of them have been so kind as to share their thoughts with me and I extend my heartfelt thanks to Gábor Erdélyi, Sam Petty, Peter Strickland, and Felicity Wilcox for giving me insights into their working methods. I'm especially grateful to Peter for being so generous with his time over the years and for letting me into the secrets of the creative and postproduction processes of the films that inspired me, and without which the conversation about the new soundtrack practices discussed in this book would be sorely lacking. My gratitude also goes to Marek Szold, who kindly provided access to the photos he made on the sets of *Katalin Varga* and *Berberian Sound Studio* and has granted permission for using his photo for the cover image.

I am immensely grateful to my colleagues from the film music community who make our conferences so friendly and the singular interests of our discipline and our obsessions more meaningful. They all contributed to the creation of this book with their own work, friendly advice, and support, especially Laura Anderson, Julie Brown, James Buhler, Carlo Cenciarelli, Maurizio Corbella, Lisa Coulthard, Annette Davison, Kevin Donnelly, Claudia Gorbman, Meghan Joyce Tozer, Miguel Mera, Aimee Mollaghan, Chris Morris, John O'Flynn, Katherine Spring, Robynn Stilwell, Tim Summers, James Wierzbicki, and Anna Windisch. My heartfelt thanks to Gillian Anderson and Ron Sadoff for creating such a productive space for our community at NYU Steinhardt's annual Music and the Moving Image conference—I would be much the poorer without the many invaluable professional experiences and friendships gained at MaMI. I'm particularly grateful to Elsie Walker for extending her kindness and generosity beyond collegiality to become a valued friend.

Although blurring the line between personal and professional was not at all part of my agenda with this project, it so happens that the themes of disruption, breakup with tradition, and evolution, which are all relevant to the practices addressed in this book, somehow also spilled into my private life. This book was

Sound Design Is the New Score: Theory, Aesthetics, and Erotics of the Integrated Soundtrack. Danijela Kulezic-Wilson, Oxford University Press (2020). © Oxford University Press.
DOI: 10.1093/oso/ 9780190855314.001.0001

conceived in a comfortable, familiar place, but completed while I was trying to find my bearings in a new, more challenging place that I'm still learning about. I'm deeply grateful to Ian for being a faithful and loving companion for a big part of my journey (not to mention for all the proofreading!), and to my friends and family for helping me find my feet in a new place, especially Tamara, the Krnajski family, and my son Adam.

I would like to thank University College Cork for assisting the realization of this book with sabbatical leave and with financial support of the College of Arts, Celtic Studies and Social Sciences Publication Fund; the CACSSS Research Support Fund; and the Departmental Research Fund. I would also like to thank my colleagues from the School of Film, Music, and Theatre for their help and advice, particularly Kelly Boyle, Ciara Chambers, John Godfrey, Colin P. McGuire, Mel Mercier (now at University of Limerick), Lijuan Qian, Laura Rascaroli, Jill Rogers, Griff Rollefson, and Gwenda Young. My thanks also to our Head of School, Jools Gilson, for her enthusiastic support of all of our School's creative endeavours. A special shout-out goes to Melanie Marshall for introducing me to Audre Lord and to John Hough for helping me prepare the illustrations. I'm grateful to my former and present students for reminding me regularly why teaching matters.

Earlier versions of the material presented in chapters 3 and 5 respectively appeared in "Soundscapes of Trauma and the Silence of Revenge in Peter Strickland's *Katalin Varga,*" *New Soundtrack* 1, no. 1 (2011): 57–71, and "Musically Conceived Sound Design, Musicalization of Speech and the Breakdown of Film Soundtrack Hierarchy," in *The Palgrave Handbook of Sound Design and Music in Screen Media: Integrated Soundtracks*, edited by Liz Greene and Danijela Kulezic-Wilson, 429–444 (Basingstoke, Hampshire: Palgrave Macmillan, 2016).

1

Introduction

In the fall of 2017, a couple of weeks before the worldwide premiere of his film *Mother!*, Darren Aronofsky announced that, in consultation with the film's composer Jóhann Jóhannsson, he had decided to eliminate the score in favour of an elaborate sound design. According to the film's sound designer Chris Henighan, some of Jóhannsson's music is still present in the film but is manipulated in different ways so that we never hear anything resembling a traditional score (bar a couple of moments of diegetic music).[1]

This announcement came almost exactly two decades after Aronofsky's debut *Pi* (1998) had introduced an audiovisual style that would become emblematic of a new aesthetics marked by an emancipation of sound effects from their "mimetic" role[2] into vividly expressive and, most of all, musicalized elements of the soundtrack. Termed "hip-hop editing" by the director, and further refined in his following film *Requiem for a Dream* (2000), Aronofsky's style of audiovisual manipulation and musicalization demonstrated in a powerful and often ostentatious manner how deeply the combination of musical sensibility and digital technology can mine the musical potential of soundtrack elements that are traditionally seen as simply functional. Despite the explicitly musical qualities of his audiovisual vocabulary, however, it was not until *Mother!* that Aronofsky considered such a radical gesture as doing away with the score altogether. *Pi* throbs throughout with techno beats, while in *Requiem for a Dream* Clint Mansell's score, performed by the Kronos Quartet, hammers home the message about the desperate pits of addiction. Aronofsky's later films *The Fountain* (2006), *Black Swan* (2010), and *Noah* (2014) all feature scores that conform to the standards of big productions.[3] So after dutifully playing by industry rules for almost two decades—at least in terms of scoring expectations—what led Aronofsky and his composer collaborator to get rid of the score? Jóhannsson himself offered an explanation:

---

[1] Chris O'Falt, "'Mother!': Why Darren Aronofsky and Jóhann Jóhannsson Scrapped the Original Score for a More Expressive Soundscape," *IndieWire*, September 9, 2017, http://www.indiewire.com/2017/09/mother-score-eliminated-johann-johannsson-darren-aronofsky-sound-design-1201874404/.

[2] Rick Altman, "Moving Lips: Cinema as Ventriloquism," *Yale French Studies*, no. 60, Cinema/Sound (1980): 67.

[3] The only exception to this approach is Aronofsky's 2008 film *The Wrestler*, which is altogether more restrained in both visual style and scoring.

Sound Design Is the New Score: Theory, Aesthetics, and Erotics of the Integrated Soundtrack. Danijela Kulezic-Wilson, Oxford University Press (2020). © Oxford University Press.
DOI: 10.1093/oso/ 9780190855314.001.0001

Mother! is a film where half measures have no place and after Darren and I had explored many different approaches, my instinct was to eliminate the score entirely. Erasure is a big part of the creative process and in this case, we knew we had to take this approach to its logical extreme.[4]

It is worth emphasizing here that in the context of Aronofsky's style, erasure does not mean a retreat to the world of Hanekean silence and expressive reticence. Choosing to present his allegory about humanity's relationship with Mother Earth in the form of a horror, Aronofsky employs the sonic conventions of the genre generously, but instead of music he uses sound design in a manner typical of horror scores, underscoring moments of surprise or terror and inducing anxiety with an impressive array of sound effects. The only element conspicuously absent is actual musical material and the affective and semantically coded content it usually provides, as Aronofsky did not want to give the audience "any relief by allowing them to lean back on something that easily gives you emotion."[5]

Aronofsky's film was released around the time when another significant audiovisual landmark, David Lynch's eighteen-part TV series *Twin Peaks: The Return*, completed its run. In a show that delighted, puzzled, frustrated, and inspired in equal measure with its idiosyncratic narrative and acting style, with stories and characters of which some dipped into the most profound questions of human existence and some simply went nowhere, one of its most astonishing accomplishments was the sound design credited to Lynch himself. Combining Lynch's trademark taste for experimentation with his knack for the unsettling, the show's sound design is embedded in the crevices of *Twin Peaks'* multidimensional universe like a score, seeping through the porous borders of its morphing subplots, connecting temporal slippages and teleportations, enticing characters to stick forks into electrical sockets, or acting as an extension of their mental processes. The noises of humming, bristling, and buzzing; radio static and wind moaning; looped sound effects and electrical interferences are just some of the sounds in an almost ubiquitous sheet of sound woven into the show's endless polyphonic dance between physical and metaphysical, diegetic and nondiegetic, nature and technology. In that sense neither the functional nor the sonic properties of Lynch's sound design, created with the assistance of sound supervisors Dean Hurley and Ron Eng,[6] differ much from a typical incidental score produced by electronic means. The "composed" nature of the sound design invites us to consider it as yet another aspect of the show's highly heterogeneous musical world

---

[4] O'Falt, "'Mother!'"

[5] Ibid.

[6] See Noel Murray's interview with David Lynch, "'I Love Winds': David Lynch on the Sound of 'Twin Peaks,'" *New York Times*, August 17, 2017, https://www.nytimes.com/2017/08/17/arts/television/david-lynch-twin-peaks-interview.html?_r=0.

ranging from the 1960s musical avant-garde appearing in the form of Krzysztof Penderecki's *Threnody to the Victims of Hiroshima* (Ep. 8) to various genres of popular music represented by regular diegetic performances in *Twin Peaks'* local tavern, the Roadhouse, as well as Badalamenti's famous credits theme.

The examples of Aronofsky's films and Lynch's TV show are just some recent ones among many that illustrate a profound shift in the understanding of and attitude towards the role of music in screen media that has affected scoring and sound design practices in recent decades. They also illuminate the heterogeneous nature of this shift and the various factors that influenced it, which include an increasing appetite for subverting the traditional functions of the musical score, the impact of digital technology, the foregrounding of audiovisual sensuousness, and the absorption of different musical practices from the avant-garde to hip-hop and electronic dance music. Substituting traditional Hollywood scoring and mixing practices with a more adventurous language and methods that recognize the interconnectedness of all soundtrack elements, this trend has produced soundtracks in which it is difficult to tell the difference between score and ambient sound, where pieces of pre-existing *musique concrète* or electroacoustic music are merged with diegetic sound, sound effects are absorbed by the score or treated as music, and diegetic sound is treated as *musique concrète*. Over the last few decades this trend has relativized the boundary between scoring and sound design and subverted long-established hierarchical relationships between dialogue, music, and sound effects, challenging the modes of perception shaped by classical soundtrack practices. This book explores the origins and theoretical and aesthetic frameworks of this trend, as well as its sensuous dimensions, arguing that the one factor that connects all the different cultural, aesthetic, and technological influences, and all manifestations of the present shift in practice, is the *musical* approach to the film soundtrack, which is conceived as an integrated whole.

While this book argues that the musicalization of a soundtrack invites us to disregard the habitual divisions between its constitutive elements in order to view them as part of the whole, it also acknowledges that these divisions have often been established out of necessity and in response to various economic or practical concerns, as will be discussed in the next chapter. For an equally practical reason my analysis will often refer to score, speech, and sound effects as distinct categories to illuminate various methods that have been devised to break down artificial barriers between them. One of these barriers is reflected in a phrase that is usually used in relation to the practices explored in this book, which is "blurring the line between music and sound design." While this phrase has become a helpful shorthand for denoting different ways in which a score can interact with a film's ambient sound or sound effects, it is also indicative of a habitual tendency to separate music from other soundtrack elements, and thus it effectively positions music outside the soundtrack's overall design. This phrase also tends to be used in contexts where original scores employ the language of contemporary electroacoustic, atonal, or ambient music. To be clear, these types of scores, which are often conceived with the intention of avoiding the semiotic and affective connotations of traditional scores, are indeed placed in films in close collaboration with the sound department, as in some films I will discuss in this book. The problematic aspect of the expression "blurring the line between music and sound design" in this context is that it does not refer to this collaboration but simply to the fact that the contemporary language of the score is not heard as "music" but rather as "sound design," even though it might have been conceived as an original score.[7] Thus, I am suggesting that the line blurred is that between *score* and sound design, a distinction that recognizes the score as a constitutive element of the soundtrack but does not exclude music being part of the sound design or the possibility of sound design being inherently musical.

Semantic nuances aside, this development in soundtrack practice is worth noting and exploring because, while numerous changes in formal and narrative strategies in contemporary cinema have prompted scholars to proclaim its postclassical identity,[8] the roles of the soundtrack's constitutive elements and the relationships between them have largely remained faithful to long-established classical principles. Jeff Smith makes the same point in his chapter "The Sound of Intensified Continuity," where he argues that numerous sound strategies employed to heighten the affective, sensory, and phenomenological dimensions of a contemporary film, which are comparable to the changes in narrative and visual style that David Bordwell calls "intensified continuity," remain "firmly anchored within the principles of unity, clarity, and linearity that still govern the transmission of narrative information to viewers."[9] This book, however, will focus precisely on case studies in which a departure from classical narrative principles is matched and its effects amplified by the erosion of classical principles in soundtrack practice.

Another term that warrants explanation is "integrated soundtrack." To make it clear from the beginning, for me integrated soundtrack is *not* synonymous with the practice of blurring the line between score and sound design; rather, I see it as a conceptual framework for the methods discussed in this book. While there

---

[7] I also discuss this phrasing in my chapter "Sound Design and Its Interactions with Music: Changing Historical Perspectives," in *The Routledge Companion to Screen Music and Sound*, ed. Miguel Mera, Ronald Sadoff, and Ben Winters (London and New York: Routledge), 127–138.

[8] See, for instance, Barry Langford, *Post-classical Hollywood: Film Industry, Style and Ideology Since 1945* (Edinburgh: Edinburgh University Press, 2010) and Eleftheria Thanouli, *Postclassical Cinema: An International Poetics of Film Narration* (London and New York: Wallflower Press, 2009).

[9] Jeff Smith, "The Sound of Intensified Continuity," in *The Oxford Handbook of New Audiovisual Aesthetics*, ed. John Richardson, Claudia Gorbman, and Carol Vernallis (Oxford and New York: Oxford University Press, 2013), 347.

are many ways in which the distinction between score and sound design can be undermined and relativized, what all of them have in common is a disregard for traditional soundtrack hierarchy and an interest in an integrated approach that recognizes the interconnectedness of all soundtrack elements—dialogue, music, and sound effects. However, it is important to distinguish between the use of this term for designating a holistic approach to the soundtrack *in practice,* as applied in this book, and the way this term has been used in scholarship to underline *an analytical approach* that considers all elements of the soundtrack in the context of the whole, without necessarily implying a breakdown of soundtrack hierarchy. A good example of the latter is David Neumeyer's most recent book *Meaning and Interpretation of Music in Cinema,* in which he announces from the start that in his approach the soundtrack as a whole "has priority over any of its individual elements" but insists that its vococentrism is the "mechanism" through which its elements come together.[10] This strategy makes perfect sense in the context of the classical film repertoire examined by Neumeyer, but in this book I deliberately focus on those methods that actively undermine the soundtrack hierarchy established during the classical era. However, the fact that these methods can be found in as aesthetically remote contexts as art house cinema and so-called torture porn indicates that not all techniques of integration have the same origin or have been devised with the same intention.

One of the main causes of and motivation for implementing the novel practices explored in this book is the excessive use of classical Hollywood conventions and clichés in film scoring that have dominated the industry since the 1930s. Their indiscriminate application both within and outside the mainstream has been for some time at the point where music's impact in film either is devalued by its overuse or can produce the reverse effect of that intended, especially when employed with the aim of manipulating audiences' affective responses. Searching for more subtle means of underscoring the narrative and its underlying messages, filmmakers have turned to less conventional musical devices that—because of their contemporary musical language—can often be mistaken for sound design or, as shown in the example of Aronofsky's *Mother!,* have eliminated nondiegetic scores altogether. These measures are typical of the type of cinema that seeks an engaged rather than a passive viewer, for whom an intellectual investment is part of the aesthetic pleasure.

New soundtrack practices have also been inspired and facilitated by the introduction of new technologies in postproduction. In the late 1960s the introduction

---

[10] David Neumeyer, *Meaning and Interpretation of Music in Cinema* (Bloomington and Indianapolis: Indiana University Press, 2015), 3. For more details about scholarship that advocates an integrated approach to the soundtrack see Liz Greene and Danijela Kulezic-Wilson, "Introduction," in *The Palgrave Handbook of Sound Design and Music in Screen Media: Integrated Soundtracks,* ed. Liz Greene and Danijela Kulezic-Wilson (Basingstoke, Hampshire: Palgrave Macmillan, 2016), 1–3.

of equipment based on magnetic sound, which allowed one person to design the soundtrack as well as mix it, marked the beginning of an era during which many boundaries between distinct tasks collapsed, opening a space for collaboration, integration, and a "democratized" approach to sound craft. In the following decade the introduction of synthesizers inspired new ways of thinking about sound and music in the context of postproduction and encouraged composers and sound editors to manipulate recordings of sound effects in a musical way. The process of musicalization was further advanced from the late 1990s on by the wide availability of digital audio workstations (DAWs) and the use of musical software for processing not only music but also dialogue and sound effects.[11]

The development of technology and the introduction of electronic musical equipment into the process of postproduction resulted in an ever-diminishing gap between what is perceived as music and what is perceived as sound effect. Once forced to compete for audibility in the mixing process, score and sound effects are nowadays partners. But their merging or interchange of functions has been facilitated not only by technology but also by a change in the language of musical scoring. Instead of the conventional orchestral sound that existed on a different level of perception and functionality than sound effects and dialogue, we now have scores where the language is in many ways much closer to noise or ambient sound. Thus, it is worth noting here the impact of the musical upheavals and trends that have transformed the contemporary musical landscape since the 1950s and 1960s avant-garde, including Cage's revolutionary ideas about indeterminacy, noise, and silence in music; the invention of electronic music; *musique concrète*; noise music; and so on. These, however, did not have a wider application in music practice outside avant-garde circles until the experiments with digital electronics in different genres of popular music such as hip-hop, techno, dubstep, and other types of "electronica" promoted the use of sampling in all its forms and spread the idea that any kind of noise or speech can potentially be regarded as music.

As this list of influences indicates, music, musical technology, and a musical way of thinking have been essential factors in facilitating the disintegration of the traditional hierarchy between dialogue, music, and sound effects in film soundtracks and blurring the line between score and sound design. Musicalized, integrated soundtracks can be found in different cultural, aesthetic, and production contexts, but as the case studies in this book suggest, the most striking,

---

[11] See Kevin J. Donnelly, "Extending Film Aesthetics: Audio Beyond Visuals," in *The Oxford Handbook of New Audiovisual Aesthetics*, ed. John Richardson, Claudia Gorbman, and Carol Vernallis (Oxford and New York: Oxford University Press, 2014), 365 and Katherine Spring, "From Analogue to Digital: Synthesizers and Discourses of Film Sound in the 1980s," in *The Palgrave Handbook of Sound Design and Music in Screen Media: Integrated Soundtrack*, ed. Liz Greene and Danijela Kulezic-Wilson (Basingstoke, Hampshire: Palgrave Macmillan, 2016), 273–288.

adventurous, and influential examples appear in the type of cinema that defies the ideology of the mainstream, its cultivation of passivity among audiences, and the rule of the box office as the only measure of success. The case studies I have chosen to support this claim are not confined to a specific continent, genre, or type of practice. A good number of them have been directed by filmmakers to whom Claudia Gorbman's expression *mélomans* fits comfortably, since music is an important element of their authorial style, but this label does not apply to all these directors indiscriminately, nor does it provide a sole explanation for all the methods employed by them.[12] An even more important common denominator for most of the films discussed in this book is an accent on collaborative practice between different members of the sound team on one hand, and between the composer, the director, and the sound team on the other. Another common thread linking many of the case studies is a stylistic and ideological eclecticism, which includes the affective engagement of the classical tradition, the intellectual curiosity of modernism, and the sensuous intensity of the avant-garde, producing an aesthetic framework that values all these facets of cinematic experience. This is a type of cinema that uses narrative form that is not forbidden from straying into the abstract or implausible, which stimulates sensuousness and musicality but within the narrative structure, and which produces affective impact without relying on the manipulation and passive absorption of classical cinema.[13] While some aspects of this cinema comply with David Bordwell's notion of "intensified continuity," the severe disruptions of linear narrative and temporal continuity in many films of this trend, and an affinity for disabling or destabilizing the audioviewer's passive position, connect this cinema with the aesthetics of European modernism. At the same time, in opposition to the

---

[12] Claudia Gorbman, "Auteur Music," in *Beyond the Soundtrack: Representing Music in Cinema*, ed. Daniel Goldmark, Lawrence Kramer, and Richard Leppert (Berkeley, Los Angeles, and London: California University Press, 2007), 149.

[13] The list of films addressed in this book is in no way comprehensive, but I believe it is substantial and diverse enough to present multifaceted and revealing insights into this practice. There are quite a few titles from the horror genre and New Extremism, for instance, that could have been included on the basis of their adventurous approach to the soundtrack, not to mention the endlessly fascinating and equally disturbing work of Philippe Grandrieux, but some of these have already received due scholarly attention. For more insights into the musicality of the soundtrack in the horror genre see Kevin Donnelly, *The Spectre of Sound: Music in Film and Television* (London: BFI Publishing, 2005) and *Occult Aesthetics: Synchronization in Sound Film* (Oxford and New York: Oxford University Press, 2014); for New Extremism see Lisa Coulthard, "Acoustic Disgust: Sound, Affect, and Cinematic Violence," in *The Palgrave Handbook of Sound Design and Music in Screen Media: Integrated Soundtracks*, ed. Liz Greene and Danijela Kulezic-Wilson (Basingstoke, Hampshire: Palgrave Macmillan, 2016), 183–193 and "Dirty Sound: Haptic Noise in New Extremism," in *The Oxford Handbook of Sound and Image in Digital Media*, ed. Carol Vernallis, Amy Herzog, and John Richardson (Oxford and New York: Oxford University Press, 2013), 115–126. For Grandrieux see Randolph Jordan, "Acoustical Properties: Practicing Contested Spaces in the Films of Philippe Grandrieux," in *The Oxford Handbook of Image and Sound in Western Art*, ed. Yeal Kaduri (Oxford and New York: Oxford University Press, 2016), 289–314.

Brechtian aesthetics of distancing, which defined European modernist cinema, this new cinema is not necessarily interested in taking the audioviewer "out of the narrative" and does not renounce the possibility of immersiveness, as long as it is not passive. As the ripples of this trend reach the "vococentric" heart of the soundtrack, undermining the narrative sovereignty of the spoken word and endorsing the interchangeability of speech and music, I believe that these new practices promote modes of perception that respond to film's musical and sensuous qualities, transforming our experience and expectations of narrative film.

A recurring issue associated with maverick sound practices throughout the history of cinema is the notion of film's "concreteness" and "completeness," the fact that unlike all other arts that depend on a certain level of imagination and stylization, "film seems to be 'all there.'"[14] And while other arts only evoke the materiality of reality and the experience or observation of movement, "cinema must express life with life itself."[15] This presents challenges that are different from those in other arts, as will be shown in chapter 3 in the context of a discussion about the aesthetics of reticence. On the one hand, film's "concreteness" can be seen as suffocating, as it defies the need for mystery that artists like Tarkovsky believe is the most captivating quality of any art.[16] On the other hand, the capacity of film to use modes of embodied experience as the substance of its language[17] provides a wide range of devices that can manifest and reach places that other arts cannot. Sound has proven to be extremely effective in negotiating the tension between the illusory realism of cinema and the need for art to tease our imagination. I argue in this book that the strategies of integrated soundtrack that blur the lines between its constitutive elements create new and exciting methods for carving out a space for mystery, imagination, and personal interpretation in our cinema experience.

Another theme connecting most of my case studies, also relevant to a good part of contemporary practice, is sensuousness. The stylistic excesses of so-called postclassical cinema and an emphasis on the materiality of the medium usually go hand in hand with the intense sensory stimulation provided by large screens, Dolby and surround sound systems, and elaborate sound and visual effects. This focus on the sensory experience rather than on traditional features of narrative such as plot structure and character development have been described as "boom," "intensified," or "impact" aesthetics, but I should underline that the

---

[14] Walter Murch, "Sound Design: The Dancing Shadow," in *Projections 4: Film-makers on Film-making*, ed. John Boorman, Tom Luddy, David Thompson, and Walter Donohue (London and Boston: Faber and Faber, 1995), 247.

[15] Jean Mitry quoted in Vivien Sobchack, *The Address of the Eye: A Phenomenology of Film Experience* (Princeton, NJ: Princeton University Press, 1992), 5.

[16] Andrei Tarkovsky, *Sculpting in Time: Reflections on the Cinema* (London: Bodley Head, 1986), 183.

[17] Sobchack, *The Address of the Eye*, 4–5.

type of sensuousness I discuss in this book (specifically in chapter 4) differs from the sensory overload associated with the "intensified" aesthetics of "impact" cinema.[18] Drawing on the feminist concept of erotics in art proposed by writers such as Susan Sontag and Audre Lorde, and on Vivian Sobchack's and Laura Marks's work in the area of sensory cinema, but broadening the focus to also include its acoustic properties, I conceptualize cinematic sensuousness as the result of employing a film's audiovisual devices in a manner that foregrounds the sensuous aspects of the medium itself. My choice of the word "sensuous" instead of "sensory" accentuates the difference between a purely physical reaction to sound on one hand and a "consensual" engagement with film on the other, an engagement that takes pleasure in the sensuousness of the form itself—its sonic and visual textures, composition, rhythm, movement, and flow—rather than sensations generally associated with advanced exhibition technology. This line of thought chimes with Sobchack's and Marks's comments about cinema viewing as an exchange between the bodies of the viewer and of the film, which Marks describes as erotic, but the role of sound is curiously neglected in their exploration of this erotic charge. Lawrence Kramer corrects this omission by discussing the erotic potential of the marriage of music and gaze, noting that the concoction of desire and projective impulses that we all respond to cinema with becomes even more interesting when we bring music in.[19] Kramer, however, focuses exclusively on the impact of classical music on the erotics of film spectatorship, while one of the purposes of this book is to demonstrate how the erotic charge in the union of music and gaze stretches not only beyond the classical musical repertoire but also even beyond any traditional notions of film scoring or indeed traditional notions of what constitutes music. To demonstrate the role of sound design in the context of cinematic sensuousness, I explore different types of musicalization of sound design and speech in chapters 4 and 5, arguing that an integrated approach to the soundtrack not only challenges the structure of classical soundtrack hierarchy but also is reflected in an overall approach to the medium that promotes audiovisual integration and the interchangeability of sonic and visual functions.

As the case studies in these chapters also demonstrate, the musical logic of the soundtrack often permeates other aspects of film form as well. While this

---

[18] In her book *Ubiquitous Listening: Affect, Attention, and Distributed Subjectivity*, Anahid Kassabian talks about "boom aesthetics" (Berkeley, Los Angeles, and London: California University Press, 2013); Carol Vernallis uses the expression "intensified aesthetics," referring to David Bordwell's concept of "intensified continuity" (*Unruly Media: You Tube, Music Video, and the New Digital Cinema* [Oxford and New York: Oxford University Press, 2013]). In his article "The Sound of Intensified Continuity," Jeff Smith uses the term "impact aesthetics."

[19] Lawrence Kramer, "Classical Music, Virtual Bodies, Narrative Film," in *The Oxford Handbook of Film Music Studies*, ed. David Neumeyer (Oxford and New York: Oxford University Press, 2014), 351–365.

is not the focus of my argument in this book,[20] it is worth noting that the practice of blurring the line between score and sound design through the use of contemporary musical language also introduced new types of film musicalization. A typical example is Gus Van Sant's Death Trilogy (*Gerry*, 2002; *Elephant*, 2003; *Last Days*, 2005), which spearheaded the trend of merging pre-existing pieces of *musique concrète*, electroacoustic, and soundscape compositions with diegetic sound. His employment of this type of pre-existing music transcends the act of appropriation, so the Death Trilogy films in many ways embody principles of these musical genres in their formal organization and in the way the characters interact with their surroundings. Most important in this context, these practices seem to resonate even in scenes that don't feature any pre-existing music. Some of the most engrossing scenes in Van Sant's *Gerry*, for instance, just show the characters walking, producing the type of musicality that can be described as *audiovisual musique concrète*.[21] I will address Van Sant's approach to the soundtrack in more depth in chapter 4, but at this point I would like to acknowledge that using the term *musique concrète* to refer to the musicalization of "concrete" sounds in an audiovisual context seems incongruous with the concept of reduced listening that Pierre Schaeffer associated with this genre. Famously Schaeffer insisted that an ideal way of encountering and appreciating the sound object (*objet sonore*) of *musique concrète* was through listening free from any visual or other associations during which the listener focuses on the inherent features of a sound disconnected from its origin. Critics of Schaeffer's concept of reduced listening have since pointed out that, whether a sound is manipulated to mask its origin or not, it is almost impossible to create a "pure" auditory sensation that is isolated from someone's personal and global experiences.[22] We could also argue that taking *musique concrète* out of its original acousmatic context and presenting it in a film either as diegetic or nondiegetic sound automatically changes the rules of engagement with it. But what is intriguing here is that Schaeffer's insistence on a particular type of listening highlights the essential traditionalism of his notion of what "real" music is and his belief that the only way *musique concrète* can be considered to belong to the same category is if it achieves the same

---

[20] For an extensive study of the musical approach to film see my monograph *The Musicality of Narrative Film* (Basingstoke, Hampshire: Palgrave Macmillan, 2015).

[21] Danijela Kulezic-Wilson, "Gus Van Sant's Soundwalks and Audio-visual *Musique concrète*," in *Music, Sound and Filmmakers: Sonic Style in Cinema*, ed. James Wierzbicki (New York: Routledge, 2012), 76–88.

[22] See for instance Don Ihde, *Listening and Voice: A Phenomenology of Sound* (New York: State University of New York, 2007), 44–45. This also brings to mind Jean-Luc Nancy's comment that listening is inevitably a self-reflexive act: music is "made to be listened to, but it is first of all, in itself, the listening of self" (*Listening*, trans. Charlotte Mandell [New York: Fordham University Press, 2007], 27).

level of abstraction as an idealized form of instrumental music.[23] Schaeffer's rigid notion of musicality may be surprising, considering how much his own work helped to transform our understanding of what music is in global terms, but it is also a useful reminder that a "creation" can often escape and outlive its creator's original intentions.[24] The point I want to emphasize is that my terminology in this case is informed by post-Schaefferian aesthetics and refers to the practice of *musique concrète* in terms of its materiality and grammar, but the ethos of my argument fundamentally leans on Cage's notion that any sound can potentially be musical without imposing any restrictions on how that sound is sourced and consumed.

Considering that the relationship between music and sound design is rather ambiguous and that the definition of the term "sound design" is associated with inconsistencies and disagreements, since it covers various job descriptions and practices, before embarking on exploring the ambiguities within the soundtrack, I will first tackle the ambiguities surrounding the concept of sound design and its connection to the idea of integrated soundtrack in postproduction practice.

Sound Design and the Integrated Soundtrack

There is no doubt that the increasing interest in exploring areas of sonic ambiguity and liminality in film soundtrack practice has been assisted by an integrated approach to soundtrack led by the idea of the interdependence of all its elements. Although the growing influence of this idea coincides with the introduction of the term "sound design" into the film vocabulary, its origins can be traced to the birth of sound cinema. Nevertheless, the concept of sound design is inextricably connected with the advancement of the holistic approach to the soundtrack that has been in many ways paralleled and facilitated by advancements in

---

[23] Strong evidence of that can be found in the 1986 interview recorded by Tim Hodgkinson in which Schaeffer insists that his work with concrete sounds never resulted in "music" and that he "wasted his life" because he didn't understand at the time that there was no other path for creating music but using the good old "DoReMi." Even though he is considered one of the most influential avant-garde composers of the twentieth century, he saw himself as an "explorer in sound" and a "good researcher" but not a "real musician" (Tim Hodgkinson, "An Interview with Pierre Schaeffer," in *The Book of Music and Nature*, ed. David Rothenberg and Marta Ulvaeus [Middletown, CT: Wesleyan University Press, 2001], 35, 43). Schaeffer's thoughts revealed in this interview are relevant here because they provide a context for his early theories, helping us to view them in a different light than when they were first proposed.

[24] Even though the concept of reduced listening became widely disputed by many creators of electroacoustic music and particularly advocates of soundscape compositions, it left a deep imprint on the global musical consciousness to the point that, as Joanna Demers argues, "Post-Schaefferian music can ... be characterized as a debate about the extent to which the semantic content of a sound can be manipulated" (*Listening Through the Noise: The Aesthetics of Experimental Electronic Music* [Oxford and New York: Oxford University Press, 2010], 14).

postproduction technology. Considering the interconnectedness of all these developments and that the term "sound design" encompasses both practical and aesthetic considerations that mean different things to different people, depending on their inclinations and the practice they come from, it is necessary to give more attention to this subject before exploring different ways of blurring the boundaries between score and sound design.

The term "sound design" was coined by Walter Murch and Francis Ford Coppola in order to credit Murch for his multifaceted contribution to the postproduction of Coppola's *Apocalypse Now* (1979). Incited by necessity, since the union would not allow Murch to be credited as sound editor because he was not a member, the new term also reflected the fact that Murch's multilayered involvement in both sound and image editing could not easily fit the strict descriptions of union job titles anyway. By that point Murch's contribution to Coppola's *The Rain People* (1969) and *The Conversation* (1974), and to George Lucas's *THX 1138* (1971) and *American Graffiti* (1973), had been credited as "sound montage"; his editing and sound editing work on *The Conversation* was uncredited, while his role on *The Godfather* (Coppola, 1971) was described as postproduction consultant. In the context of *Apocalypse Now*, the term "designer" referred to the fact that Murch was responsible not only for picture editing and sound rerecording but also for developing a "design for the use of the film's quadrophonic sound in the three dimensions of the theatre."[25] Although the historical path leading to *Apocalypse Now*'s lauded sound design and even the story about its technical and aesthetic innovations are a bit more complex than as habitually described in the "Dolby myth" surrounding the film's release,[26] the notion of one person planning and taking responsibility for the whole sound of a film had a significant impact on changing the perception of sound personnel as "expendable technicians."[27] According to Murch, whose definition of the role was based on his experience of working in the American Zoetrope studio, a sound designer is "someone who plans, creates the sound effects and mixes the final soundtrack, and thereby takes responsibility for the sound of a film the way a director of photography takes responsibility for the image."[28] As Benjamin Wright points out, the coordinative function of this role was not entirely different from that performed by the sound director in the studio era. The crucial difference, though, was that in contrast to the sound director's merely administrative responsibility, Murch's approach introduced a new way of conceptualizing the soundtrack that

---

[25] Murch, "Sound Design: The Dancing Shadow," 246.
[26] See Eric Dienstfrey's argument in "The Myth of the Speakers: A Critical Reexamination of Dolby History," *Film History* 28, no. 1 (2016): 167–193, doi:10.2979/filmhistory.28.1.06.
[27] Ibid., 181.
[28] Murch, "Sound Design: The Dancing Shadow," 246.

emphasized its expressive potential and a generally more collaborative approach to the postproduction process.[29]

American Zoetrope studio was founded by Coppola and Lucas in 1969 with the intention of producing "inexpensive, independent films" without being "bogged down in the bureaucratic/technical swamp" of Hollywood's big studios.[30] Nurtured by Zoetrope's ethos of innovation and collaboration, Murch developed a taste for a noncompartmentalized approach to film postproduction that recognized the interdependence of all soundtrack elements and their relevance to the overall design of the film. He opposed the practice of addressing sound in the last stages of postproduction, arguing that sound is not "something that you can only sprinkle over a film at the end of the process, but it's a force that can be used from the beginning in the telling of the story."[31] This approach, supported by the success of his groundbreaking work on Coppola's films from the 1970s, contributed immensely to raising awareness about the soundtrack's expressive potential within the industry and helped elevate the perception of sound postproduction from a "below the line" craft to artistry.[32]

While Murch's erudition, wide-ranging interests, and ability to eloquently explain his methods in written form made him the most famous representative of the holistic approach to the soundtrack, his efforts in defying Hollywood's compartmentalized approach to sound to expand its expressive range were by no means unique at the time. In his book on sound design in science fiction, William Whittington cites Stanley Kubrick's *2001: A Space Odyssey* (1968) as one of those groundbreaking films that showed "the potential of image and sound design to both describe and transform subjectivity," marking the "dawn of sound design."[33] One year before Kubrick's masterpiece, Jacques Tati released one of the most celebrated experiments from his audiovisual "laboratory,"[34] *PlayTime*, rethinking the cinematic relationships between sound and space and transforming familiar sounds of the urban landscape into "abstract rhythmic codes."[35] Another sound

---

[29] Benjamin Wright, "What Do We Hear? The Pluralism of Sound Design in Hollywood Sound Production," *New Soundtrack* 3, no. 2 (2013): 139, doi:10.3366/sound.2013.0043.

[30] Murch, "Sound Design: The Dancing Shadow," 244.

[31] Gustavo Constantini, "Walter Murch Interviewed by Gustavo Constantini," *New Soundtrack* 3, no. 1 (2010): 42.

[32] Wright also points out that Murch's concept of sound design is not opposed to the principles of classical narration and continuity, as could be inferred from some comments on why sound design "never really took hold in Hollywood." Rather, Murch's use of sound creates opportunities for the audience to see the image differently and encourages a more reflective engagement with the film ("What Do We Hear," 141–142).

[33] William Whittington, *Sound Design & Science Fiction* (Austin: University of Texas Press, 2007), 17–18.

[34] Commenting on the French director's innovative approach to sound, Michel Chion argues that "there is something of the laboratory to Tati's world" where "relationships between sounds and their visual sources are studied under the most advantageous conditions of hygiene and isolation" (*Film, A Sound Art*, trans. Claudia Gorbman [New York: Columbia University Press, 2003], 192).

[35] Chion, *Film, A Sound Art*, 243.

designer who contributed to the resurgence of an artistic approach to the sound-track in the 1970s, and who was associated with Bay Area sound and the culture of a collaborative approach to postproduction, was Alan Splet. The soundscapes he created for David Lynch's *Eraserhead* (1976) by manipulating raw, organic sounds he and the director recorded together over a seven-week period, and the eerie presence they lend to the film, count among the most remarkable achieve-ments of the era in terms of the prominence given to sound and its apparent independence from narrative content. Splet and Lynch's methods of sound re-cording and postproduction not only evoked the techniques of *musique concrète* but also would have a lasting influence on Lynch, who became one of the fore-most innovators in this area as both a director and a sound designer.

However, one of the reasons the terms "sound design" and "sound designer" are still regarded with suspicion in some scholarly circles, as well as in practice, is because the methods of Zoetrope and designers such as Murch and Splet never became the standard in the Hollywood industry. As Jay Beck argues, the highly compartmentalized process of sound postproduction supported by union policy and the technological requirements associated with the emerging Dolby tech-nology in the 1970s ensured that the idea of sound designer as a "sound auteur" never took root in big studio productions. Instead, as Randy Thom bemoans, the role of sound designer became associated with the craft of creating sound effects, "a kind of hired gun who is brought in because he or she knows how to operate samples and synthesisers and create rocket ship sounds and space alien vocali-sations."[36] Another reason for the lack of opportunity for exploring uncharted territories in the interaction between image/story and sound is the habitual perception of sound as an ingredient that is added to the story once the picture is settled. Thom argues that to obtain an expressive sound design, filmmakers have to recognize its importance in advance and make "space" for it. Or as Thom puts it, to get great sound design, film has to be designed for great sound.[37] This requires that the collaborative process takes place before postproduction and might involve extensive consultations, recording sessions, the presence of the sound designer on the set, and so forth. While the type of collaborative prac-tice described by Thom is atypical of big studio productions, prompting com-ments that in Hollywood "there is no sound designer,"[38] plenty of collaborative

---

[36] Randy Thom, "Designing a Movie for Sound," in *Soundscape: The School of Sound Lectures 1998–2001*, ed. Larry Sider, Diane Freeman, and Jerry Sider (London and New York: Wallflower Press, 2003), 122.

[37] Thom, "Designing a Movie for Sound," 122.

[38] Most recently this statement has been associated with Jay Beck, whose turn of phrase is also a reference to Michel Chion's assertion that "there is no soundtrack" (Jay Beck, "The Sounds of 'Silence': Dolby Stereo, Sound Design and *The Silence of the Lambs*," in *Lowering the Boom: Critical Studies in Film Sound*, ed. Jay Beck and Tony Grayeda [Urbana and Chicago: University of Illinois Press, 2008], 68–83). Beck's comment also echoes Larry Sider's statement that sound design as a

processes take place in smaller productions in the American independent sector, not to mention the rest of the world, where the workflow is often more flexible than in Hollywood. A creative approach to sound in European art house cinema has long been an inspiration to American filmmakers aspiring to work outside Hollywood. The process of sound postproduction in Australia is similar to that in Europe because, as sound designer Sam Petty points out, smaller budgets mean smaller crews that are used to doing multiple jobs. According to Petty, such a working environment encourages a collaborative approach to any task so that instead of asking "how best can we do this job of effects editor?" the question becomes "how best can we do this job?," which generally leads to crossing or simply disregarding barriers typical of departmentalized productions.[39] As Petty explains, having an opportunity to talk to the director early, long before he or she is thinking about filming, is an ideal situation for the sound designer. Consultations should also include the writer (who is sometimes the same person) and the producers to work out what type of opportunities the script opens up for sound. Petty explains the advantages of coming into this process quite early on using the example of his work on *War Machine* (2017) directed by his long-term collaborator David Michôd.

War Machine is based on events journalist Michael Hastings recorded while travelling with US Army General Stanley McChrystal during his posting in Afghanistan in 2010. Since lots of exteriors were shot in the United Arab Emirates doubling as Afghanistan, Petty worked out with the director and convinced the producers that he should be an official part of that shoot as sound recordist so that he could plan ahead and avoid using library sounds. He coordinated with the production manager to have access to the extras who spoke the right Afghan dialect and recorded a number of sound effects, atmospheres, musics, calls to prayer, dialogue, incidental dialogue, and sounds that he scripted in conjunction with the director. "Once logged and categorized we made up this terrific library which was a key resource all through the film," says Petty, "and this is a sort of thing that you can't do if you don't fight for it."[40]

Petty's experience echoes Randy Thom's argument that an expressive sound design can only be created in a context where its significance is recognized in advance and is facilitated by the film's overall design.[41] Examples of this type of approach are numerous, as will be shown in the case studies discussed in this book, since noncompartmentalized teamwork is essential for the kinds of practices

concept "never really took hold" in Hollywood (Larry Sider, "If You Wish to See, Listen: The Role of Sound Design," *Journal of Media Practice* 4, no. 1 [2003]: 6).

[39] Sam Petty, Skype interview with the author, August 11, 2016.
[40] Ibid.
[41] Thom, "Designing a Movie for Sound," 122.

examined here. The next section explores the relationship between musical sensibility and soundtrack integration, arguing that the musical approach to soundtrack is an essential factor in promoting the fusion of soundtrack elements and their interchangeability.

The Musicality of the Integrated Soundtrack

We live in an age where the notion of what art is exists and evolves beyond the constraints of academic definitions and criteria that have been in the past cultivated by the ruling class or the church. No other art has been affected by this change more than music. Musical modernism from the first half of the twentieth century, futurism, the rise of electronic music and *musique concrète*, and various strands of the twentieth-century musical avant-garde transformed our perception of music irrevocably. Ideas about music and musicality have expanded to include a new vocabulary of sounds produced by nature, objects, machines, tape recorders, turntables, and computers, demonstrating that music does not have to be performed on traditional instruments and can exist outside the rules of traditional hierarchical structuring, harmony, and orchestration. Thanks to composers and philosophers of sound such as John Cage and R. Murray Schafer, the divisions between music and sound fell away, teaching us to listen in a new way and to discover music in nature and our everyday environments. Even the notion of noise lost its traditionally negative connotations and was subsumed into this inclusive approach to music to become just another category or subgenre.

In this context where every sound can be perceived as inherently musical, the act of listening is no less musical than the act of performing music, because a sound can be heard as musical only if there is someone to perceive it as such. Or, as Paul Hegarty observes, when the world is "revealed as infinitely musical," musicality is "about our attentiveness to the sounds of the world."[42] The same logic applies to film soundtrack: to hear its musicality, one has to approach the soundtrack as a potentially musical entity. In the context of compartmentalized and highly industrialized film production where the value of the soundtrack is measured purely by its narrative functionality, its musical properties are limited to the score itself. Its hierarchy is based on the primacy of the spoken word, while the placement of music and sound effects is conditioned by the requirements of the narrative context. But when film soundtrack is considered in its totality as a

---

[42] Paul Hegarty, *Noise/Music: A History* (New York, London, New Delhi, and Sydney: Bloomsbury, 2007), 6.

composition of speech, music, and sound effects, it is easier to recognize its musicality and the different ways in which it can be generated.[43]

As Walter Murch points out, the musicality of the soundtrack stems from the fact that film itself is musical. Emphasizing the importance of creating balance between story, emotion, and rhythm in the process of film editing, he says:

> You can tell a story intelligently and with emotion and not do it rhythmically.... But that's a dangerous place to be for very long because film, I think, is very close to music in how it works. In editing pictures I am constructing images that have a flow back and forth that's very similar to visual music. And, of course, in the construction of a soundtrack we actually use real music, but we also use sounds and voices rhythmically, interrelating to each other and the music, but also relating to the musical rhythm of the images.[44]

There are a couple of points Murch makes here that are relevant for the argument of this book: first, the idea of interconnectivity that applies to all levels of storytelling, concerning not only the craft and rhythm of storytelling and an abstract concept of emotion but also the interaction between different elements of the soundtrack; second, the idea of the musical nature of the soundtrack and of film itself. We will see over the course of this book that Murch's sentiments are echoed by many other practitioners involved in various stages of the filmmaking process. The musical quality of film soundtrack has been noted by many scholars as well, but the development of its musical potential was not always connected with a "unified" approach to soundtrack, partly because the latter idea is still somewhat contentious, prompting a wide range of reactions, from enthusiastic advocacy to the denial of its possibility. Some of the earliest remarks on how soundtrack elements can interact by circumventing the Hollywood hierarchical model were offered by Noël Burch in his book *Theory and Film Practice*. Starting from the position that there should be no real distinction between music, dialogue, and sound effects in pursuit of a dialectical interaction between auditory and visual spaces, Burch cites Kenji Mizoguchi's *The Crucified Lovers* (1954) as a successful example. Burch rightly observes that the "open quality of Japanese music," which is not "subject to the 'tyranny of the bar-line,'" is "infinitely more adaptable to the eminently nonmeasurable rhythms of film 'action' and film editing" because its

[43] See for instance Philip Brophy, *100 Modern Soundtracks* (London: British Film Institute, 2004); James Buhler, "Analytical and Interpretative Approaches to Film Music (II): Analysing Interactions of Music and Film," in *Film Music: Critical Approaches*, ed. K. J. Donnelly (Edinburgh: Edinburgh University Press, 2001), 39–61; Donnelly, *Occult Aesthetics*; Kulezic-Wilson, *The Musicality of Narrative Film*; Vernallis, *Unruly Media*; James Wierzbicki, "Sound as Music in the Films of Terrence Malick," in *The Cinema of Terrence Malick: Poetic Visions of America*, ed. Hannah Patterson (New York: Columbia University Press, 2007), 112–124.
[44] Constantini, "Walter Murch interviewed by Gustavo Constantini," 42.

free flow is closer to that of the film image.[45] But he also illuminates the decisions that further facilitate this interaction through the use of diegetic sound effects, such as the clang of a wooden bowl, or a ladder banging against a wall as the first note of a musical phrase, or ending a musical phrase with the diegetic sound of a door closing. These "organic" links established between "functional" sound effects and music not only create effective moments of synchronized interaction but also result in the interaction between "the images and the entire sound tissue of the film, which at times shifts without a break from an off-screen to an on-screen 'presence.'"[46] Although many contemporary films from different parts of Asia nowadays opt for scores that evoke conventions of Hollywood scoring in terms of harmonic language, orchestration, and narrative cueing, we will see in chapter 4 with the example of Hou Hsiao-Hsien's film *The Assassin* that Burch's comments still resonate strongly with certain practices.

Burch's comments about the interrelatedness of all soundtrack elements are built into his argument about the dialectical relationship between auditory and visual aspects of film, which, of course, has its roots in the first film sound manifesto issued by Eisenstein, Pudovkin, and Aleksandrov only one year after recorded sound was introduced in cinema. But unlike the Soviet masters of montage, whose "Statement" is mostly concerned with the relationship between sound and image, Burch also considers the features of an integrated film sound-track in the context of contemporary musical practice. He gives the example of Michel Fano, a composer-turned-sound engineer and filmmaker famous for his collaboration with Alain Robbe-Grillet, who incorporated off-screen sounds into the soundtrack organizing them into "musical" structures or stylizing them in a manner evocative of contemporary art music.[47]

These two lines of enquiry—the dialectic relationship between image and sound and the musicality of the soundtrack—are also brought together in James Buhler's 2001 chapter "Analytical and Interpretative Approaches to Film Music."[48] Buhler, however, criticizes Burch's view of a unified soundtrack as a structure in which dialogue, music, and sound effects "dissolve into one another," arguing that the erosion of the distinctiveness between the individual components is "too dear a price" to pay because it "surrenders the possibility of forging an internal dialectic of sound."[49] Of course, recent developments in the

---

[45] Noël Burch, *Theory of Film Practice* (Princeton, NJ: Princeton University Press, 1981), 99.

[46] Burch, *Theory of Film Practice*, 95. Sensitivity to the musical quality of sound effects might also be connected to the influence of Japanese kabuki theater practice, which employs a wide range of percussive instruments, a tradition that carried over into early Japanese cinema, as explained by Alexander Binns, "'Sounding Japanese': Traditions of Music in Japanese Cinema," in *The Routledge Companion to Screen Music and Sound*, ed. Miguel Mera, Ronald Sadoff, and Ben Winters (London and New York: Routledge, 2017), 428–439.

[47] Burch, *Theory of Film Practice*, 97.

[48] Buhler, "Analytical and Interpretative Approaches to Film Music (II)."

[49] Ibid., 54.

practice designed to dissolve the boundaries between soundtrack elements, as in Gus Van Sant's *Elephant* and *Paranoid Park* (2007) or Peter Strickland's *Katalin Varga* (2009) and *Berberian Sound Studio* (2012), demonstrate that Buhler's fear of losing the soundtrack's inner dialecticism in the process was unfounded. That detail aside, in his analysis Buhler also campaigns for the cause of a "unified soundtrack" by proposing that music should be viewed as a "subsidiary element in the sound design." He explains that, however provocative his choice of words might seem, its purpose is not to "undermine the undeniably important role that music plays in film" but to argue that "a musical sensibility can thus be extended to the soundtrack as a whole."[50] Citing the concept of *mise-en-bande* proposed by Rick Altman, McGraw Jones, and Sonia Tatroe, which argues for recognizing the coherence of a soundtrack in its entirety, Buhler argues that "the complex interplay of music, dialogue, ambient sound, effects, silences and so forth, can be understood—indeed is perhaps best understood—as a kind of musical 'composition.' "[51]

While Buhler questions the ability of integrated soundtrack to facilitate a dialectical relationship between image and sound, Michel Chion essentially denies its existence, citing the idea of the "unification of sounds" as one of those frequently advocated by film visionaries that failed to manifest in practice.[52] According to Chion, considering that Dolby and digital technology are indispensable tools in contemporary film production and exhibition, producing highly defined sounds with a wide range of contrast, "film should abandon, at least for now, any dreams of *fusion* among sonic elements."[53] Chion admits, though, that there are rare exceptions to this rule and cites *Blade Runner* (Ridley Scott, 1982) as a "magnificent realization of the ideal."[54] The interesting detail worth quoting here is Chion's observation that the organic unity of speech, music, and sound effects in this film is partly achieved due to the "material analogy" between Vangelis's electronic music and the sound effects, which is not surprising considering that Vangelis used his Yamaha CS-80 to create various diegetic and nondiegetic sound effects for the film. Chion also states that

---

[50] Ibid., 39–40.

[51] Ibid., 58. Buhler demonstrates the analytical value of his approach in a case study of *Casablanca* (Michael Curtiz, 1942) coauthored with David Neumeyer for Neumeyer's book *Meaning and Interpretation of Music in Cinema*. While the authors admit that viewing *mise-en-bande* as a musical composition requires a particular type of musical sensibility, they propose that their analytical strategy, which examines the soundtrack as a whole, its relationship to the image, the narrative, and the act of narration itself, results in a way of reading film that is more "musical" than treating the score as a relatively independent component written *for* a film (*Meaning and Interpretation of Music in Cinema*, 100).

[52] Chion, *Film, A Sound Art*, 203–205.

[53] Ibid., 205.

[54] Ibid., 204.

the whole film is conceived rhythmically, as a sort of rhythmic pyramid that extends from big waves of sound in low registers to rapid electronic beepings in the ultrahigh range—and it is also conceived symphonically, organically, through the admirable mix created by the British sound engineer Graham Hartstone.[55]

This is an interesting point to note because Chion's description implies a musical logic behind the unification of the sonic elements in this film, which is exactly the argument I pursue in this book.

Finally, while most scholars interested in this topic recognize the growing taste for the dissolution of the boundaries between soundtrack elements, they don't always view its musicalization as a root of the change but rather as a side product, or they tend to emphasize different aspects of filmmaking or postproduction practice. Carol Vernallis, for instance, attributes the musicalization of the soundtrack to the general influence of music videos on film. Her argument is mostly focused on illuminating the musicality of "intensified" cinema in terms of structuring and audiovisual aesthetics, although she also points to the promotion of sound effects to "leading roles" in this context and the shaping of dialogue and sound effects into musical phrases alongside the composed music.[56] Anahid Kassabian views the roots of evaporating boundaries between sound and music through the prism of power relations, stating that the rise of rock and rap as "noise" encourages us to "hear the history of music in the twentieth century as an increasing absorption of noise into music":

> In providing the raw material of both hip-hop and techno, sampling technologies have turned music into sound and back again, treating previously recorded music as the functional equivalent of industrial sounds and noises for composers of *musique concrète* and for groups like Kraftwerk.[57]

Using the soundtrack of *The Cell* (Tarsem Singh, 2000) as an example, Kassabian comments that its noises and sounds, which are treated "compositionally," are "neither music nor not music, but rather a textural use of sound that disregards most, if not all, the 'laws' of classic Hollywood film scoring technique."[58]

In their nuanced analysis of the stylistic heterogeneity of European cinema, Miguel Mera and David Burnand identify the influence of modernism as a relevant factor in strengthening the alliance of music and sound design in an

---

[55] Ibid., 139.
[56] Vernallis, *Unruly Media*, 69–75.
[57] Anahid Kassabian, "The Sound of a New Film Form," in *Popular Music and Film*, ed. Ian Inglis (London and New York: Wallflower, 2003), 92.
[58] Kassabian, *Ubiquitous Listening*, 38.

integrated approach to soundtrack that opposes the hierarchical structure of the classical soundtrack. However, in the same breath they admit that it would be wrong to conclude that this is a direct result of "more open attitudes" typical of European or avant-garde filmmakers because they recognize the same approach to "total sound design" in certain aspects of mainstream American cinema such as the work of David Fincher.[59] This is an important point because it reminds us that interaction between music and sound design is not exclusive to nonmainstream cinema, nor is it, as I mentioned earlier, associated with one single type of practice. In recent years even the work of one of the industry's most influential composers at the moment, Hans Zimmer, has been leaning in the same direction.[60] While his working methods, which value collaboration on different levels of postproduction, will be addressed in more detail in the next chapter, the reason none of Zimmer's output is included among this book's case studies is because even though his techniques often result in a blurring of the line between score and sound design aurally, the employment of his material generally does not challenge any of the conventions typical of classical scoring practices, an approach aptly described by Nicholas Reyland as "corporate classicism."[61]

Nevertheless, a signature aspect of the aural style applied by Zimmer and many other composers interested in exploring the sound world in between score and sound design is the use of digital technology, which can involve any aspect of composing including recording/improvising sessions, the use of sample libraries, sound processing, editing, and so forth. According to Kevin Donnelly, the use of digital technology is among the main factors encouraging an increasingly "aesthetic" rather than representational conception of the soundtrack that results in "a unified aural field of music and other sounds in many films."[62] As Donnelly argues, the use of synthesizers in the 1980s and then digital audio workstations from the 1990s for processing both dialogue and sound effects inspired film sound personnel to think about soundtrack in musical terms. As was noted in the aforementioned example of *Blade Runner*, the pioneers of electronic film music scores like Vangelis blurred the line between composing and sound design production by using their own musical equipment to create sound effects. Another figure of interest who predates Vangelis is Frank Serafine, who put his composing career on hold when he was asked to produce sound effects for *Star*

[59] Miguel Mera and David Burnand, "Introduction," in *European Film Music*, ed. Miguel Mera and David Burnand (Furnham, Surrey: Ashgate, 2006), 5.
[60] For more details about this aspect of Zimmer's work see Benjamin Wright, "Sculptural Dissonance: Hans Zimmer and the Composer as Engineer," *Sounding Out!*, July 10, 2014, https://soundstudiesblog.com/author/wrightonfilm/.
[61] Nicholas Reyland, "Corporate Classicism and the Metaphysical Style: Affects, Effects, and Contexts of Two Recent Trends in Screen Scoring," *Music, Sound and the Moving Image* 9, no. 2 (Autumn 2015): 115–130, doi:10.3828/msmi.2015.8.
[62] Donnelly, "Extending Film Aesthetics," 358.

Trek: The Motion Picture (Robert Wise, 1979) and ended up forming his own company specializing in sound postproduction. The use of musical technology in postproduction also undermined the differences between composers and film sound practitioners and the relevance of their background and musical knowledge, allowing people with no classical musical training to compose music for film while also encouraging composers, especially those using electronic equipment, to become involved in the production of sound effects. Donnelly's point is particularly resonant today considering that some of the most sought-after composers whose work relies on the use of digital technology come from a popular music background without any substantial classical musical training, including Hans Zimmer and Clint Mansell.

However, the musical way of thinking about sound effects predates all these developments in technology. Filmmakers like Dziga Vertov and Rouben Mamoulian anticipated the aesthetics of *musique concrète* with their approach to diegetic sound in early sound films such as *Enthusiasm: Symphony of the Donbass* (1930) and *Love Me Tonight* (1932), respectively. As Mark Mancini tells us, one of the early heroes of film sound and the magician behind the sound effects in many Disney films since the late 1930s, Jimmy MacDonald, drew on his experience as a drummer when creating sound effects and used a music staff to "score" them first, "each note denoting the duration of a sound and each note annotated to indicate its identity or source."[63] These are just some of the examples that indicate the influence of the musical way of thinking when approaching "nonmusical" aspects of the soundtrack, which will be discussed at length in the next chapter. Throughout the history of cinema, many filmmakers—*mélomanes* and mavericks—exhibited attentiveness to film sound, an attentiveness that, as Hegarty suggests, is the most important step in discovering the soundtrack's musicality. My intention in this book is to show that, even though the musical potential of the soundtrack has been championed by filmmakers and practitioners in the past, what has brought this potential into focus more recently is the growing tendency to dissolve the boundaries and hierarchical relationships between music and other elements of the soundtrack, giving rise to new aesthetic tastes and modes of perception.

Outline of Contents

Scholarly approaches entrenched in particular theoretical or ideological frameworks tend to emphasize one aspect of our experience of engaging with cinema

---

[63] Mark Mancini, "The Sound Designer," in *Film Sound: Theory and Practice*, ed. Elisabeth Weis and John Belton (New York: Columbia University Press, 1985), 364.

while overlooking others. Those concerned with intellectual engagement who explore meaning from different positions of hermeneutics, psychoanalysis, or cultural theory are inclined to neglect the sensuous aspect of cinema, while sensory-based theories focus on phenomenological experiences and the representation of corporeality without always giving enough attention to aesthetic or intellectual dimensions of spectatorship. Or, as Kevin Donnelly notes in relation to cognitive film theory, the analysis tends to get atomized to "minute subcomponents, while avoiding the 'bigger picture.'"[64] It is impossible, of course, for any approach to be as comprehensive as to cover all areas of potential interest, let alone to do it in depth. But in concordance with the idea of integration as one of the running themes of this book, and because I am personally drawn to cinema that embraces the interdependency of intellectual, affective, and sensory stimuli, I have tried to capture the multifaceted nature of the experience encouraged by such practice by giving attention to its different aspects in individual chapters. Thus, in terms of their general functions in the overall argument, chapter 2 provides the basis for exploring the integrated soundtrack in the digital era by setting up the historical context for the contemporary methods that define it; chapter 3 delves into issues of aesthetics, arguing that the need to resist the conventions of classical scoring played an important part in encouraging blurring of the line between score and sound design; chapters 4 and 5 address sensuous aspects of this practice, the former by exploring the notion of the erotics of film sound in general and the latter by emphasizing the connection between sensuousness and the musicality of speech. Each chapter also focuses on one of the main methods associated with erasing the boundaries between soundtrack elements, and each method will be explored in relationship to those influences that have been most dominant in shaping it: thus, the discussion about the sonic overlaps between score and sound design and the musicalization of sound effects in chapter 2 emphasizes the importance of new technologies and the influence of popular music; in chapter 3, the merging of electroacoustic music and *musique concrète* with ambient sound is discussed in relation to issues of aesthetics; in chapter 4, the notion of *audio-visual musique concrète* is explored in connection to the musical avant-garde and contemporary art practice; chapter 5 illuminates the connection between musicality and sensuality as a driving principle in the musicalization of speech in this practice. Finally, I should point out that the order of chapters also charts the progression of the breakdown of the classical soundtrack hierarchy, from the musicalization of sound effects, through the employment of *musique concrète* and electroacoustic music as sound design, to the musicalization of speech as the most radical manifestation of this trend. This

---

[64] Donnelly, *Occult Aesthetics*, x.

narrative arc also captures the gradual transformation of the audience's increasing tolerance of strategies typical of nonmainstream cinema and the growing affinity for the sensuous aspect of the cinematic experience, as can be inferred from the ensuing, more detailed overview of chapter content.

Chapter 2 explores various ways in which the relationship between score and sound design and their functions can overlap under the influences of technology and the musical approach to the soundtrack. It looks at different ways in which contemporary scoring interacts with or moves in the direction of sound design, as well as at the musicalization of sound effects. Positing the latter as the oldest and most basic type of musical approach to the soundtrack, early examples of which coincide with the introduction of recorded sound in cinema, this chapter also explores the relationship between the impact of technology and the idea of musicality as the two dominant inspirations for this trend.

Chapter 3 argues that the practice of replacing diegetic sound with preexisting electroacoustic music and/or *musique concrète*, or their seamless merging, represents a significant development in the practice of erasing the line between score and sound design. It focuses on the work of British director Peter Strickland (*Katalin Varga,* 2009; *Berberian Sound Studio,* 2012; *The Duke of Burgundy,* 2014), one of the most exciting and musically adventurous representatives of soundtrack practices discussed in this book who has pushed the musically conceived soundtrack firmly into the area of the avant-garde and experimental music. His methods of "scoring with sound design" are viewed in the context of an *aesthetics of reticence* that deliberately rejects the conventions of traditional scoring to encourage active intellectual and emotional engagements with the text.

Chapter 4 explores the sensuous dimension of contemporary soundtracks through examples of soundtrack musicality drawn from ordinary diegetic sounds such as walking, physical activities, or environmental sounds. This chapter asserts that the overall musical effect produced by the interaction between repetitive sound and rhythmicized visual movement creates musicality of an inherently cinematic nature, a type of *audio-visual musique concrète.* This approach is theorized through the concept of the erotics of art, contending that the mode of aural engagement with cinema facilitated by the integrated approach to the soundtrack and the practice of blurring the boundaries between music and the soundtrack's other elements is intimately connected to the emergence of a trend that emphasizes the sensuousness of film form without confusing it with sensory overload.

The most compelling evidence that recent changes in soundtrack practice have been influenced by a musical way of thinking can be found in the fact that even the use of speech has been affected. As chapter 5 argues, the musical approach to the spoken word undermines classical soundtrack hierarchy more than any other method discussed in the preceding chapters, since the dominance and narrative sovereignty of speech are the pillars of cinema's "vococentrism."[65] As a consequence of the musical approach to the soundtrack, the unwritten laws regarding speech intelligibility and redundancy are broken, the familiar hierarchy is replaced by a more fluid relationship in which music and speech alternately come in and out of focus, and information is often conveyed through nonverbal means—*mise-en-scène*, editing, characters' body language, expressive close-ups—thus emphasizing musicality as the primary guiding principle of this practice.

Finally, while the method of blurring the line between scoring and sound design is widely acknowledged as an intriguing new and increasingly popular development of soundtrack practice, not everyone will agree that its underlying principles can and should be "explained" by the musical approach to the soundtrack. It is difficult to deny, though, that the various manifestations of this practice, including the use of electroacoustic music and *musique concrète* as sound design, the musical emancipation of sound effects, the musical use of speech, and the deliberate foregrounding of musical material at the expense of audible dialogue, have disrupted soundtrack conventions by giving priority to musicality over narrative functionality and to sensuous experience over intelligibility. I hope to demonstrate in this book that, owing to this new practice, the traditionally stable categories of originally composed or compiled scores, dialogue, and sound effects, and familiar binaries such as diegetic/nondiegetic and music/sound design, have not simply dissipated but have been adjusted to the principles of editing and signification that are strongly influenced by musical logic.

---

[65] Michel Chion, *The Voice in Cinema*, trans. Claudia Gorbman (New York: Columbia University Press, 1999), 5–6.

2

"The Most Beautiful Area"

Soundtrack's Liminal Spaces

"The borderline between sound effects and music is the most *beautiful* area," proclaimed David Lynch.[1] Sonically intriguing and rich with ambiguities, this area has been successfully explored by many composers and sound designers throughout the history of cinema. As this chapter will show, access to this area can be gained from different aesthetic and practical positions. Here I will focus on the two main approaches: that in which the score moves towards the realm that is usually covered by the sound department, including ambient sound, sound effects, and Foley sounds, and that which involves the musicalization of sounds that are traditionally tasked with a purely mimetic role and the creation of a "realistic" sound environment. Although the plurality of methods and motivations for blurring the lines between music and sound effects demonstrates that the forces behind the ongoing processes of soundtrack integration are too complex to be reduced to a single influence or explanation, two factors are repeatedly associated with the trend. One of them—which is also the running theme of this book—is a musical sensibility behind the affinity for soundtrack integration in general, and in this case specifically behind the methods that emphasize the affective and rhythmical qualities of sound effects. The other is the influence of technology. As the limitations of and innovations in technology played an important part in the processes of departmentalization and integration in soundtrack postproduction throughout the history of cinema, it is worth looking closer at the evolution of this relationship.

Technology and the Forces of Departmentalization and Integration

American Zoetrope's ethos of encouraging cross-departmental collaboration and avoiding Hollywood's strict division of labour was in many ways enabled by the development of technology in the 1960s that allowed one person to design

---

[1] Chris Rodley, ed., *Lynch on Lynch* (London: Faber and Faber, 2005), 242 (emphasis in the original).

Sound Design Is the New Score: Theory, Aesthetics, and Erotics of the Integrated Soundtrack. Danijela Kulezic-Wilson, Oxford University Press (2020). © Oxford University Press. DOI: 10.1093/oso/ 9780190855314.001.0001

the soundtrack and mix it. Conversely, the habitual separation of different soundtrack elements during production had also been influenced by technology and its limits at the time when recorded sound was introduced in cinema.

The dominance of dialogue is in soundtrack's DNA, since the art of storytelling cultivated by filmmakers even before the introduction of recorded sound generally depends on the clarity of the story, the relationships between the characters, and their motivations. Once the intertitles of so-called mute cinema[2] were replaced by spoken words, dialogue became the primary carrier of narrative action while the necessity of providing sufficient narrative information became entangled with enjoyment of the medium's sonic reinvention and a desire to participate in the "illusion of real people speaking real words."[3] Considering that in the early ages of the "talkies" intelligibility of dialogue equalled intelligibility of the story, its dominance in the soundtrack hierarchy was inevitable. It was apparent not only in the level of dialogue being prioritized over the levels of music and sound effects but also, as Mary Ann Doane points out, in the fact that dialogue became "the only sound which remains with the image throughout the production" and is edited with it.[4]

Apart from the reason of intelligibility, the seeds of further segregation between dialogue and other elements of the soundtrack in the first few years following the introduction of recorded synchronized sound were sown due to the limitations of the available technology. On the one hand, as Rick Altman explains, nondirectional microphones used between 1927 and 1933 for recording sound were fragile and sensitive to all ambient noises and required special recording conditions; on the other, the technology of sound mixing was underdeveloped and did not allow postmixing of multiple tracks without audible loss of quality. As a result, it was quite rare for dialogue and music to appear simultaneously on the soundtrack unless they were recorded at the same time. And if they were recorded together on the set, the music was usually played from a previously recorded track to solve the problems caused by the different reverberation and amplification requirements for recording music and dialogue.[5]

This so-called playback system not only created the division between music and the rest of the soundtrack but also, as Altman argues, separated the

---

[2] Gillian B. Anderson argues that "mute" is a more appropriate term than "silent" because it "emphasizes the absence of talking rather than of sound" ("The Shock of the Old: The Restoration, Reconstruction, or Creation of 'Mute'-Film Accompaniments," in *The Routledge Companion to Screen Music and Sound*, ed. Miguel Mera, Ronald Sadoff, and Ben Winters [London and New York: Routledge, 2017], 201).

[3] Rick Altman, "The Evolution of Sound Technology," in *Film Sound: Theory and Practice*, ed. Elisabeth Weis and John Belton (New York: Columbia University Press, 1985), 47.

[4] Mary Ann Doane, "Ideology and the Practice of Sound Editing and Mixing," in *Film Sound: Theory and Practice*, ed. Elisabeth Weis and John Belton (New York: Columbia University Press, 1985), 58.

[5] Altman, "The Evolution of Sound Technology," 46.

soundtrack from the image while facilitating the illusion that the sound is produced by it.[6] But that was not the only issue resulting from the use of recorded music on the set. As Gianluca Sergi explains in his study of the organization of departmentalized labour in Hollywood, since the use of so-called canned music started to threaten the jobs of musicians employed by the industry, this caused an organized protest that further soured the relationship between musicians and those responsible for the rest of the soundtrack. During the 1920s, the place of sound practitioners in the production process and within the industrial structure was far from settled, meaning that "nobody truly 'owned' cinema sound in the run up to the swift change that would see Hollywood go from silent to sound at the end of the decade."[7] Composers and musicians, on the other hand, enjoyed organized support and representation, and responded to the increasing use of "canned music" with an aggressive propaganda battle led by the American Federation of Musicians to protect jobs during their Music Defence League campaign. Arguing that "the talkies brought with them the risk of the demise of refinement, quality and variety in music and beyond,"[8] this campaign "slammed the door on closer integration of music and sound in the cinema right at the very moment when sound departments were being established."[9]

During the 1930s significant advancements in production technology improved the quality of sound, such as the introduction of better microphones and speakers, quieter cameras and lights, and sound-on-film recording becoming standard for the industry. One practice that had a particular impact on the development of scoring conventions was the widespread use of rerecording in postproduction, allowing sound technicians on the set to focus on recording dialogue.[10] The ability to mix separately recorded music with the synchronous dialogue track without audible loss of quality facilitated more liberal use of background music[11] and paved the way for establishing the conventions of classical Hollywood scoring. Even though by this time score production had again become fully dependent on the availability of orchestral musicians to perform originally composed scores, the division of labour in soundtrack production was fully departmentalized, separating music, dialogue, and sound effects into three distinct categories.

---

[6] Ibid.
[7] Gianluca Sergi, "Organizing Sound: Labour Organizations and Power Struggles That Helped Define Music and Sound in Hollywood," in *The Palgrave Handbook of Sound Design and Music in Screen Media: Integrated Soundtracks*, ed. Liz Greene and Danijela Kulezic-Wilson (Basingstoke, Hampshire: Palgrave Macmillan, 2016), 47.
[8] Ibid., 50.
[9] Ibid., 54.
[10] James Buhler, David Neumeyer, and Rob Deemer, *Hearing the Movies: Music and Sound in Film History* (Oxford and New York: Oxford University Press, 2010), 308–311.
[11] Barry Salt, "Film Style and Technology in the Thirties: Sound," in *Film Sound: Theory and Practice*, ed. Elisabeth Weis and John Belton (New York: Columbia University Press, 1985), 43.

The employment of magnetic recording techniques in the 1950s was another major technological development that revolutionized the production of sound for film. Although the industry initially resisted the use of magnetic sound equipment in theatres, the magnetic recording technology was widely applied in sound recording, dubbing, mixing, and remixing, replacing the use of optical technology. On the one hand, the newly available technology further encouraged departmentalization of production; on the other, according to Murch's recollections of the late 1960s/early 1970s period in Zoetrope, this opened up new creative possibilities and a space for experimentation.[12] The crucial feature of the new technology that "democratized" the craft of film sound and allowed practitioners to develop a more holistic approach to it was the fact that it could potentially remove the barrier between the creation of sound effects and mixing: "The director would then be able to talk to one person about the sound of the film the way he was able to talk to the director of photography about the look of the film."[13]

Blurring the lines between different postproduction duties or their merging encouraged by the advancements in technology was to become a consistent pattern in the narrative of soundtrack innovation and integration. The introduction of synthesizers to postproduction in the 1980s, followed by the widespread use of digital audio workstations (DAWs) in the 1990s, facilitated the beginning of a new stage in soundtrack practice that undermined the separation between music and other elements of the soundtrack. Eight years before the invention of the Moog synthesizer, Bebe and Louis Barron used their own ring modulators to produce the score for *Forbidden Planet* (Fred Macleod Wilcox, 1956), their futuristic vision of sci-fi sound deeming the distinction between music and sound effects irrelevant. In the years that followed, the expansive sonic palette of synthesizers inspired new ways of thinking about sound and music in the context of film soundtrack, allowing composers to create sound effects and inspiring sound editors to manipulate sound recordings in a musical way.[14] The introduction of electronic instruments into film sound production and postproduction encouraged the move of professionals from the audio and music trade into film and video production, part of a broader phenomenon that Paul Théberge termed "transectorial migration"—"the movement, from one industry sector to another, of individuals with particular forms of technical knowledge

[12] Walter Murch, "Sound Design: The Dancing Shadow," in *Projections 4: Film-makers on Film-making*, ed. John Boorman, Tom Luddy, David Thompson, and Walter Donohue (London and Boston: Faber and Faber, 1995), 244.

[13] Ibid., 245.

[14] Kevin J. Donnelly, "Extending Film Aesthetics: Audio Beyond Visuals," in *The Oxford Handbook of New Audiovisual Aesthetics*, ed. John Richardson, Claudia Gorbman, and Carol Vernallis (Oxford and New York: Oxford University Press, 2014), 365–366.

and expertise."[15] Commenting on transectorial migration from music to the film industry, Katherine Spring contends that this process "inspired some sound editors to adopt a new understanding of his or her job in musical terms—specifically as 'sound composers.'"[16] Both Spring and Donnelly cite the examples of Frank Serafine and Alan Howarth, who started their musical careers playing in rock bands but ended up applying their musical craft and knowledge of synthesizers to the production of sound effects, predominantly in sci-fi and horror. After creating sound effects for *TRON* (Steven Lisberger, 1982) and *Star Trek: The Motion Picture* (dir. Robert Wise, 1979), Serafine formed a company for sound postproduction, providing services in sound editing and sound design. As Spring explains, Serafine's proficiency with Moog synthesizers, acquired during his early musical career, allowed him to not only create sound effects but also "*perform* the effects to picture in 'real time', in much the same way that a studio orchestra or Foley artist performs while simultaneously watching a video monitor during a recording session."[17] Mark Mancini emphasizes this point in his analysis of Serafine's contribution to modern sound design practice, saying that seeing Serafine work is "not to watch someone calibrating and tooling sound effects; it is to watch someone who composes and performs them."[18] And while Serafine's migration from music to film led him to focus on a career in sound postproduction, Alan Howarth remained active as a composer, dividing his time between scoring (John Carpenter's *Halloween II*, 1981; *Christine*, 1983; *Big Trouble in Little China*, 1986; *Prince of Darkness*, 1987) and sound effects production (*Star Trek: The Motion Picture*; *Poltergeist*, Tobe Hooper, 1982; *Stargate*, Roland Emmerich, 1992) or doing both (*Escape from New York*, John Carpenter, 1981; *The Dentist*, Brian Yuzna, 1996).

The introduction of digital tools for music production into film postproduction pushed the overlap between composition and sound design even further. By the end of the 1990s, DAWs such as Pro Tools and Cubase were being used by sound designers for the processing of both dialogue and sound effects, allowing sound designers and editors to manipulate those in the same way that composers might approach musical material.[19] Donnelly finds that exploring the material and sensuous qualities of sound through processing by using, for instance,

[15] Paul Théberge, *Any Sound You Can Imagine: Making Music/Consuming Technology* (Hanover and London: Wesleyan University Press, 1997), 59.

[16] Katherine Spring, "From Analogue to Digital: Synthesizers and Discourses of Film Sound in the 1980s," in *The Palgrave Handbook of Sound Design and Music in Screen Media: Integrated Soundtrack*, ed. Liz Greene and Danijela Kulezic-Wilson (Basingstoke, Hampshire: Palgrave Macmillan, 2016), 279.

[17] Ibid., 280.

[18] Mark Mancini, "The Sound Designer," in *Film Sound: Theory and Practice*, ed. Elisabeth Weis and John Belton (New York: Columbia University Press, 1985), 363.

[19] Donnelly, "Extending Film Aesthetics," 365; *Occult Aesthetics: Synchronization in Sound Film* (Oxford and New York: Oxford University Press, 2014), 125.

reverb and filters corresponds to a "sound for sound's sake" approach in much contemporary music that is less interested in traditional features of composition such as harmony, motivic development, and orchestration.[20] Thinking about music in terms of sound is also encouraged by a widespread use of sample-based digital instruments that emulate or expand the sound of real instruments. The combination of sampled and synthetic instruments, real live recording sessions, and sound processing available through digital instruments constitutes a virtual ensemble known as a hyperorchestra, which, as Sergi Casanelles asserts, is particularly well suited for screen composing and sound design as it allows the composer to respond quickly to the ever-changing content of re-edits with a tailor-made sound.[21] The use of hyperinstruments and hyperorchestra not only facilitates collaboration between composer and sound designer, which will be discussed at greater length in the next section, but also encourages collaboration on other levels as well. Hans Zimmer, the king of sample libraries and the person most responsible for turning hyperorchestration into an essential device of mainstream scoring, stresses that for him the collaborative process starts even before any music is written, with a recording session during which improvisation, unconventional playing of traditional instruments, the use of exotic instruments, and accidental "wrong notes" create a pool of ideas from which a motif or a timbre is chosen for further development.[22]

Access to vast collections of sample libraries as one of the features of hyperorchestra has also provoked some more reserved reactions. Frank Serafine, for instance, bemoans the replacement of synthesizers by digital tools claiming that "DAWs such as Pro Tools encourage the simple insertion of library sound effects rather than the manipulation of sampled sounds with hardware controllers" and "all the fun stuff" they had back then.[23] Commenting on the wide application of digital instruments in film and game scoring, Ronald H. Sadoff observes that the access to diverse sound libraries has diminished the gulf between conservatory-trained composers and those from a popular music background, and has encouraged experimentation and cross-pollination of genres and culture, but he also

---

[20]   Donnelly, *Occult Aesthetics*, 125.

[21]   Sergi Casanelles, "Mixing as a Hyperorchestration Tool," in *The Palgrave Handbook of Sound Design and Music in Screen Media: Integrated Soundtrack*, ed. Liz Greene and Danijela Kulezic-Wilson (Basingstoke, Hampshire: Palgrave Macmillan, 2016), 69.

[22]   An insight into Zimmer's working methods can be easily gained thanks to the numerous YouTube clips in which he talks about the origin of his scores for various blockbusters, including *The Dark Knight* (Christopher Nolan, 2008), *Man of Steel* (Zack Snyder, 2013), and others. Focusing on the most innovative aspects of Zimmer's scoring techniques, Benjamin Wright concisely captures the importance of his engagement with various collaborators and the relevance of digital equipment in contemporary film scoring in "Sculptural Dissonance: Hans Zimmer and the Composer as Engineer," *Sounding Out!*, July 10, 2014, https://soundstudiesblog.com/author/wrightonfilm/.

[23]   Spring, "From Analogue to Digital," 284.

points out that the repeated reuse of digital sound libraries can lead to clichéd solutions and ultimately may stifle creativity.[24]

It is worth emphasizing, though, that the use of musical software in film post-production does not automatically or necessarily translate into a musical approach to the soundtrack. Many examples discussed in this book are infused with a musical logic that goes beyond the fact that sound effects can be produced by musical software, which means that one still has to be musically inclined to apply technology in a musical manner. Also, in the final section of this chapter I will discuss a number of examples that demonstrate that what makes us perceive certain sound effects as musical is less to do with the equipment that assisted their creation and more to do with the fact that they are given a distinctly musical and/or percussive function in both musical and nonmusical contexts.

Score and Sound Design

While technological developments and the transectorial migration of professionals from audio and music production into film and video production certainly played a role in erasing the distinction between music and sound effects over the years, Kevin Donnelly argues that the "clinical" separation between the two has always been "impossible" since scores "regularly have mimicked, emphasized, or suggested certain sound effects in the diegesis," while sound effects "often have symbolic or emotional valences that outweigh their representational status."[25] That music "has spent a lot of time and energy in attempting to approximate ... the natural world and human ambiences, from birdsong to the rhythmic sounds of machinery,"[26] is partly due to the fact that this type of mimetic representation was exactly what was expected from the early scores for silent films that tried to compensate for the absence of sound effects. The connection between music and narrative action remained an important aspect of classical scores' stylistic vocabulary throughout the Hollywood Golden Era, which was manifested most explicitly in the form of Mickey Mousing.[27] It is also worth noting that the language of late Romanticism favoured by film composers of the Golden Era was especially suitable for evoking the spirit of mimesis since one of the defining features of much nineteenth-century instrumental music was composers' interest

---

[24] Ronald H. Sadoff, "Scoring for Film and Video Games: Collaborative Practices and Digital Post Production," in *The Oxford Handbook of Sound and Image in Digital Media*, ed. Carol Vernallis, Amy Herzog, and John Richardson (Oxford and New York: Oxford University Press, 2013), 672.

[25] Donnelly, *Occult Aesthetics*, 129.

[26] Ibid.

[27] Kathryn Kalinak, *Setting the Score: Narrative Film Music* (Madison: University of Wisconsin Press, 1992), 84–85.

in giving musical form to their extramusical inspirations through highly sophisticated musical means.

For films that deliberately distanced themselves from the classical approach in terms of both narrative style and scoring, choosing the language of twentieth-century music instead of the sound of the late Romantic orchestra opened up many new options for exploring the relationship between music and sound design. The use of electronic instruments was one obvious step in that direction, with scores such as those for *Forbidden Planet*[28] and the electronically generated bird noises in Hitchcock's *The Birds* (1963)[29] creating new soundscapes and establishing new standards for their evaluation. Outside of the sci-fi and horror genres, a particularly imaginative use of electronic music and its integration into the soundtrack resulted from the collaboration between director Andrei Tarkovsky and composer Eduard Artemiev[30] in films such as *Solaris* (1972), *The Mirror* (1975), and *Stalker* (1979). An interesting example of their approach can be found in *Solaris*, which, set in the distant future, uses the context of a sci-fi drama to explore the nature of consciousness and the power of guilt in shaping one's reality.

Solaris opens with the sound of water gurgling and birds chirping, and images of water plants and grass floating in a stream. Sounds and images of nature dominate the first half of the film, introducing us to the protagonist Kris Kelvin (Donatas Banionis) at his childhood home. One of those images—long blades of grass floating in a river—becomes a visual refrain symbolizing natural life on Earth, marking also the beginning of the film's coda. The lake and green fields surrounding Kelvin's home, clouds of mist hanging above the river, and sudden summer showers all evoke the vibrancy of natural life on Earth, in contrast to the confining, sterile interiors of the space station where the second half of the film takes place. Dividing these two parts of the film is a scene showing retired space pilot Henri Berton (Vladislav Dvorzhetskiy) returning home from visiting Kelvin, his taxi traversing the motorways, bypasses, and tunnels of some future city [00:31:47–00:36:29].[31] The scene symbolizes a transition both literally, depicting the endless stream of vehicles on the road, and symbolically, announcing the story's transition from a place of natural life to an interstellar station

---

[28] For a detailed analysis of the score see James Wierzbicki, *Louis and Bebe Barron's* Forbidden Planet: *A Film Score Guide* (Lanham, MD: Scarecrow Press, 2005).

[29] Most sound effects in *The Birds* were produced by a monophonic electronic instrument called a Trautonium. For a detailed analysis of the soundtrack in *The Birds* see Elisabeth Weis, "The Evolution of Hitchcock's Aural Style and Sound in *The Birds*," in *Film Sound: Theory and Practice*, ed. Elisabeth Weis and John Belton (New York: Columbia University Press, 1985), 298–311.

[30] The anglicized spelling of his name also appears in the version "Artemev."

[31] This is the timing of the scene in the DVD release of *Solaris*, Dream Plus Company, PAL, 2011. The duration of films and timings of quoted scenes may differ between PAL and NTSC formats and also depending on which programme is used to play the DVD.

orbiting the oceanic planet Solaris.[32] From the beginning, diegetic sounds of cars racing through the urban landscape and whooshing through tunnels merge with Eduard Artemiev's electronic score. However, Artemiev's interventions, especially at the beginning, are very subtle and do not immediately register as a score because he treats diegetic sounds as core material that, augmented and amplified by electronic means, is stretched into a resonant sonic body. What is particularly intriguing about this example is that the electronic manipulation of diegetic sounds is not perceived as the addition of a nondiegetic score because diegetic sounds maintain the quality of *musique concrète*. The result is strikingly musical insofar as we are inclined to perceive the sounds of traffic as musical in themselves.

Artemiev's approach is closely aligned with Tarkovsky's fascination with the innate musicality and dramatic potency of diegetic sound as described in his book *Sculpting in Time*:

> For strictly speaking the world transformed by cinema and the world as trans-formed by music are parallel, and conflict with each other. Properly organised in a film, the resonant world is musical in its essence—and that is the true music of cinema.[33]

Tarkovsky gives examples of evocative treatments of sound by Ingmar Bergman, Robert Bresson, and Michelangelo Antonioni, concluding with a Cageian obser-vation: "Above all, I feel that the sounds of this world are so beautiful in them-selves that if only we could learn to listen to them properly, cinema would have no need of music at all."[34] He explains how in *The Mirror* he instructed Artemiev to create his electroacoustic score around the sounds of nature, responding to "earthly echoes, rustling and sighing."[35] The motorway scene indicates that the same principle was applied to diegetic sounds symbolizing the future in a sci-fi context—the sounds of urbanscapes, technology, and speed.

However, it is not only electronic scores that allow the seamless merging of music with sound design. In recent decades a similar fusion results from the use of a musical language that can slip into or emulate noise through the em-ployment of various compositional and performing techniques or the elec-tronic processing of acoustic sounds. This is the type of score that foregrounds the materiality of sound, where the use of microtones, clusters, and extended

---

[32] We return once more to Kelvin's childhood home after the motorway scene in a sort of coda to his life on Earth that will afterwards exist only in his memory.

[33] Andrei Tarkovsky, *Sculpting in Time: Reflections on the Cinema* (London: Bodley Head, 1986), 159.

[34] Ibid., 160.

[35] Ibid., 162.

performing techniques produces a haptic quality that Miguel Mera, referring to Laura Marks's concept of visual hapticity, has termed "haptic music."[36] The sensuous impact of this type of score takes us into territory that is discussed in more detail in chapter 4, but for the purposes of this chapter I will comment on the collaborative aspect of the context in which integrated soundtracks with scores like these are able to flourish.

Mera illustrates the notion of haptic music through an illuminating analysis of Jonny Greenwood's scores for Paul Thomas Anderson's films *There Will Be Blood* (2007) and *The Master* (2012), focusing on sounds that approximate noise and performative techniques that emphasize their haptic "dirtiness."[37] Anderson himself revealed his *méloman* credentials and taste for nonconventional scoring in his previous films scored by Jon Brion, such as *Magnolia* (1999) and *Punch Drunk Love* (2002), while Greenwood produced exciting scores with a similar haptic quality while working with Lynne Ramsay on *We Need to Talk About Kevin* (2011) and *You Were Never Really Here* (2017). Other notable collaborations include those between composer Jóhann Jóhannsson and director Denis Villeneuve (*Sicario*, 2015; *Arrival*, 2016) and composer Mica Levi and director Jonathan Glazer (*Under the Skin*, 2013). These partnerships grew in environments that encouraged adventurousness and originality,[38] enabled the composer to be involved in the early stages of preproduction, eliminated the dictates of a temp track so typical of many productions,[39] and facilitated close collaboration between all key figures in the sound team.

According to sound designer Johnnie Burn, the creation of the soundtrack for *Under the Skin* was based on the ongoing communication between him, Levi, and music supervisor Peter Raeburn.[40] Part of Burn's working process involved "adjusting" the sounds of the environment in the sound design to the incoming and outgoing music by using equalization.[41] At other times it was Levi who responded to the sound design, as in the scene in the cabin in the woods

[36] Miguel Mera, "Materializing Film Music," in *The Cambridge Companion of Film Music*, ed. Mervyn Cooke and Diona Ford (Cambridge: Cambridge University Press, 2017), 157–172.
[37] Mera, "Materializing Film Music," 158.
[38] Jóhann Jóhannsson stated that while working on *Arrival*, director Denis Villeneuve challenged him to produce "something he hasn't heard in the cinema before." Matt Grobar, "'Sicario' Composer Jóhann Jóhannsson on Creating Propulsive Sound of Drug War Drama—AwardsLine," *Deadline*, December 23, 2015, http://deadline.com/2015/12/johann-johannsson-sicario-composer-oscars-best-score-1201664692/.
[39] For a discussion about the impact of temp tracks on scoring, see Miguel Mera and Ron Sadoff, "Shaping the Soundtrack? Hollywood Preview Audiences," in *The Routledge Companion to Screen Music and Sound*, ed. Miguel Mera, Ron Sadoff, and Ben Winters (New York and London: Routledge, 2017), 299–301.
[40] John Hough, "Under the Skin of Film Sound—An Interview with Johnnie Burn," in *The Palgrave Handbook of Sound Design and Music in Screen Media: Integrated Soundtracks*, ed. Liz Greene and Danijela Kulezic-Wilson (Basingstoke: Palgrave Macmillan, 2016), 381.
[41] Ibid.

where the music is built around the diegetic sound of wind (track "Bothy" on the soundtrack CD). According to Burn, it took a year of back and forth between the key members of the soundtrack team before they reached the mix stage to make sure "that every single thing was in some way sympathetic to the music around it."[42]

Although Jóhannsson's work on Villeneuve's films *Sicario* and *Arrival* was constrained by tighter postproduction schedules, it was still highly collaborative, built around his style of writing "around the sound design," which included trying to anticipate what the sound team will do and incorporate that into the score so it "doesn't feel like the music is a layer that's tacked on."[43] Conversely, there were instances where the sound design team provided ambient sounds and effects to fit the music that was already locked in, as in the scene in *Arrival* where Amy Adams's character Dr. Banks is flown to a military base and where the sounds of helicopters were adjusted in frequency and rhythm to support the "hypnotic," "dreamy" quality of Jóhannsson's music.[44]

Crucially, though, what enables the effectiveness of this type of collaboration is the musical language of Greenwood's, Jóhannsson's, and Levi's scores, which can easily blend with sound design; or it can be so harsh, abrasive, or percussive that it can be mistaken for a Foley. In Jóhannsson's case, his signature sound of visceral, sinister, dark rumbling timbres comes from an imaginative employment of instruments at the low end of the orchestral register—basses, contrabasses, low woodwinds, contrabassoons, contrabass clarinets, and contrabass saxophones—enhanced by the use of extended techniques. Contributing to the otherworldly nature of these sounds is the subtle processing of various acoustic instruments to create a hybrid sound that blurs the line between orchestral and electronic.[45] A similar approach of fusing the materiality of "haptic dirtiness" with electronic manipulation is applied by Levi in her score for *Under the Skin*. She uses a broad range of idiomatic writing for strings, including glissandos, rhythmic use of tremolos, microtonal screeches in the highest register, and harmonic clustering, but the most sinister touches are brought by slowing down the recorded melodies already warped through the use of microtones or glissandos, or manipulating the pitch "to make it feel uncomfortable."[46] Jonny Greenwood's

[42] Ibid.

[43] Grobar, "'Sicario' Composer Jóhann Jóhannsson on Creating Propulsive Sound of Drug War Drama."

[44] "The Making of Arrival's BAFTA-Winning Sound Mix," BAFTA Guru, April 1, 2017, https://www.youtube.com/watch?v=tvW1dSWNEqQ.

[45] Hrishikesh Hirway, "Song Exploder: Jóhann Jóhannsson on the Secrets of *Arrival*'s Score," *Vulture*, November 17, 2016, http://www.vulture.com/2016/11/arrival-score-johann-johannsson-song-exploder.html.

[46] Mica Levi, "How Mica Levi Got Under the Skin of Her First Film Soundtrack," *The Guardian*, March 15, 2014, https://www.theguardian.com/music/2014/mar/15/mica-levi-under-the-skin-soundtrack.

score for Lynne Ramsay's *You Were Never Really Here* (2017) goes even further in emphasizing the sonic hapticity of music, which often morphs into noise, and the visceral effect of using strings and piano as percussive instruments. Violent plucking or sawing of strings, detuned arpeggios, tapping the bodies of string instruments, and various other percussive effects are considerably augmented by subtle electronic manipulation, creating noises that can be mistaken for diegetic. This ambiguity creates a particularly intense and even uncanny effect in the scene where Joe (Joaquin Phoenix) is about to find out the terrible truth about who murdered a paedophile politician in his own home [01:11:50].[47] As he slowly walks through the house, the thuds of his footsteps and the creaking of the floorboards are intermittently mixed with faint noises of an unidentifiable source. When Joe stops at the top of the stairs, observing the ground floor, it is suggested that he is trying to determine the origin of the noises. At the ground floor he hesitates for a moment before heading towards the front door, then suddenly turns around and walks in the opposite direction, seemingly alerted by loud, vibrating thumps. While he passes rooms in which he sees his recently deceased mother and then his younger self, the thumps become more frequent and intense, accompanied by dissonant, scraping sounds in the strings. The noise culminates at the moment he discovers Nina (Ekaterina Samsonov), the abducted girl he was trying to save, eating dinner, her hands covered with blood, a blood-encrusted cutthroat razor resting beside her plate (see Figures 2.1 and 2.2). As Joe approaches Nina, the noise gradually disappears, giving way to the sounds of Nina eating. Only at this point does it become clear that all the acousmatic sounds in the scene that Joe apparently reacted to were actually part of Greenwood's score, the disorienting effect of blurring diegetic and nondiegetic sounds indicative of Joe's disturbed state of mind affected by grief, violence, and his childhood trauma.

While the line between score and sound design in previous examples is often crossed due to the nature of the musical language employed by composers such as Greenwood, Levi, and Jóhannsson, in other cases this approach can be required by the narrative context, as in Richard Ayoade's *The Double* (2013), a black-comedic take on identity crisis set in the dystopian world of a bureaucratic, totalitarian society that evokes the bleakness of Terry Gilliam's *Brazil* (1985) and Orson Welles's film adaptation of Kafka's *The Trial* (1962). For the most part Andrew Hewitt's original music for Ayoade's film keeps within the traditional vein of a theme score subject to variations and performed by solo violin, piano, and strings. However, the first time we see the troubled protagonist Simon (Jesse Eisenberg) at work, the soundtrack is dominated by percussive sounds

---

[47] This is the timing of the scene on *You Were Never Really Here* DVD, Studiocanal, PAL, 2018.

Figures 2.1 and 2.2. *You Were Never Really Here*: Joe (Joaquin Phoenix) finds Nina (Ekaterina Samsonov) eating dinner after murdering her kidnapper.

that seem to be generated by office equipment, suggesting a highly mechanized and controlled working environment [00:04:28].[48] Increasingly rhythmicized, the buzzes, clicks, bleeps, and hisses surrounding Simon eventually form a consistent stream of metrically regular noises, making it difficult to discern where the sound design stops and the originally written score starts.

In some cases musical material that treads the line between score and sound design is provided through the combination of original and pre-existing music as in David Michôd's *The Rover* (2014). The original motion picture soundtrack for *The Rover* features pieces written by the film's composer Antony Partos and sound designer Sam Petty, as well as pre-existing pieces by experimental rock band Tortoise, saxophonist and multi-reedist Colin Stetson, and Italian composer Giacinto Scelsi. All the pieces are very atmospheric, enveloping the apocalyptic world of poverty and lawlessness with a gloomy, melancholic mood. The

---

[48] This is the timing of the scene in the DVD release of *The Double*, Studiocanal, PAL, 2014.

pre-existing pieces by Scelsi and Stetson, however, push the moodiness of the score into a sound world in which the accent on timbre and extended silences produce rather unconventional audiovisual combinations underlined by the interaction between the score and the sound design. Scelsi's distinctive musical language, built around the exploration of sonorities of individual instruments and the whole orchestra through extended performing techniques, does not lend itself easily to film because of the composer's penchant for long pauses and compositions that revolve around just one pitch, which prevents his scores from performing some of the fundamental film music roles, such as providing a sense of continuity and forward movement. Previously employed only in Martin Scorsese's *Shutter Island* (2010) and Luca Guadagnino's *A Bigger Splash* (2015), with an accent on the affective impact of its rich and unusual orchestral textures, in *The Rover* Scelsi's music is absorbed into a harsh dystopian soundscape where "everything rasps, drags, grates, and grinds."[49]

The Rover's story revolves around protagonist Eric's (Guy Pearce) attempts to retrieve his stolen car from a gang of thieves on the run, accompanied by the brother of one of the gang members, Rey (Robert Pattinson), who was left wounded at the site of the robbery. It is clear from the beginning that the societal infrastructure in *The Rover*'s world is broken, that there are no regular supplies of food or petrol, and that in many places money has no value. Thus, the question of why Eric is risking everything to retrieve his battered Rover hangs unanswered until the very end, providing the fuel for a story about the growing connection between the two adversaries played by Pearce and Pattinson. *The Rover* has also been described as a modern western and in that sense Eric fits the bill of an antihero with unclear motivation and a dubious moral compass who nevertheless engenders a certain sympathy. The score, however, counters the genre conventions with its harsh quality and the unpredictability of both the diegetic and nondiegetic choices, and by resisting any identification or empathy with the characters, constructing a world "where everything is rusty and corroding, and held by gaffer tape, or wire, or not being held together, just sort of creating vibrations and sounds—a very uneasy, broken, damaged environment."[50]

The excerpt from Scelsi's piece "Ko-Tha, Three Dances of Shiva" is first heard early in the film when Rey escapes the site of the robbery after being abandoned by his brother Henry's (Scoot McNairy) gang (see Figure 2.3) [00:12:17].[51] The music connects this scene with the image of Eric waking up in the desert after receiving a blow to the head while pursuing Henry's gang, which stole his car. Originally composed for guitar and heard in *The Rover* in the transcription for

---

[49] Sam Petty, Skype conversation with the author, August 11, 2016.
[50] Ibid.
[51] This is the timing of the scene on *The Rover* DVD, Entertainment One, PAL, 2015.

double bass, "Ko-Tha" features some of the signature elements of Scelsi's single-pitch pieces, such as a focus on timbre and rhythm, microtonal oscillations, harmonic allusions, and subtle or sudden changes in dynamics. According to sound designer Sam Petty, who also authored some of the musical cues in the film, Scelsi's music was slightly edited at places to fit the narrative requirements, but its distinctive, nonmetric flow is not only preserved but also used as an opportunity for musical interaction between the score and the sound design.

Treating the double bass as a percussive instrument, Scelsi's piece unfolds through a succession of rhythmic figures based on the note E. Melodically static, the piece is nevertheless highly engaging as it encourages the listener to follow the "life cycle" of every sound until it perishes, each sound different from the previous one due to the use of various performing techniques and rhythmic variations. There are moments in the scene where the editing underlines the rhythmic and affective synergy between the image and the score, most notably when Eric, waking up after his concussion, lifts his face towards the camera (as seen in Figure 2.4), which is accompanied by a crescendo produced by thumping on the body of the double bass. But more interesting is how the *mise-en-scène* takes in and occasionally highlights the music's irregular flow, foregrounding its lingering decrescendos and lengthy pauses as if asserting its refusal to engage with more conventional functions of film music. Instead, the lack of melodic phrasing or development and the focus on the instrument's pure sonority in Scelsi's piece seem to merge with the spacious sound design filled with silence and the subdued buzzing of insects punctuated with the occasional cry of an eagle.

Describing his approach to sound design, Petty compares sonically diverse and yet interdependent aural lines in film to "musical voices" and the process of constructing a soundtrack to composing and arranging:

> You have all of these musical voices to work with. Some are more tonal than others. There's a lot of percussion, all effects are percussion, as are Foley.... [S]ometimes you can leave things unresolved just as you would as a composer— resolve things with a major chord, or leave them unresolved or sustained.[52]

The scene described here illustrates convincingly the relevance of approaching the soundtrack with such a musical sensibility, especially when dealing with delicate musical material like Scelsi's piece. Petty confirms that this scene in particular was one that encouraged lots of "fiddling, sliding and slipping," "two frames that way, one-and-a-half frames back,"[53] in an effort to create a seamless interaction between image, score, and sound design. The result is distinctly musical in

[52] Petty, Skype conversation with the author.
[53] Ibid.

Figures 2.3 and 2.4. *The Rover*: Rey (Robert Pattinson) escapes the site of a robbery while Eric (Guy Pearce) wakes up after being assaulted by the thieves who took his car.

the sense that the sound design reflects the type of musicality imposed by Scelsi's score so that a car door opening sounds like a sonic accent and the flapping of a bird's wings like a coda to a rhythmic phrase performed on the double bass. The soundtrack absorbs the spirit of Scelsi's music to the point that even the cuts in the score—as when Eric is looking for the keys of the truck left behind by the thieves—are perceived as musical pauses created to give way to the Foley sounds of Eric's crunching footsteps and the cries of an eagle.

A similarly musically executed interaction can be found in *Arrival* in the scene where Dr. Banks visits the alien ship for the first time [00:27:41].[54] During her ascent into the ship's low-gravity zone, metrically regular rhythmic thumps and rumbling glissandos in the score are separated by long pauses and punctuated by Dr. Banks's heavy breathing. As the crew approaches the meeting point with the

---

[54] This is the timing of the scene on *Arrival* DVD, Entertainment One, PAL, 2017.

aliens, foghorn-like chords based on clusters of semitone and whole tone intervals flood the audiovisual space with textural density and frequency, which, especially in a cinema auditorium, has an immensely visceral effect, and are rounded off with low-register thunderous noises that could be part of the score but could also be the sounds of the approaching creatures. The same chords are heard again just before the alien Heptapods emerge from a thick cloud of smoke, followed by their whooshes and whale-like groans. The line between sound design and score, which is in *The Rover* disregarded by the musical merging of Scelsi's music with Foley sounds, is here further blurred by drawing on and emphasizing the timbral similarities between the sound effects and the score, and the harmonization of their dynamic and rhythmic pacing. The approach to the sound design is inherently musical in both cases, the main difference being that the *Arrival* scene is distinguished by its textural density and the visceral quality of its low-frequency, organic-based sounds, while in *The Rover* the source from which both musical and Foley sounds rise is silence.

The Musicalization of Sound Effects

The previous section explored different ways in which the score can be integrated into the sound design, sometimes reaching the point where the line between them is so blurred that one can be mistaken for the other. But this same result can be achieved by treating sound effects in a musical way. Donnelly's observations quoted at the beginning of the previous section suggest that the symbolic and emotional potency of sound effects, which "outweigh their representation status," make the function of effects comparable to those of the score. James Wierzbicki makes the same point when he states that "affective" filmic sound "has the potential to trigger in its listeners emotional responses, or affects, at least as deep as those stirred by a film's extra diegetic music."[55] Commenting on the function of the diegetic sounds in Malick's *The Thin Red Line* (1998), Wierzbicki connects their affective quality with their association with certain characters or situations:

> The rustle of grass, whether in the swamp or on the hillside, becomes a symbol
> for action; the whistle of wind, whether on land or sea, suggests fear.... [T]he
> sound of water—dripping from canoe paddles, trickling over blood-stained

---

[55] James Wierzbicki, "Sound Effects/Sound Affects: 'Meaningful' Noise in the Cinema," in *The Palgrave Handbook of Sound Design and Music in Screen Media: Integrated Soundtracks*, ed. Liz Greene and Danijela Kulezic-Wilson (Basingstoke, Hampshire: Palgrave Macmillan, 2016), 156. See also James Wierzbicki, "Sound as Music in the Films of Terrence Malick," in *The Cinema of Terrence Malick: Poetic Visions of America*, ed. Hannah Patterson (New York: Columbia University Press, 2003), 110–122.

stones, splashing wildly under the feet of members of a reconnaissance mission—seems always to be linked with the character of Private Witt.[56]

According to Wierzbicki, though, Malick's use of sound in *Days of Heaven* (1978) is not only affective but also "demonstrably musical."[57] Noting the prominence of environmental sounds such as the repetitive thumps of mill machinery, the rhythmic whirring of a wind gauge, and various sounds associated with the elemental forces of wind, earth, and fire, Wierzbicki compares their organizational logic and the effect of their placement to *musique concrète* compositions, which resonates with my argument in chapter 4.

The affective impact of sound effects can be augmented by emphasizing their sensuous attributes and even by a strategic use of volume increase or decrease, but it is even more dependent on the context, in both narrative terms and the overall sensory stimulation. The crackling of breaking glass when the protagonist's wife, who committed suicide by swallowing liquid oxygen, is brought back to life by the mysterious planet Solaris in Tarkovksy's eponymous film (1972);[58] the incessant ringing of the phone in *Once Upon a Time in America* (Sergio Leone, 1984) haunting the character tortured by a guilty conscience; the rumble of the train in *Anna Karenina* (Joe Wright, 2012) announcing the unstoppable momentum of fate carrying the eponymous heroine towards her end—all these sounds are as deeply affective as any provided by the score. But apart from the affective value bestowed on sound effects through the narrative context, the line between them and the score can also be blurred by emphasizing musical qualities of those sounds, most often achieved through the use of repetition, rhythmic accentuation, and musical editing.

Although this practice has become particularly noticeable in recent decades, examples of the musical use of sound effects can be found throughout the history of cinema. In one of the famous scenes in *Delicatessen* (Jean-Pierre Jenet and Marc Caro, 1991), the interconnectedness of all the characters living in a dilapidated building in postapocalyptic France is evocatively conveyed through a rhythmic audiovisual montage. The repetitive actions and sounds of the tenants painting walls, practising cello, beating a carpet, and pumping up a bike tyre are all synchronized with the sound of the building's landlord Clapet (Jean-Claude Dreyfus) having sex with his lover, the squeaking of the bedsprings dictating the tempo of all the actions in the same way Clapet and his butcher shop dominate the lives of his tenants. This scene from *Delicatessen* is reminiscent of

---

56 Wierzbicki, "Sound as Music in the Films of Terrence Malick," 115.

57 Ibid., 110.

58 See Michel Chion's insightful analysis of this scene in *Audio-Vision: Sound on Screen* (New York: Columbia University Press, 1992), 39.

(and possibly an homage to) the opening scene of Rouben Mamoulian's *Love Me Tonight* (1932), also set in Paris, which shows a montage of road workers, housewives, carpenters, street vendors, and repairmen working in sync, producing an increasingly complex counterpoint of road drilling, sweeping, carpet beating, knife sharpening, banging, hammering, and traffic noise. In a comedy where the main plot points are drawn from the class gulf between the two would-be lovers, this scene not only is strikingly musical but also comments eloquently on the idea of a finely tuned working-class machine that keeps the city running.

The rhythms of urban life were the inspiration for a musical approach to sound effects even before Mamoulian's carefully staged and choreographed opening scene. In his pioneering sonic portrait of Berlin, *Weekend* (1930), Walter Ruttmann offered a model for thinking about quotidian, "documentary" sounds in a musical way decades before Luc Ferrari pursued that idea in the field of *musique concrète* with his landmark collection *Presque Rien* (1967–1998). Technically a radio piece, *Weekend* is known as "a film without an image" because it was created by using an optical sound film. Ruttmann's recordings made in the apartments, factories, train stations, and the city's busy streets are rhythmically edited, emphasizing the musicality and musical combinations of different pitches, textures, and tone colours derived from those places. *Weekend* was greeted by the directors of the Soviet montage school as an example of their dialectical editing principles transposed to sound, while in turn the musicality of Ruttmann's approach was echoed in Dziga Vertov's documentary *Enthusiasm: Symphony of the Donbass* (1930), an ode to the Soviet Union's rapid industrialization. Refusing to rely on the conventions of scoring and synchronous dialogue that had started to take hold in sound film, Vertov was determined to "move over from the velvet coffin of the soundless studio and to plunge into the terrible thunder and iron clanging of the Donbass" with newly developed mobile sound equipment.[59] The central part of the film, recorded in Ukrainian factories, mines, quarries, and foundries, is a particularly striking example of the aesthetics of Futurism and the utopian spirit of socialism, an audiovisual symphonic poem of industrial progress in which the sounds of machines, furnaces, engines, industrial carts, pumps, and giant hammers dominate the soundscape. Their musical qualities are emphasized through rhythmic editing and combined with segments of audiovisual asynchrony where the musicality of sound is implied in the workers' repetitive actions or images of machinery. Vertov's focus on repetitive actions and sounds that are rhythmicized through mechanization or just plain repetition emphasizes the latent musicality of such scenes, which

---

[59] For a detailed analysis of Vertov's film sound aesthetics, see Lucy Fischer, "*Enthusiasm*: From Kino-Eye to Radio-Eye," in *Film Sound: Theory and Practice*, ed. Elisabeth Weis and John Belton (New York: Columbia University Press, 1985), 250.

would inspire imaginative explorations of this potential in feature films of all
genres. The opening scene showing creaky coal buckets moving on cable wires
from Béla Tarr's *Damnation* (1988), which will be addressed in more detail in
chapter 4, looks as if it could have been taken directly from Vertov's film, except
that in Tarr's universe of depression and hopelessness, the repetitive rattling and
scraping sounds of buckets travelling up and down the wires, accompanied by a
slightly ominous electronic background, project a sense of lethargy rather than
working zeal.

French director Robert Bresson, whose motto "What is for the eye must not
duplicate what is for the ear"[60] echoes the Soviet montage school's call to explore
the independence of sound's narrative and expressive powers in film, was particularly drawn to the rhythmic quality of soundtrack. Insisting on the use of
the word "composition" rather than "construction" when talking about his films,
Bresson stated that he listens to his films "the way a pianist listens to the sonata
he is performing," adjusting picture to sound rather than the other way round.[61]
In his 1974 film *Lancelot du Lac*, his focus on the rhythmic effect of the diegetic
sounds is such a prominent component of the film's macro-rhythmic organization that it prompted Jay Plaat to comment that

> the foregrounding rhythms of doors that are opened and shut, the contin-
> uous walking towards or away from something and the rattling sounds of the
> knights' armors, are taken to such an extreme that the film's central action, the
> legend of Lancelot, Camelot et cetera almost appears to be little more than a
> coat rack upon which these rhythms can be hanged.[62]

Lancelot du Lac opens with images of violence that wouldn't be out of place in a
Tarantino film, considering the graphic representation of a methodical slaughter,
with decapitated, hung, burned, and slain bodies gushing with blood, swaying
from trees, or still sizzling in a fire. There is no dialogue in the prologue and no
attempt to establish the context for the killings or the identities of the knights
whose heads are covered by helmets, because the focus is deliberately placed on
the action and the affective impact of the images of corpses and the sounds of
swords clashing, armour rattling, and horses galloping. Only after being exposed
to this onslaught of violence are audioviewers informed that they have witnessed

---

[60] Robert Bresson, "Notes on Sound," in *Film Sound: Theory and Practice*, ed. Elisabeth Weis and
John Belton (New York: Columbia University Press, 1985), 149.

[61] Robert Bresson quoted in Michel Ciment, "I Seek Not Description but Vision: Robert Bresson
on *L'Argent*," in *Robert Bresson*, ed. James Quandt (Bloomington: Indiana University Press, 2011),
499–511.

[62] Jay Plaat, "The Rhythm of the Void: On the Rhythm of Any-Space-Whatever in Bresson,
Tarkovsky and Winterbottom" (Master's thesis, Radboud University Nijmegen, 2015–2016), 38.

King Arthur's knights in action, returning to Camelot from their unsuccessful mission to retrieve the Holy Grail. Such a dynamic opening is in stark contrast with the rest of the film, where all significant action either takes place off screen or is completely eschewed in favour of scenes that focus on "transition spaces" showing characters going from one place to another.[63] However, considering that the male characters are almost never seen without their armour, or protective leg plates at least, their comings and goings are accompanied by the incessant sounds of rattling and clanking. Omnipresent almost to the point of absurdity, even in scenes of intimate conversations such as those between Lancelot (Luc Simon) and Queen Guinevere (Laura Duke Condominas), the clanging of the metal plates becomes like an obstinate *musique concrète* reminder of the opening scene and what the armour symbolizes.

Another genre where sound effects tend to be approached with a heightened sense for their rhythmic and musical potential is martial arts films, or action films that feature martial arts combat, especially since Lana and Lilly Wachowski's (formerly known as the Wachowski brothers) innovative approach to audiovisual rhythm and a musical use of diegetic sounds and silences in *The Matrix* (1999) set new standards for staging and editing fight scenes.[64] The balletic choreography of the fight scenes in *The Matrix*, overseen by Yuen Woo-Ping, one of the most celebrated Chinese martial arts choreographers and film directors, is emphasized additionally through editing owing to the rhythmical combination of bullet-time effects with slow motion. The focal points of these scenes are the moments of stasis that punctuate the action, often accentuated with diegetic sounds of fighting or strategic use of silences. What made *The Matrix* look so innovative[65] was how its audiovisual language reflected the underlying musicality inherent to martial arts and the fact that rhythm and sound are key to the effectiveness of its attack and defence strategies. Colin McGuire emphasizes this aspect of martial arts and the role of sound in establishing the combative rhythm when he talks about "the thud of strikes landing or being defended, the whizz of armed or unarmed attacks cutting through the air, the clash of weapons against each other, the patter of footwork, and the snap of clothing from vigorous motion," which are accompanied by noises made by the fighters and punctuated by their vocalizations, slaps, claps, and stomps. What is interesting to note here is

---

[63] For an insight into how the rhythm of *Lancelot du Lac* relates to Gilles Deleuze's concept of "any-space-whatever" see Plaat, "The Rhythm of the Void," 37–48.

[64] For more detailed comments on the musicality of the Wachowskis's approach see Danijela Kulezic-Wilson, "The Music of Film Silence," *Music and the Moving Image* 2, no. 3 (Fall 2009): 1–10, https://www.jstor.org/stable/10.5406/musimoviimag.2.3.0001?seq=1#page_scan_tab_contents.

[65] Soon after *The Matrix*, other films such as *Crouching Tiger, Hidden Dragon* (Ang Lee, 2000), *The Matrix* sequels *The Matrix Reloaded* (2003) and *The Matrix Revolutions* (2003), and *Kill Bill* (Quentin Tarantino) vols. 1 (2003) and 2 (2004) followed its lead and even used the same choreographer, Yuen Woo-Ping, to stage their fight scenes.

that, according to McGuire, what is generally thought of as "music," like percussion or a song of Brazilian capoeira, in the martial arts context is simply understood as part of the "martial sound," which is "any sonic material that is ... a component of training, competition, combat, ritual, and/or performance in any type of martial art whatsoever," including instruments like the gong and drum of kung fu, as well as the rhythm of combat. Thus, when in films such as *Crouching Tiger, Hidden Dragon* (Ang Lee, 2000), *Hero* (Yimou Zhang, 2002), and *House of Flying Daggers* (Yimou Zhang, 2004) fight scenes are paired with percussive accompaniment, they evoke the customs of those traditions in which percussion and other instruments are considered an inherent part of the "martial sound" rather than "music."

At the same time, all combative rhythms and sounds associated with martial arts have a potential musical quality about them that some films deliberately emphasize. The battle in the bamboo forest in *House of Flying Daggers* [01:00:28–01.07:07][66] is an illustrative example of this approach as the sound design here is particularly elaborate and certain sounds are accentuated to convey the point of audition of the female protagonist Xiao Mei (Zhang Ziyi), who is supposedly blind. The choreography of the combat is based on the *Wudang* style of martial arts, which combines physical skill and strength with spiritual practice, allowing real masters of this art—according to legend—to defy the laws of physics, climb walls and roofs, skim across water, and battle at the tops of trees. The action, which unfolds with balletic gracefulness between and on top of densely packed bamboo trees, is rhythmically punctuated with shouts, grunts, thumps, and audiovisual accents of sharpened combat sticks piercing bamboo trees or being sliced into strips (see Figure 2.5). A distinctly musical touch is provided by the sound of bamboo vibrating, which, amplified to convey the blind protagonist's sense of focus, sounds like an Ondes Martenot travelling through hollow bamboo stalks. Halfway through the scene, when Xiao Mei is joined by her partner who she thinks has abandoned her, the soundscape is transformed by the introduction of nondiegetic music. As if responding to the metallic timbre of organ-like keyboard and voice, the bamboo stick combat gives way to a sword fight punctuated by the hiss and clash of steel blades.

This type of interaction between sound effects and score is often based on using the timbral or rhythmic quality of sound effects as a starting point for developing the musical cue, as suggested by Johnnie Burn in his comments about working with Mica Levi on *Under the Skin*. Another common approach includes the musicalization of sound effects through their repetition, leading to their incorporation into the score: the steady footsteps of a man (Lee Marvin) betrayed

---

[66] This is the timing of the scene on *House of Flying Daggers* DVD, Focus Features, PAL, 2004.

Figure 2.5. *House of Flying Daggers*: Battle in the bamboo forest.

by his partner on his way to get revenge in *Point Blank* (John Boorman, 1967) becoming a rhythmic ostinato in Johnny Mandel's electronic score; the ride in an open railway handcar towards the "Zone" in Tarkovsky's *Stalker*, blending seamlessly with Artemiev's subtle electronic augmentations; the percussive sounds of typing and paper stumping in Joe Wright's *Atonement* (2007) and *Anna Karenina,* respectively, absorbed into Dario Marianelli's orchestral scores.[67] In some cases the musicalization of sound effects amplifies their affective impact as well. In *Point Blank*, the shot of Lee Marvin's character pacing, his footsteps reverberating through an underground tunnel, is intercut with images of his wife who was unfaithful to him with the man who left him for dead. The juxtaposition of the protagonist's purposeful stride with images from his unsuspecting wife's daily routine endows his footsteps with a sense of urgency and determination fuelled by his thirst for revenge. In *Atonement*, the sound of typing precedes all the scenes narrated from protagonist Briony's (Saoirse Ronan/Romola Garai) perspective, becoming a symbol of her literary aspirations but also a potent comment on the power of projection, the unreliability of a single person's perspective, and the potentially devastating consequences of misinterpretation.

[67] The opening of Fritz Lang's *The Testament of Dr. Mabuse* (1933) offers a memorable example of a reverse approach in which music morphs into sound effects. Following the title credits accompanied by a short orchestral overture, the opening scene shows a man with a gun hiding in what looks like a storage room that is shaken by the vibrations of an unknown sonic source. The intensity of the sound is reinforced visually by showing the ceiling lights swinging and numerous bottles rattling from the tremors. Its penetrative force owes some of its power, however, to the sounds of the timpani, which bled seamlessly from the overture into the opening credits (see Chion, *Film, A Sound Art*, 204). This haunting sonic fusion and Lang's early exploration of acousmetre in this film are some of the reasons *The Testament of Dr. Mabuse* is revered as an example of pioneering experiments in sound design, while its one-minute-long symphony of car horns in a traffic jam—also the setting of a successful assassination attempt—looks and sounds like a scene that would also be equally at home in a Tati or a Hitchcock film.

Musicalized sound effects can be the result of an approach to film that extends the application of musical principles to its overall structure, *mise-en-scène*, editing, and so on. The aforementioned films by Joe Wright—*Atonement* and especially *Anna Karenina*—are examples of a musical approach that informs every aspect of the film's organization, rhythm, and flow. A distinctive type of musical approach to film is also found in Sergio Leone's spaghetti westerns scored by Ennio Morricone. Described as "operatic" because of the way music takes centre stage in key scenes, overriding the conventions of narrative and action development, Leone's musical style also encompasses the treatment of sound effects and soundtrack in its totality. No scene illustrates this better than the opening of *Once Upon a Time in the West* (1968), where the buzzing of insects, gurgling of water in a trough, creaking of a rocking chair, and ticking of a telegraph machine weave a fine linear counterpoint to the ostinato of repetitive windmill squeaks, adding to a slow buildup of tension after three bandits take over a train station to set up an ambush. When one of the bandits, annoyed by the sound of the telegraph, pulls out its wires, the diegetic *musique concrète* weave is suddenly interrupted, only to start again with new "voices" of water dripping, knuckle crackling, a fly buzzing, and a train approaching, culminating with the arrival of the train and the first sounding of Harmonica's (Charles Bronson) famous "Judgment" motif.

While the musical flow of Joe Wright's films scored by Dario Marianelli is attuned to the language of Western classical music, and Leone's "operatic" style combines *bel canto* sensibility with pop-song hooks,[68] the musicality of Edgar Wright's and Darren Aronofsky's early films is unmistakably informed by more contemporary popular music genres. Wright's *Baby Driver* (2017) is one of the more recent examples of a systematically applied musical approach to film inspired by a wide range of genres, from alternative rock to early classics like The Champs' "Tequila." Wright revealed that the screenplay was written around a collection of songs chosen in advance, originally inspired by the Jon Spencer Blues Explosion's song "Bellbottoms," which accompanies the opening bank robbery/getaway sequence. His interest in setting action to music was already apparent in his previous films *Shaun of the Dead* (2004) and *Scott Pilgrim vs. the World* (2010), but *Baby Driver* pushes the bar much higher, with every aspect of the action presented through the perspective of the protagonist whose experience of the world is defined by the music he constantly listens to in order to drown out his tinnitus. Like Joe Wright's *Anna Karenina*, which was conceived in the director's close collaboration with composer Dario Marianelli and choreographer Sidi Larbi Cherkaoui, *Baby Driver*'s musicalization involved composer Steven Price, who helped Wright organize the pre-existing musical material, and

[68] See Jeff Smith's inspired analysis of Morricone's scoring style in *The Sounds of Commerce: Marketing Popular Film Music* (New York: Columbia University Press, 1998), 131–153.

choreographer Ryan Heffington, who was responsible for the dance-like quality of the on-screen movement, from big action scenes right down to the protagonist Baby (Ansel Elgort) tapping his hands on the table.[69] The result is exhilaratingly stylish and sensuous, with music governing every aspect of the *mise-en-scène* and the sound design, resulting in the musicalization of sound effects across the board, from minor details such as incorporating the beeping of an ATM machine into a song being listened to by Baby, to synchronizing the gunshots in a major shootout with the music.

Amongst all these memorable examples, Darren Aronofsky's hip-hop editing and the resulting musicalization of sound effects in his first two films *Pi* (1998) and *Requiem for a Dream* (2000) are arguably still among the most groundbreaking and influential stylistic innovations of recent decades. Although Aronofsky's self-proclaimed fascination with hip-hop is generally cited as the main inspiration behind the innovative audiovisual style of his first two films, I have argued elsewhere that techno music is another popular music genre that contributed to their distinctive stylistic profiles.[70] The influence of hip-hop undoubtedly accounts for Aronofsky's decision to apply principles of sampling to editing, repeatedly punctuating the narrative with audiovisual segments that represent the protagonists' battle with obsessive behaviour.[71] His internalization of the aesthetics of hip-hop can also be observed in the emphasis on the rhythmic qualities of sound, and the use of repetitions and breaks in the flow on both micro- and macro-levels. The principles of integration that erase the boundaries between diegetic and nondiegetic sound effects, and the dissolution of hierarchical relationships between voice, score, and sound effects—especially in *Pi*—seem equally, if not more so, indebted to techno's disregard for the origins of sonic sources and their assimilation into a continuous musical flow.[72]

[69] Clark Collis, "How Director Edgar Wright Steered *Baby Driver* to Global Success," *Entertainment,* December 4, 2017, http://ew.com/movies/2017/12/04/edgar-wright-baby-driver-success-sequel-spacey/.
[70] For a detailed analysis of the influence of hip-hop and techno on *Pi*'s formal structure and soundtrack see Danijela Kulezic-Wilson, "A Musical Approach to Filmmaking: Hip Hop and Techno Composing Techniques and Models of Structuring in Darren Aronofsky's *Pi*," *Music and the Moving Image* 1, no. 1 (2008): 19–34, https://www.jstor.org/stable/10.5406/musimoviimag.1.1.0019.
[71] Although the origins of music sampling can be traced back to the first experiments with manipulating recordings in *musique concrète*, Aronofsky has repeatedly insisted that the inspiration for his editing style derives from his fascination with hip-hop culture, which permeated his experience of growing up in Brooklyn in the 1980s. See, for instance, John Anderson, "The Many Worlds of Darren Aronofsky," *DGA Quarterly*, Fall 2013, https://www.dga.org/craft/dgaq/all-articles/1304-fall-2013/darren-aronofsky.aspx.
[72] In his diary about making *Pi* Aronofsky mentions that for a long time his affinity for hip-hop was quite exclusive to the point of making fun of his friend and future producer Eric Watson because he was "into the early electronic music scene." His eventual realization that "electronica was on its way to replacing hip hop as the new underground" was possibly one of the reasons *Pi*'s soundtrack is utterly infused by techno music, from the original score composed by Clint Mansell to tracks by other artists like Autechre, Orbital, Banco de Gaia, and Spacetime Continuum (Darren Aronofsky, π: *Screenplay & The Guerilla Diaries* [London: Faber & Faber, 1998], 5).

In *Pi*, the samples representing addiction show the protagonist Max (Shaun Guilette) taking drugs prescribed for his debilitating migraine attacks and obsessively locking his front door. The addictive behaviour in *Requiem for a Dream* encompasses all four characters, three young drug addicts and the mother of one of them, whose obsession with food and trash TV causes her physical and psychological downfall. What makes these segments striking in musical terms is the audiovisual editing in which images symbolizing the characters' addictions—opening a bottle of pills, popping pills into the mouth, powder hitting a table or sizzling in a spoon, flicking a lighter, opening a box of chocolates, turning on a television, and so on—are matched with sound effects that are exaggerated and rhythmicized. Staccato versions of swallowing, snorting, sipping, pouring, and buzzing are organized into metrically regular patterns that prioritize their musicality over traditional mimetic purpose. Even images of eyes moving or pupils dilating are given their inflated sonic equivalents. Technically diegetic but unabashedly unrealistic, these sounds are rhythmically interspersed with noises such as the blaring of a car alarm, ringing of a cash register, and a sampled human voice, which don't even have visible diegetic sources but are symbolically connected to the actions represented on screen. Short, sharp, and loud, all these rhythmicized sounds come with a percussive quality that brings to mind effects and stylistic devices typical of hip-hop music: scratching, punching, and rupturing the flow with unexpected breaks.[73] The reappearance of these "hip-hop samples" throughout the film has a clear narrative function, underlying the compulsive behaviour of the characters and the overwhelming nature of their habits. However, by drawing attention to stylistic devices and downplaying the traditional mimetic role of sound effects to emphasize their musical and percussive quality, Aronofsky endows these hip-hop samples with additional dramaturgical and affective quality.

While the recurrence of audiovisual samples is reminiscent of the function of cuts and breaks in hop-hop music, the scores in both films are more techno oriented, interacting with sound effects in a manner typical of electronic music that erases the limits of what can be considered a "legitimate" musical source, allowing any noise, vibration, or even a binary code to become music. This is particularly apparent in *Pi*, where nondiegetic sounds of screeching, scraping, drilling, and whizzing associated with Max's headaches are integrated into Mansell's electronic score accompanying the scenes of Max's migraine attacks. While these sound effects might very well be part of the score, the setting of these scenes in an

---

[73] Tricia Rose points out that the musical flow of rap music, which is based on repetition, loops, and circulating rhythms, is systematically ruptured by cuts or breaks, but since these cuts and breaks are themselves looped, their repetitions "reposition" them as "equilibrium inside the rupture" (*Black Noise: Rap Music and Black Culture in Contemporary America* [Hanover, NH: Wesleyan University Press, 1994], 70).

underground station and Max's apartment respectively [00:32:28–00:33:01 and 00:49:55–00:51:20][74] imply that the noises interwoven with the pulsing score are actual diegetic sounds as heard from Max's perspective, distorted and amplified by his pain. Sometimes sound effects and music become interchangeable, as in one of the hallucination scenes in *Pi* when it turns out that the amplified sound of drops of blood hitting the ground actually comes from Banco de Gaia's track "Drippy" [00:23:45], or in *Requiem for a Dream* when Mansell uses the sound of a building alarm triggered mischievously by Marion Silver (Jennifer Connelly) as the beginning of a musical cue [00:12:40].[75] In all these examples, as well as in hip-hop editing, the use of digital technology is, of course, essential in the manipulation of sound effects and their incorporation into scores, but in the same way it is essential in the popular musical genres that inspired those approaches.

Conclusion

The examples discussed in this chapter capture the richness of the various guises in which integrated soundtrack can manifest itself in contemporary cinema and the confluence of influences that inspired them. They also confirm that some of the most notable attempts at pushing against the constraints of a departmentalized approach to soundtrack and scoring conventions defined by the language of late Romanticism were inspired by musical logic and tendencies informed by the spirits of both contemporary art and popular music.

Although for large part of its history the language of mainstream film scoring was famously immune to the adventurous spirit that defined twentieth-century music, the tide of innovation carried by continuous progress in technology, the growing influence of various musical genres and trends, and the hunger for new solutions to old aesthetic problems eventually broke down the pillars of classical soundtrack aesthetics set up during the Golden Era, disrupting the established modes of production and the hierarchy between soundtrack elements. Considering Hollywood's affinity for more traditional forms of music, it is not surprising that attempts to blur the lines between soundtrack elements were initially manifested in the musicalization of sound effects, which did not automatically challenge the traditional roles of the score. Early examples of cinematic experimentation with the musicality of soundtrack, like those by Rutmann, Mamoulian, and Vertov, reflect some of the spirit of Futurism and a musical approach to everyday sounds recorded on the streets of metropoles or in mines and factories, anticipating the rise of *musique concrète* and twentieth-century music's

---

[74] This is the timing of the scenes in the *Pi* DVD, Pathé, PAL, 1999.
[75] This is the timing of the scene in *Requiem for a Dream* DVD, Momentum Pictures, PAL, 2001.

fascination with noise, but these films also include various types of diegetic music and, in the case of Mamoulian's film, orchestral nondiegetic music and musical numbers. Only decades later would we see more explicit and focused attempts at interchanging the roles of sound effects and the score. Lynch's description of the borderline between music and sound effects as "the most beautiful area" efficiently captures this shift, reflecting the influence of contemporary music that expanded its traditional notions of music as "man-made" and "performed" to include the vast universe of sounds vibrating everywhere around us.

Technological innovations have certainly played an important role in the evolution of this trend. The availability of new postproduction equipment at the end of the 1960s facilitated the move towards less rigid and compartmentalized workflow, while the introduction of synthesizers and musical software in sound postproduction gave rise to new practices that would increasingly contribute to the erasure of the barriers between music and sound effects. The score for *Forbidden Planet* demonstrated effectively the ability of electronic music to effortlessly cross that barrier as early as the mid-1950s. Although other electronic scores that followed were unsurprisingly mostly confined to sci-fi or horror genres, Artemiev's music for Tarkovsky's *The Mirror* and *Stalker* revealed that their boundary-busting potential could equally successfully be applied in the service of aesthetic principles that resist the conventions of manipulative or genre-defined scoring, aiming instead for soundscapes that emphasize the musical quality of diegetic sound. On the other hand, in more contemporary film scores, technology has been used by composers such as Greenwood, Jóhannsson, and Levi to give an edge to sounds performed by orchestral instruments and enrich their timbral range. It is also worth noting the influence of popular music on these developments: hip-hop, techno, and other types of "electronica" popularized the use of sampling in all its forms so that all kinds of quotidian noises came to be regarded as potential "music."

In most of the examples discussed in this chapter the musical use of sound effects and the scoring styles that enter the territory of sound design fulfil both narrative and aesthetic roles. The emphasis on one or the other depends on the type and demands of the film, but they all promote the aesthetics of sonic integration, undermining the hierarchy of the classical soundtrack and compartmentalized labour in order to realize the full expressive potential of sound. This interplay between narrative and aesthetic concerns is equally relevant in the examples discussed in the next chapter where the line between sound design and score is blurred to the point that differentiation between the two is often impossible.

3

Scoring with Sound, the Aesthetics of Reticence, and Films of Peter Strickland

The widespread musical use of sound effects explored in the previous chapter demonstrates how fine the line is that separates nonmusical elements of the sound-track from the score. What has made this line even hazier in recent decades is the approach where diegetic sound is combined with, or completely replaced by, pre-existing pieces of electroacoustic music or *musique concrète*. This approach was famously applied by Gus Van Sant in his Death Trilogy (*Gerry*, 2002; *Elephant*, 2003; *Last Days*, 2005) and *Paranoid Park* (2007), creating one of the most influ-ential models of interaction between sound design and music since the turn of the century. In these films pre-existing pieces that feature sounds of nature, the urban environment, and electronically produced noises are generally mixed with diegetic sound in such a way that it is difficult to tell whether what we hear emanates from the diegesis or the score.

Although Van Sant here takes advantage of the fact that the language of some contemporary music is not necessarily always perceived as music, a seamless merging of electroacoustic music and diegetic sound is not his ultimate purpose. In fact, there is no attempt to avoid or cover up the origins of some sounds that appear as "foreign" in the diegetic context, such as the forest sounds in the killing-spree scene in *Elephant*, which are sourced from Hildegard Westerkamp's *Beneath the Forest Floor* and Frances White's *Walk Through Resonant Landscape #2*. In other cases nondiegetic sounds from *musique concrète* pieces are emphasized for affective purposes, a good example being the shower scene in *Paranoid Park*, where the sounds of a waterfall and birds chirping, also from Frances White's *Walk Through Resonant Landscape #2*, are mixed with the diegetic sound of the shower.[1] This approach not only makes the distinctions between diegetic and nondiegetic or between music and noise obsolete but also, as Randolph Jordan points out, inverts sound design's traditional function as a contextualization device.[2]

[1] See Danijela Kulezic-Wilson, "Gus Van Sant's Soundwalks and Audio-visual *Musique con-crète*," in *Music, Sound and Filmmakers: Sonic Style in Cinema*, ed. James Wierzbicki (London and New York: Routledge, 2012), 80–81.

[2] Randolph Jordan, "The Work of Hildegard Westerkamp in the Films of Gus Van Sant: An Interview with the Soundscape Composer (and Some Added Thoughts of My Own)," *Offscreen* 11, nos. 8–9 (2007), accessed December 12, 2010, http://offscreen.com/view/jordan_westerkamp.

Sound Design Is the New Score: Theory, Aesthetics, and Erotics of the Integrated Soundtrack. Danijela Kulezic-Wilson, Oxford University Press (2020). © Oxford University Press.
DOI: 10.1093/oso/ 9780190855314.001.0001

Van Sant's work has received a fair amount of attention in recent years,[3] but it will be examined further in the next chapter with the intention of addressing the sensuous aspect of methods pioneered in his soundtracks. In this chapter I will focus on the work of British writer and director Peter Strickland, who has taken Van Sant's methods one step further, not only combining pre-existing pieces of electroacoustic music and *musique concrète* with a film's environmental sound but also even building whole scenes around them, treating these pieces as diegetic sound. Another example of the musical approach to the soundtrack, Strickland's work will be viewed in the context of an aesthetics that deliberately shuns the conventions of traditional scoring and its traps of affective overstatement and passive absorption, encouraging instead both intellectual and emotional engagement with the text. By examining the history and main principles of the *aesthetics of reticence*,[4] I hope to shed more light on the ideological and aesthetic background of the practices explored in this book.

Peter Strickland, Filmmaker and Acoustic Auteur

Strickland first attracted public and critical attention in 2009 with his debut *Katalin Varga*, the story of a woman who is banished from her home when her husband finds out that their son was the result of a rape, which sends Katalin on a journey through the Carpathian Mountains seeking vengeance. The film was deservedly praised for its sensitive approach to the subjects of trauma and

---

[3] In addition to already referenced articles by Jordan and Kulezic-Wilson, see also Randolph Jordan, "The Ecology of Listening While Looking in the Cinema: Reflective Audioviewing in Gus Van Sant's Elephant," *Organised Sound* 17, no. 3 (Special Issue, Sound, Listening and Place II) (2012): 248–256, https://doi.org/10.1017/S1355771811000458 and Danijela Kulezic-Wilson, "Sound Design Is the New Score," *Music, Sound and the Moving Image* 2, no. 2 (2008): 127–131.

[4] While this term captures well the aesthetic principles that provide a context for the practices discussed in this and the following chapter, it does not necessarily apply to the whole of art cinema, even though its implications of "sparse," "restrained," or "suppressed" resonate with many of the narrative strategies that David Bordwell associates with art cinema narration (*Narration in the Fiction Film*, [London and New York: Routledge, 1985]). In the case of Andrey Tarkovsky and Alexander Sokurov, whose comments quoted later inspired my coining of the term, "reticent" applies to practically every aspect of their expressive vocabulary. The same could be said for representatives of the Romanian New Wave also discussed in this section, as well as directors such as Nuri Bilge Ceylan, Jim Jarmusch, Abas Kiarostami, and others. Soundtrack practices associated with reticent narration are less uniform, however, and range from complete musical abstinence to elaborate strategies devised to avoid empathetic scoring, as will be demonstrated by the analysis of Strickland's films. For a detailed analysis of Sokurov's films see Ira Jaffe, *Slow Movies: Countering the Cinema of Action* (London and New York: Wallflower Press, 2014). For more insight into Tarkovsky's work see his book *Sculpting in Time: Reflections on the Cinema* (London: Bodley Head, 1986). For more insight into Jim Jarmusch's aesthetics and his use of music see Ludvig Hertzberg, ed., *Jim Jarmusch: Interviews* (Jackson: University Press of Mississippi, 2001), Danijela Kulezic-Wilson, "The Musicality of Film and Jim Jarmusch's *Dead Man*," *Film and Film Culture* 4 (2007): 8–20, and Elsie Walker, *Understanding Sound Tracks Through Film Theory* (Oxford and New York: Oxford University Press, 2015), 52–85.

revenge, its visual aesthetics, and the poignant leading performance by Hilda Péter, but even more important in this context, also for its striking soundtrack, which won the film a Silver Bear for outstanding sound design at the 2009 Berlin Film Festival. Strickland's follow-up to *Katalin Varga*, *Berberian Sound Studio* (2012), emphasized even more the director's fervent interest in aural aspects of the medium, focusing on the character of an English sound engineer Gilderoy (Toby Jones), who comes to 1970s Italy believing that he has been hired to work on a film about horses but ends up providing sound effects for a *giallo* film.

Both *Katalin Varga* and *Berberian Sound Studio* afford great opportunities for exploring the fluidity between different soundtrack elements as they are both representative of Strickland's unique approach to film soundtrack informed by his interest in contemporary musical language and his direct experience of creating *musique concrète* with the Sonic Catering Band. Despite many obvious differences between these two films in terms of their themes, genres, and visual aesthetics, they also share many similarities. Both use a specific genre defined by violence as their starting point—rape-revenge thriller and horror, respectively—and yet in both cases Strickland refuses to play by the rules, denying the audience explicit images of sexual violence and torture. *Katalin Varga* deliberately eschews the depiction of the protagonist's rape, while in *Berberian Sound Studio* the torture scenes that Gilderoy is providing Foley for are presented exclusively through sound, drawing the audience's attention to its often overlooked power but also making a clear statement about the sensationalist nature of horror cinema. Both films are unequivocally critical of violence against women but they also explore territories of moral ambiguity, *Katalin Varga* questioning the actions of a victimized woman who becomes a murderer and *Berberian Sound Studio* exposing the exploitative nature of violence in horror cinema and the audience's complicity in it while at the same time paying homage to the flamboyant style of Italian *giallo* films.[5] This interest in gray areas of morality and the fine line that divides artistic interrogation from exploitation also makes both films suitable case studies for investigating the relationship between film soundtrack and the aesthetics of art cinema, which encourages audiences' engagement instead of passive absorption.

As one of those writers/directors for whom sound is a vital element of his personal film aesthetics, Strickland is both a *mélomane* and an "acoustic

---

[5] The term *giallo*, which means "yellow" in Italian, was originally given to pulp mystery novels with characteristic yellow covers that were published in the 1930s and 1940s in Italy. The cinematic equivalent appeared in the 1960s, expanding the themes of murder mystery to include elements of slasher and supernatural horror, psychological thriller, and eroticism. Despite its pulp origins, taste for gory violence, and exploitation, the genre developed a cult following due to its distinctive visual style and adventurous soundtracks that embraced the influences of free jazz, prog-rock, and Italian modernism.

auteur."[6] His diverse musical tastes define the way in which he approaches the films he writes and directs, making music "the code for entering" their sometimes puzzling narratives.[7] Strickland's methods can best be described as "scoring with sound design," which on one hand seems like a natural choice for a director comfortable with contemporary musical language. On the other hand, though, his conscious decision not to use any conventional scoring or even any traditional (tonal, instrumental) type of music in scenes dealing with intense emotional content can also be interpreted as a reaction to the overindulgent conventions of classical scoring. As his approach is representative of a growing tendency in transnational cinema and television dramas,[8] it is worth shedding more light on the main characteristics of this trend and its roots before exploring Strickland's methods in detail. Generally associated with the art cinema ethos, which values reticence over transparency and ambiguity over narrative redundancy, this approach is facilitated by soundtrack methods that range from complete musical abstinence to various other strategies devised to avoid conventional nondiegetic scores. Considering the correlation between these methods and certain principles of art cinema, it is worth taking a closer look at the aesthetic and ideological parameters that informed the new soundtrack practices discussed in this and the following chapter. Using this framework as a starting point, the ensuing analysis of Strickland's films will show how the affective and narrative functions of score and sound design became irrevocably blurred in the process of forging a new path in soundtrack practices,

---

[6] Referring to Claudia Gorbman's notion of *auteur music* ("Auteur Music," in *Beyond the Soundtrack: Representing Music in Cinema*, ed. Daniel Goldmark, Lawrence Kramer, and Richard Leppert [Berkeley and Los Angeles and London: University of California Press, 2007], 149–162), Jay Beck uses this term for directors who choose nonmusical or rather nonconventional musical means and sound design over traditional scores to "construct personal sound aesthetics that rework the rules of commercially driven audiovisual relations" ("Acoustic Auteurs and Transnational Cinema," in *The Oxford Handbook of Sound and Image in Digital Media*, ed. Carol Vernallis, Amy Herzog, and John Richardson [Oxford and New York: Oxford University Press, 2013], 732).

[7] Peter Strickland, "Special Features, Director's Commentary," *Berberian Sound Studio* DVD, Artificial Eye, 2012.

[8] For the most extensive and insightful studies on the effects and meaning of silences, specifically in Michael Haneke's films, see Elsie Walker, "Hearing the Silences (as Well as the Music) in Michael Haneke's Films," *Music and the Moving Image* 3, no. 3 (Fall 2010): 15–30, doi:10.5406/musimoviimag.5.3.i, and *Hearing Haneke: The Sound Tracks of a Radical Auteur* (Oxford and New York: Oxford University Press, 2018). See also Beck, "Acoustic Auteurs in Transnational Cinema"; Annette Davison and Nicholas Rayland, "The Janus Project: Cristobal Tapia de Veer's *Utopia*, Anempathic Empathy and the Radicalization of Convention," in *The Palgrave Handbook of Sound Design and Music in Screen Media: Integrated Soundtracks*, ed. Liz Greene and Danijela Kulezic-Wilson (Basingstoke, Hampshire: Palgrave Macmillan, 2016), 305–307; Kulezic-Wilson, "After Excess—Abstinence: Notes on a New Trend in Music Scoring (and Its Absence) in Film and TV" (paper presented at the Film Music Conference, University of Leeds, November 6–9, 2009); Kulezic-Wilson, "Soundscapes of Trauma and the Silence of Revenge in Peter Strickland's *Katalin Varga*," *New Soundtrack* 1, no. 1 (2010): 57–71.

establishing "scoring with sound design" as a crucial stage in the breakdown of soundtrack hierarchy.

The Aesthetics of Reticence, Interrogative Text, and Soundtrack

Although art is often sought out because we believe that this is where "the flames of truth and beauty" burn the strongest,[9] many artists argue that art should nevertheless retain a certain level of mystery. According to the Russian director Alexander Sokurov, "art is only where ... reticence exists. A limitation of what we can actually see and feel."[10] His statement echoes Tarkovsky's belief that in a work of art "something must always be left secret"[11] because a certain level of elusiveness is its "air" and "its most captivating quality."[12] These sentiments have a particular resonance in the context of the post-Saussurean view that meaning is not inherent in a work of art but is rather created in the meeting between text and reader. What a reader or spectator takes from a piece of art is informed by his or her social and cultural background in the same way the reader's general outlook on the world is ideologically constructed, rooted in a specific historical situation, and informed by his or her background and previous experiences.[13] Tarkovsky takes this train of thought even further, saying that, since every person responds to art in light of his or her individual experience, every piece of art thus becomes a mirror in which the perceiver sees himself or herself.[14]

Creating mystery and encouraging individual readings of the text is, however, not a popular approach within the mainstream industry, not least because the dominant practice of storytelling follows the tradition of classical realism, which promotes clarity of motivation and narration to secure the audience's immersion into the narrative world. Mainstream film's affinity for transparent intentions and satisfying closures is well served by the nature of the medium itself, which encourages expectations of realistic representation. But this concreteness of film representation is that very thing that "can suffocate its subjects," noted Walter Murch, echoing Tarkovsky's comment about elusiveness being the "air of art." The fact that film "doesn't possess the built-in escape valves of ambiguity

---

[9] Karl Ove Knausgård, *A Man In Love: My Struggle: Book 2*, trans. Don Bartlett (London: Harvill Secker, 2013), 145.

[10] Alexander Sokurov quoted in Jaffe, *Slow Movies*, 35.

[11] Tarkovsky, *Sculpting in Time*, 110.

[12] Ibid., 183.

[13] Catherine Belsey, *Critical Practice*, 2nd ed. (London and New York: Routledge, 2002), 3.

[14] Tarkovsky, *Sculpting in Time*, 184.

that painting, music, literature, radio drama and black-and-white silent film automatically have, simply by virtue of their sensory incompleteness," makes it that much more difficult for filmmakers to engage their viewers' imaginations, argues Murch.[15] The "suffocation" that Murch refers to applies not only to the perceived realism of the film sound and image that create an illusion of a "real" world with "real" characters but also, even more, to the fact that all storytelling devices, including sound and music, are employed with the intention of avoiding any potential causes of confusion in order to facilitate passive spectatorship. But precisely because film is "all there," as Murch says, it is "the responsibility of film-makers ... to find ways within that completeness to refrain from achieving it."[16]

Filmmakers who share the same view of the medium have used different methods to make sure that their work retains a certain level of reticence, but only a handful of them have commented on the role that sound can play in this context. Tarkovsky eloquently argued:

> As soon as the sounds of the visible world, reflected by the screen, are removed from it, or that world is filled, for the sake of the image, with extraneous sounds that don't exist literally, or if the real sounds are distorted so that they can no longer correspond with the image—then the film acquires a resonance.[17]

Murch's advocacy for the metaphoric use of sound emphasizes the same necessity for finding alternatives to the practice of the classically constructed soundtrack: "by choosing carefully what to eliminate, and then adding sounds that at first hearing seem to be somewhat at odds with the accompanying image, the film-maker can open up a perceptual vacuum into which the mind of the audience must inevitably rush."[18]

This urge to resist the methods of classical realism in the use of soundtrack, which has dominated the industry since the invention of recorded sound, was first articulated as early as 1928, when Eisenstein, Pudovkin, and Alexandrov issued a "Statement" calling for the contrapuntal use of sound in film, arguing that sound is supposed to have a life and purpose of its own, separate from delivering sounds implied by the images.[19] Since then, many other filmmakers and theorists commented on the possibilities of diversifying functions of sound and opening

---

[15] Walter Murch, "Sound Design: The Dancing Shadow," in *Projections 4: Film-makers on Film-making*, ed. John Boorman, Tom Luddy, David Thompson, and Walter Donohue (London and Boston: Faber and Faber, 1995), 247.

[16] Ibid.

[17] Tarkovsky, *Sculpting in Time*, 162.

[18] Murch, "Sound Design," 247.

[19] S. M. Eisenstein, V. I. Pudovkin, and G. V. Alexandrov, "A Statement," in *Film Sound: Theory and Practice*, ed. Elisabeth Weis and John Belton (New York: Columbia University Press, 1985), 83–85.

text for multiple readings, including Robert Bresson, David Lynch, Randy Thom, and Larry Sider.[20]

Similar sentiments have been expressed in the domain of film music practice and scholarship. In the first book to tackle the issue of film music aesthetics head on, *Composing for the Films*, Theodor Adorno and Hanns Eisler dissected Hollywood scoring practice with surgical precision, criticizing many of its conventions, including the rule of "unobtrusiveness," the need to "illustrate" that leads to duplication, the exaggeration of expression, and the use of clichéd melodic, harmonic, and instrumental connotative devices, pronouncing them "tired." These conventions notwithstanding, music has also served as one of the key devices employed to eliminate discomfort or confusion among spectators and facilitate passive spectatorship, as was eloquently argued by Claudia Gorbman, Caryl Flinn, Royal S. Brown, and others.[21] From the first shows in which music masked the sound of the projector and provided the sense of continuity, to the snippets of the story put together through editing, to the elaborate orchestral scores emphasizing dramatic moments and lending their affective power to the images on screen, music was charged with drawing the audience into film's narrative world. And in the same way sound is used in film to buttress its sense of realism, scoring eliminates any potential semiotic gaps that might exist between visual and musical content, directing the viewer towards only one interpretation or type of experience. As Royal S. Brown points out, "popular film industries worldwide and the critical establishments that have been built up around them have a massive distaste for ambiguity and multivalence,"[22] which is why throughout the history of cinema, music has played a significant role in preventing "the displeasure of ambiguity."[23]

In opposition to this prevalent practice, advocates of what could be called the aesthetics of reticence insist that restraint and a certain level of ambiguity are the basic conditions for allowing individuated responses to film and encouraging

---

[20] See Robert Bresson, "Notes on Sound," in *Film Sound: Theory and Practice*, 149; David Lynch, "Action and Reaction," in *Soundscape: The School of Sound Lectures 1998–2001*, ed. Larry Sider, Diane Freeman, and Jerry Sider (London and New York: Wallflower Press), 49–53; Randy Thom, "Designing a Movie for Sound," in *Soundscape: The School of Sound Lectures 1998–2001*, 121–137. Adding to the discussion of the employment of sound within a film, Larry Sider addresses the influence of projection technology on the nature of spectatorship, arguing that surround sound systems facilitate immersive experience while mono systems encourage spectatorship of engagement ("Mono," lecture presented at the Synch/Non-synch Symposium on Sound and Film, NUI Galway, February 19, 2014).

[21] Claudia Gorbman, *Unheard Melodies: Narrative Film Music* (London: BFI Publishing/ Bloomington: Indiana University Press, 1987); Caryl Flinn, *Strains of Utopia: Gender, Nostalgia and Hollywood Film Music* (Princeton, NJ: Princeton University Press); Royal S. Brown, *Overtones and Undertones: Reading Film Music* (Berkeley: California University Press, 1994).

[22] Brown, *Overtones and Undertones*, 10.

[23] Gorbman, *Unheard Melodies*, 58.

more active involvement with the text. This engagement with the text is a crucial
part of the equation because, as Sokurov says:

> Confronted with a true cinematographic work of art, the viewer is never a pas-
> sive contemplator, but someone who participates in the creation of this artistic
> world. All works of high art are built on confidence in the delicate considera-
> tion and intuition of this person. They always leave something unsaid, or con-
> versely, say too much, thereby concealing some simple truth.[24]

Considering, however, that music is habitually employed in film to ensure
that nothing is left unsaid and no truths remain concealed, it is not surprising
that in reaction to the practice of excess, a notable number of films and TV pro-
grammes in recent years have responded with drastic musical frugality. The first
manifest gesture of this kind came in the mid-1990s when filmmakers gathered
around the Dogme 95 movement announced as one of their ten essential rules
that "music must not be used unless it occurs where the scene is being shot." In
the following decades the rejection of nondiegetic scoring became a noteworthy
choice for many European directors, including the Dardenne brothers, Michael
Haneke, Götz Spielmann, Nuri Bilge Ceylan, Andrew Haigh, Joana Hogg, and
representatives of the Romanian New Wave, as well as Asian directors such as
Lee Chang-dong and Anthony Chen, the Argentinian director Lucrecia Martel,
the Mexican director Michel Franco, American independent directors such as
Kelly Reichardt and Joe Swanberg, the TV show *The Wire* (2002–2008), and so
on.[25] Another response to the practice of musical excess that will be discussed in
more detail later in this chapter is the shift of focus from scoring to sound design,
which includes the employment of musical pieces that can be perceived as part of
the ambient sound and/or sound design.

It should be noted, however, that although a restrained use of nondiegetic
music might seem like a radical choice in the context of mainstream cinema and
our broader culture saturated with music, this is indeed just another wave in the
natural cycle of stylistic fluctuations that happen periodically, reflecting corre-
sponding changes in other arts. In cinema, the dynamic of these fluctuations has

---

[24] Sokurov quoted in Jaffe, *Slow Movies*, 35.

[25] Examples include Haneke's *The Time of the Wolf* (2003) and *Caché* (2005); Nuri Bilge Ceylan's
Uzak (2002) and *Three Monkeys* (2008); Luc and Jean-Pierre Dardenne's *The Child* (2005), *Lorna's
Silence* (2008), and *Two Days, One Night* (2014); Andrew Haigh's *Weekend* (2011) and *45 Years* (2015);
Joanna Hogg's *Unrelated* (2008), *Archipelago* (2010), and *Exhibition* (2013); Cristi Puiu's *The Death
of Mr. Lazarescu* (2005); Cristian Mungiu's *4 months, 3 weeks, 2 days* (2007); Cristian Nemescu's
California Dreamin' (2007); Götz Spielmann's *Revanche* (2008); Lucrecia Martel's *The Headless
Woman* (2008); Lee Chang-dong's *Poetry* (2010); Anthony Chen's *Ilo Ilo* (2013); Kelly Reichardt's
Wendy and Lucy (2008); Joe Swanberg's *Art History* (2011) and *The Zone* (2011); and Michel Franco's
Chronic (2015). See also Beck, "Acoustic Auteurs."

SCORING WITH SOUND 63

always been affected by the opposition and interaction between Hollywood and European practices. The resistance to using music to induce emotional responses is by no means the product of recent times and practices—James Wierzbicki notes a similar tendency in the 1950s, particularly in European and more specifically British films. He quotes the Austrian-born British columnist of *The Music Review*, Hans Keller, who in November 1952 commented on George Auric's work in the United Kingdom:

> [Auric's] quarter of an hour's music for a British film, placed at important junctures, was noticed by everyone, whereas some of his continuous French scores went entirely unnoticed; one can make film without music and indeed will soon do so out of disgust at the exaggerated use of film music.[26]

Judging by his other reviews, Keller's aesthetic affinities would fit quite well with the contemporary practice discussed in this book. In 1951 he praised Pat Jackson's film *White Corridors* for having a soundtrack that "does not harbour any film music" and, by avoiding any musical "nonsense," "actually achieves some definite and well-defined poetic realism on the acoustic side *by dint of thematic, indeed, almost musicalized noises.*"[27] Wierzbicki points out that filmmakers' deliberate decisions to avoid music, regularly praised by Keller, "were more common in 'understating' England than elsewhere," but by the end of the 1950s "the fashion for musical understatement had spread even to Hollywood."[28] One example would be the views of the Austrian-born American composer Ernest Gold published in the *Los Angeles Times* in 1958. Commenting on his work on *The Defiant Ones* (1958), he singles out one scene that, according to him, was suggested by the film's director, Stanley Kramer:

> Its [music's] value lay primarily in the effect it had on the scenes dealing with the convicts, which contained no music whatsoever. The sudden stark silence and the naturalistic sound effects were made more eloquent and the plight of the convicts more terrifying by the sudden withdrawal of music. The value of the music lay not in its presence in the film's most meaningful scenes but in its absence.[29]

The next decade and the birth of the French New Wave would see even more dramatic changes in the approach to scoring as music was suddenly considered

---

[26] Hans Keller quoted in James Wierzbicki, *Film Music: A History* (London and New York: Routledge, 2009), 175.
[27] Ibid., 176 (emphasis in the original).
[28] Ibid.
[29] Ernest Gold quoted in Wierzbicki, *Film Music*, 182.

not only a useful accompaniment and source of affective power but also a constitutive element of the medium. One of the most revolutionary figures of this movement, Jean-Luc Godard, created an aesthetics infused with the Brechtian idea of detachment that was emphatically "political" and intellectual rather than sensuous.[30] Godard's visionary ideas subverted the Hollywood conventions of production and continuity-style narration and enlisted sound and music as important tools of his vision. His use of "direct" sound inspired by *cinema vérité*, "dirtied" by the employment of omnidirectional microphones; his complete disregard for the soundtrack hierarchy that privileged dialogue over other aspects of soundtrack; and his unpredictable use of music induced tectonic changes in how the role of sound was perceived by both filmmakers and audiences. Instead of eschewing nondiegetic music, Godard showed how it can be employed without succumbing to the conventions of Hollywood scoring. Analysing the role of Beethoven's String Quartet in *Prénom: Carmen* (1983), Annette Davison points out that its purpose seems "to embody a locus of confusion: it lacks narrative motivation; and, it undermines the role(s) of music as defined by classical Hollywood scoring and exposes such scoring practices as 'conventional' rather than established by 'natural law.'"[31] That doesn't mean that Godard's approach to music was in any way crude—on the contrary. As both Royal S. Brown and Claudia Gorbman argue, by thinking about music as an integral part of his audiovisual toolkit—"like another sound, but in a different form"[32]—and by negating music's role as a narrative signifier, Godard stressed "instead its presence both aesthetically and as raw, affective morphology."[33]

The European influence in terms of novel approaches to sound design and scoring was felt in American cinema particularly during the era of New Hollywood in the 1970s, and then again in the second half of the 1980s, at the beginning of the first golden decade of independent cinema. As I mentioned in the introduction, the Bay Area sound played an important role in introducing new ways of thinking about the use and functions of music and sound. In some cases, as in the Coppola-Murch or Lynch-Splet collaborations, the accent was on elaborate interaction between scoring and sound design. In others, the ripples of the French New Wave were felt in the insistence on "the dramatic absence of nondiegetic music and the striking imposition of the vérité-ists' mandate of

---

[30] See Alan Williams, "Godard's Use of Sound," in *Film Sound: Theory and Practice*, ed. Elisabeth Weis and John Belton (New York: Columbia University Press, 1985), 332–345; Annette Davison, *Hollywood Theory, Non-Hollywood Practice: Cinema Soundtracks in the 1980s and 1990s* (Farnham, Surrey: Ashgate, 2004), 78.
[31] Davison, *Hollywood Theory*, 83.
[32] Godard quoted in Brown, *Overtones and Undertones*, 188.
[33] Ibid., 192. See also Gorbman, "Auteur Music."

'source music only.' "[34] A decade later, however, nonconventional scoring practices in American independent film were manifested more in the excessive use of auteur soundtracks than in the affinity for musical abstinence. While this is a somewhat sweeping generalization that does not apply to sworn "independents" like Jim Jarmusch—whose resolutely reticent aesthetics accounts for his highly controlled approach to all expressive aspects of the film vocabulary, including scoring—high-profile directors with origins in indie culture, such as Quentin Tarantino and Wes Anderson, became as famous for their hands-on approach to compilation scoring as for the distinctive features of their narrative and visual styles. At the same time, American independent cinema of the 1980s gave birth to "acoustic auteurs" like Gus Van Sant, whose debut *Mala Noche* (1986) announced the director's taste for expressive sound design. On the other hand, the inspiration that led Van Sant back to his independent roots, after his short stint with Hollywood in the 1990s, came again from European cinema, specifically after watching the films of Hungarian director Béla Tarr, whose influence will be discussed in more detail in the next chapter.

The renouncement of the traditional nondiegetic score is, first, a matter of aesthetic choice and a return to one of the main Bressonian principles: "What is for the eye must not duplicate what is for the ear."[35] Bresson was not talking only about music in film but about sound in general, insisting that "image and sound must not support each other, but must work each in turn through *a sort of relay*."[36] This proclamation is, of course, an echo of the first famous statement about the contrapuntal use of sound issued by Eisenstein, Pudovkin, and Alexandrov mentioned earlier. What they both imply is not that sound has to contrast or contradict the image in some way, as the term "counterpoint" was then interpreted, but rather that the film soundtrack is supposed to have a life and purpose of its own, apart from delivering sounds implied by the images. If this aesthetic stance involves self-imposed limitations in the use of nondiegetic music, it usually results in increased attentiveness to diegetic sound, an approach that will be discussed in more detail in the next chapter.

Apart from the obvious aesthetic purpose, eschewing a nondiegetic score is also closely related to the intention of avoiding the ideological prerequisites of classical narration—the suture, the predictability of narrative, the evasion of discomfort and ambiguity. The main objective of Hollywood film is to tell a story in a straightforward manner, avoiding anything that might prevent the pleasure of passive comprehension, and this agenda accounts for a consistently

---

[34] Julie Hubbert, "'Whatever Happened to Great Movie Music?': *Cinema Vérité* and Hollywood Film Music of the Early 1970s," *American Music* 21, no. 2 (Summer 2003): 194.

[35] Bresson, "Notes on Sound," 149.

[36] Ibid., emphasis in the original.

unadventurous use of music. Of course, it would be misleading to suggest that traditional scores always simply duplicate visual and narrative content. However, while they often bring to light less obvious aspects of the narrative, emphasize the subtext, or might even contradict the text, creating anempathetic emphasis,[37] they never enter into a relationship with the image that might cause what Roland Barthes dramatically dubbed "the terror of uncertain signs."[38]

In opposition to this ideology of facilitating the culture of noncritical spectatorship and catering for a passive audience is the notion of what Barthes calls a *writerly* text or what Elsie Walker, borrowing terminology from Catherine Belsey's literary theory, calls an *interrogative* text in film.[39] The goal of writerly text is to "make the reader no longer a consumer but a producer of the text," says Barthes.[40] Also in reference to a literary context, Belsey explains that an interrogative text is one that discourages a stable, single-point-of-view position and interpretation, prevents the passive stance of the viewer, and invites him or her to "produce answers to questions it implicitly or explicitly raises."[41] Both concepts emphasize the agency of the "reader," which can apply to any artistic context or a medium, except that Belsey's term puts additional stress on the notions of elusiveness and ambiguity explored through the concept of interrogation.

Conventional scoring, of course, supports the principles of classic realism that values nonchallenging narratives and facilitates the stable position of the reader. Its tendency is to eliminate any space that might leave scenes open to interpretation and instead insists on directing the viewer towards only one reading and particular type of emotional experience. The absence of empathetic scoring, on the other hand—whether manifested through the lack of any scoring or an elaborate sound design that might involve some contemporary musical pieces—allows the creation of a potentially more ambiguous soundscape and an interrogative text.

This connection between interrogative form and the aesthetics of reticence can be recognized, for instance, in many of the Romanian films that emerged at the beginning of the noughties, exposing the complexities of communist and postcommunist society through intimate dramas. Many of these films achieve an almost documentary feel and give the impression of a purely observational style through the extreme rigour of the dialogue, the framing, and the editing choices, including the absence of nondiegetic music. As Cristian Mungiu, director of *4 months, 3 weeks, 2 days* (2007), says, the reason he doesn't use any music in

---

[37] Michel Chion, *Audio-vision: Sound on Screen*, ed. and trans. Claudia Gorbman (New York: Columbia University Press, 1994), 8.

[38] Barthes quoted in Gorbman, *Unheard Melodies*, 58.

[39] See Roland Barthes, *S/Z*, trans. Richard Miller, preface by Richard Howard (Oxford: Blackwell Publishing, 1974/2002); Belsey, *Critical Practice*; Walker, "Hearing the Silences."

[40] Barthes, *S/Z*, 4.

[41] Balsey, *Critical Practice*, 84.

that film, unnecessary camera movements, or cuts is because he does not want to impose either his style or his message on the viewer, an approach emblematic of this style in general.[42] Instead, he offers carefully assembled material as close to reality as possible, tuned to the inner states of his protagonists, and invites the viewer to form his or her own opinion about both.

Commitment to the aesthetics of reticence in narrative or scoring terms, however, does not mean that the aspect of "interrogation" has to be the dominant feature of a film. It is indeed an important part of Michael Haneke's films, which consistently strive to make strong political, social, or cultural statements as "an alternative to the hermetically sealed-off illusion which ... deprives the spectator of the possibility of critical participation."[43] As Elsie Walker points out in her article about Haneke's *Caché* (2005) and *Funny Games* (2007), the director's decision not to use any nondiegetic music in some of his films plays a significant part in his attempt to make those films the "productive centre of an interactive process."[44] However, the determination to pose socially and politically provocative questions can be less apparent in films concerned with intimate dramas, like Nuri Bilge Ceylan's *Climates* (2006), Haneke's *Amour* (2012), and Andrew Haigh's *45 Years* (2015). These films are nevertheless marked not only by a similarly rigorous control of expressive means and sparse scoring—*45 Years* eschews a nondiegetic score altogether—but also by a delicate interrogation of the nature of intimate relationships, the bonds that sustain them, and the weaknesses that undo them.

It should also be mentioned that this aesthetics of reticence that conceives film as a plural, interrogative text is not solely dependent on the absence of nondiegetic scoring and has been associated in the past with various formal or narrative strategies typical of art cinema, including narrative ellipses, an insistence on ambiguous characters/situations/endings, striking formal patterns, and so on. What is worth noting here is that in the last two decades the absence of a nondiegetic score has become an important part of those strategies, as Walker argues in relation to Haneke, Jay Beck notes in connection to sound design in Latin American cinema, and I have discussed in relation to broader tendencies of contemporary cinema to embrace the aesthetics of reticence.[45]

[42] Patrick Z. McGavin, "Q&A: Cristin Mungiu," *StopSmiling*, February 26, 2008, accessed November 2, 2015, http://stopsmilingonline.com/story_detail.php?id=985.

[43] Michael Haneke, "71 Fragments of a Chronology of Chance: Notes to the Film," in *After Postmodernism: Austrian Literature and Film in Transition*, ed. Willy Riemer (Riverside, CA: Ariadne, 2000), 172.

[44] Walker, "Hearing the Silences," 15–16. For an additional insight into Haneke's approach to music see also Lisa Coulthard, "From a Whisper to a Scream: Music in the Films of Michael Haneke," *Music and the Moving Image* 5, no. 3 (Fall 2012): 1–10, accessed January 17, 2013, doi:10.5406/musimoviimag.5.3.i.

[45] Beck, "Acoustic Auteurs in Transnational Cinema"; Kulezic-Wilson, "After Excess Abstinence"; Walker, "Hearing the Silences."

While this type of aesthetics is sometimes associated with the Brechtian "distancing effect"—certainly both Belsey and Walker make explicit the connection between an interrogative text and Brechtian principles of *Verfremdungseffekt*[46]— my view is that the films I discuss here and many others that resist the tropes of classical narration do so not with the intention of pulling the viewer out of the narrative, as was the case with Godard, for instance, who championed Brechtian aesthetics. Rather, they do so in order to create a space where ambiguity is accepted and narrative strategies encourage both emotional and intellectual engagement with the text, an engagement that allows a certain "internal distance" from the prevalent ideology, to use Louis Althusser's term,[47] but does not prevent emotional commitment. Then again, the question of what someone finds distancing or engaging depends on many factors, including the viewer's personal experience, background, and taste. Claudia Gorbman recently pointed out that what she has in the past dubbed as the inaudibility of classical scoring certainly wouldn't be described as such by contemporary audiences because the high level of synchronization between music and visual movement once favoured by classical composers is inevitably noticed by contemporary audiences who are used to more subtle scoring methods.[48] Looking at the ideas of engagement, immersion, and alienation from this perspective, I don't think it's too far-fetched to claim that, to some, it is the persistence of classical scoring that is alienating rather than any other type of practice that avoids those conventions.

Finally, practising musical abstinence is also about charting a particular emotional landscape in film that is *not* aided by music. This too could be understood as part of the general package of art cinema strategies aimed at engendering a sense of ambiguity, but I would argue there is more to it than that. Although music is generally used to enhance the viewer's emotional response to a film, its conventional deployment is often so predictable that it prevents the exact thing it was meant to do. To quote Claudia Gorbman again, "the strictures and underlying aesthetics of the classical rules of film music simply no longer hold" and "melodies are no longer unheard,"[49] and yet the industry seems reluctant to

[46] Translated either as "alienating effect" or "distancing effect," *Verfremdungseffekt* was coined by Bertolt Brecht to describe an approach to theatre that disrupts stage illusion and audiences' identification with characters, prompting them instead to become critically engaged with the play. See Belsey, *Critical Practice*, 84–85, and Walker, "Hearing the Silences," 15. It's worth noting, though, that in her book *Hearing Haneke*, Walker expands her original references to Brecht's *Verfremdung* in the context of Haneke's films into a more nuanced argument, explaining that, even though Haneke's approach to music is Brechtian in the sense that he resists its use for merely "aestheticizing drama," the purpose of it is not necessarily to "'antagonize' or 'detach' the audience entirely but, rather, to create a sense of 'surprise' or 'astonishment' at the everyday or normalized experience" (*Hearing Haneke*, 11–12).

[47] Althusser quoted in Belsey, *Critical Practice*, 85.

[48] Claudia Gorbman, "Music and Character" (Keynote Lecture presented at the 4th Music and Media Study Group Conference, Universita di Torino, June 28–29, 2012).

[49] Gorbman, "Auteur Music," 151.

accept that the old ways of scoring aimed at influencing our emotional response to film have not only become self-defeating but also even turned music into an obstacle to experiencing film more intensely. In response, directors who are very conscious of the mainstream tendency to exploit music for prompting affective responses deliberately employ music with great restraint, avoiding the full narrative and emotional alignment between sound and image that can be insistent in a standard film score.

Although not all the examples discussed in this chapter comply neatly with the aesthetic criteria associated with the idea of reticence, I think this concept is prevalent enough to provide a useful framework for examining types of scoring and sound design that resist the "tired" clichés of excessive scoring. This topic is all the more intriguing now when it has become obvious that complete musical abstinence and an extremely restricted use of nondiegetic music are not the only ways to defy the existing conventions. As directors like Gus Van Sant and Peter Strickland demonstrate, the world of contemporary music is sufficiently vast and diverse to produce new ideas and audiovisual relationships that can stimulate new modes of perception and a more engaged spectatorship. The ensuing sections will shed light on the various strategies involved in this new practice.

Breaching the Boundary Between Score and Sound Design: *Katalin Varga*

Described as a mixture of folk tale, rape-revenge thriller, and road movie, Strickland's multiply awarded debut, *Katalin Varga*, tells the story of a woman who loses her husband and the life she knows when it is revealed that her son is the result of a rape. When Katalin starts her journey through the Carpathian Mountains looking for revenge, this releases destructive forces that claim the lives of two persons—neither of whom was the direct perpetrator of the crime— and it ends with Katalin being murdered herself. Katalin's first victim is a man who was the accomplice to her rape; the other casualty of her revenge is a completely innocent person, the wife of the rapist who commits suicide after finding out the truth about her husband. Strickland further complicates things by presenting the rapist as a devoted husband haunted by the memory of his crime. At the end Katalin herself is killed by the family of her first victim in another act of retribution, which suggests that once the demons of revenge are unleashed they are impossible to stop. The underlying question, though, is whether the cycle of revenge was triggered by Katalin when she set out on her vengeful trip or a long time before that, by the original crime. The film brings up a number of issues concerning gender relations in rural Romania and its characters' understandings of morality and religion, but Strickland's most commendable achievement must be the fact that not only does he tell this harsh, unsettling, and suspenseful story with obvious disdain for the explicit and gratuitous representation of violence but also he does it with haunting audiovisual beauty.

When *Katalin Varga* won a Silver Bear for "outstanding artistic contribution" in sound design at the 2009 Berlin Film Festival, the jury stated that "there's a tremendous originality and risk in the experimental and original way this film builds up its sombre narration around its powerful sound design."[50] Similar praise could be given to the soundtracks of Strickland's ensuing films, *Berberian Sound Studio* and *The Duke of Burgundy*, affirming sound and music to be among the most potent tools of his creative vocabulary that developed through long experience of making *musique concrète* with the Sonic Catering Band. Strickland's methods of incorporating pre-existing pieces of electroacoustic music and *musique concrète* into sound design on one hand, and his musical use of diegetic sounds in these films on the other, not only make him a frontrunner in developing new strategies for an integrated approach to soundtrack but also highlight the importance of the musical logic that governs this process.

Strickland says that while working on the script for *Katalin Varga* he "had a rough sense of needing heightened natural sounds for the film," hoping to "do to rustic sounds what Alan Splet did to industrial sounds for *Eraserhead* and *The Elephant Man*." At the same time, he wanted to avoid library sounds as much as possible because he felt they were "prefab" and "off the shelf":

> Those sounds have too much baggage yet no baggage at the same time. Once you hear enough of those sound effects CDs, you begin to recognise the samples when watching other films. It was very important that every sound in *Katalin Varga* was not so much "innocent" but free of any unwanted association.[51]

As a result, most sound effects heard in the film were recorded on location by different people at different times, some even while the script was still in its early drafts, while others were provided by Gábor Erdélyi and György Kovács, who used their own field recordings during the mixing. Many of the birdsongs come from Strickland's own record collection, while others were carefully researched and obtained from more unexpected places, including the National Sound Archive at the British Library where Strickland spent hours looking for just the right sound of a Scops owl, which was meant as an homage to his favourite *musique concrète* record, *Presque Rien*, by Luc Ferrari. However, the most interesting aspect of *Katalin Varga*'s sound design is the fact that it is often hard to identify the acoustic or visual origin of the sounds because the field sound effects and

---

[50] "Berlinale Awards," IMDb, February 17, 2009, https://www.imdb.com/news/ni0682319.
[51] Peter Strickland, email message to author, January 23, 2010.

pieces of electroacoustic music and *musique concrète* are either combined or find themselves in exchanged roles. Of course, the sounds of sheep, frogs, dogs, birds, wind, and thunder that punctuate Katalin's journey are perceived as a natural part of the soundscape, but occasionally, as in the montage sequence during which Katalin dreams about her first murder, foregrounded sounds of sheep and goat bells accompanied by a strong wind have a strangely "metallic" feel, giving the impression that we're hearing a piece of *musique concrète* [00:35:02–00:36:33].[52]

On the other hand, Strickland uses a number of pre-existing pieces of *musique concrète* as diegetic sound, the most striking example being the scene in which Katalin's assailant, Antal (Tibor Pálffy), searches for his wife, who committed suicide after learning the truth about her husband [01:05:33–01:09:35]. At the beginning of the scene, gentle, indistinct noises of nature are mixed with distant, muffled sounds of bells and singing. After Antal realizes his wife is missing and, driven by a feeling of dread, starts running through the fields, the sense of suspense and desperation increases as the "heightened natural sounds"—the steady hammering of woodpeckers pierced by bird cries and wind rumbling in the distance—become more intense, almost threatening. The soundscape changes once more when Antal, after finding his hanging wife, stumbles through a field carrying her dead body—the sound of clacking wood deepens and the bird cries are here accompanied by distant noises that could be either wind or some exotic animals roaring (see Figures 3.1, 3.2, and and 3.3). And yet, the soundtrack for this scene from beginning to end is provided by a single piece of pre-existing music, Nurse with Wound's "Ciconia."[53]

"Some people regard this ['Ciconia'] as the highlight of the film's sound design," wrote Strickland in his blog, "but it is actually a 'song' from my record collection used in the film in the same manner as say, Kenneth Anger using The Paris Sisters for his *Kustom Kar Kommandos*."[54] This scene in particular attests to the degree to which the difference between music and sound design can become indistinct when a contemporary musical language is involved in pre-existing recordings. The extraordinary and quite intense sounds of wood-pecking, birds screeching, insects scratching, and distant singing that constitute "Ciconia" are not questioned as being foreign to the environment even though there is a sense that they are intensified compared to the generally more docile background

---

[52] This is the timing of the scene in the DVD release of *Katalin Varga*, Artificial Eye, PAL, 2010.

[53] The content of the scene was determined prior to shooting and Strickland played the track to Tibor Pálffy (who plays Antal) in advance, to give him the "feel" of the scene. The excerpt from "Ciconia" heard in the film is slightly edited, though, matching different sections of the track to the changes in visual content (the section starting at 2.48 of the track accompanies Antal running though the fields; the section starting around 6.00 is heard at the beginning of the scene, and the beginning of the track accompanies the shot of Antal carrying his dead wife).

[54] Peter Strickland, "Bear Necessities," Peter Strickland Blog, February 16, 2009, http://peterstrickland.blogspot.com.

Figures 3.1, 3.2, and 3.3. *Katalin Varga*: Antal (Tibor Pálffy) finds his wife, who has committed suicide after learning the truth about her husband's crime.

sounds of nature. Thanks to the *concrète* aspect of the recording, these sounds bypass the "blood/brain" barrier that, as Murch argues, conventional nondiegetic music usually has to deal with.[55] Nevertheless, these sounds are indeed more dense and forceful than one would expect to hear in a field seen on the screen, which brings to mind the relationship between image and sound that Murch calls "metaphoric."[56]

As was mentioned earlier, Murch argues that, to avoid the tendency of cinema to "suffocate its subjects" by its very ability to represent them in realistic terms, sound should be somewhat "at odds with the accompanying image."[57] Similar to the Russian formalists' argument about the necessity to create a counterpoint between image and sound, or Tarkovsky's call for "distorting" real sounds so that they "no longer correspond with the image,"[58] Murch advocates the *metaphoric* use of sound to create "a perceptual vacuum into which the mind of the audience must inevitably rush" and allow film to become "more 'dimensional.' "[59] Like the sounds of nature in the massacre scene in Gus Van Sant's *Elephant* or the sounds of birds chirping in the shower scene of *Paranoid Park*, or indeed in the iconic match of the sound of helicopter blades with the image of a ceiling fan in *Apocalypse Now*—the resulting "perceptual vacuum" encourages deeper engagement with and multiple readings of the text. The interesting part is that, no matter how peculiar or striking the sounds constituting the perceptual gap are, if it is implied that they originate from the diegetic world, it is more than likely that they will be accepted as an inherent part of it, due to the phenomenon that Chion calls *synchresis*—"the spontaneous and irresistible weld" that is produced between an image and a sound when they occur at the same time.[60] The purpose of this approach is to avoid the explicit musical commentary usually provided by empathetic or dramatic scoring, opting instead for an emotionally ambiguous soundscape.

In *Katalin Varga*, the stunningly pure and beautiful landscapes of the Carpathian Mountains constitute a strong visual and sonic presence throughout the film, but the sounds of "Ciconia" urge us to see nature as being something other than indifferent to the plight of the people who inhabit it. Its turmoil is not necessarily reflective of Antal's own, but can be interpreted as a direct reaction of the "powers from above" to a disturbance in the natural order. The

[55] Murch quoted in Michael Ondaatje, *The Conversations: Walter Murch and the Art of Editing Film* (New York: Alfred A. Knopf, 2002), 172.
[56] Murch, "Sound Design"; See also Liz Greene, "Ambiguity: Walter Murch and the Metaphoric Use of Sound in *The Godfather, The Conversation* and *Apocalypse Now*," *Film and Film Culture* 3 (2004): 107–113.
[57] Murch, "Sound Design," 247.
[58] Tarkovsky, *Sculpting in Time*, 162.
[59] Murch, "Sound Design," 247.
[60] Chion, *Audio-Vision*, 63.

personification of nature as an active participant in the narrative is first revealed when, in the lake scene, Katalin tells Antal and his wife how her son was conceived and how rain and wild animals came to comfort her after she had been left in the forest by her attackers. At that point, though, nature's magical powers are presented "second hand" so to speak, through Katalin's recounting of the event, although some of its magic seeps into the scene through the appearance of rain, which actually and miraculously started to fall while shooting the single take of Katalin's monologue.[61] At the point where Antal is running through the field to recover his dead wife's body, however, the commotion we hear in nature is in no way comforting, since there are no innocents left to console.

Another dimension to the reading of this scene is rendered by the fact that its soundtrack, even though perceived as enhanced diegetic sound, comes from a single piece of *musique concrète*. The overt blurring of the lines between music and sound design and between diegetic and nondiegetic is not accidental here, and according to Strickland, it reflects the moment in which the film enters the grayest area concerning the moral issues of revenge since Katalin's actions lead to the death of a completely innocent person.[62] The ambiguity surrounding this "fantastical gap"[63] between the diegetic and nondiegetic is reinforced by adjustments to the volume levels of the musical track, which are increased in the outdoor scenes and decreased within the house, to encourage the perception that the sounds of nature heard in this scene are indeed diegetic rather than "composed."

The scene with "Ciconia" was not the only one that used a pre-existing track of *musique concrète*—many other similar tracks were created specifically for the film by friends of the director including Roy (Richard Stevens), Tim Kirby, RR Habarc, én (Pál Tóth), James Blackhouse, and Jean-Michel Van Schouwburg. According to Strickland, using music by people he knows in the context of the sound design was liberating because it allowed him to play with the tracks to the point of "defacing them," in order to respond to the particular need of a scene.[64] As a consequence some of the tracks are hidden in the background, some are used

[61] Strickland, email message to author, January 23, 2010.
[62] Ibid.
[63] Robynn Stilwell's term alludes to the "fantastical," unstable, and ambiguous nature of the process that crosses the barrier between diegetic and nondiegetic, "piercing the skin that explodes the two 'universes'" ("The Fantastical Gap Between Diegetic and Nondiegetic," in *Beyond the Soundtrack: Representing Music in Cinema*, ed. Daniel Goldmark, Lawrence Kramer, and Richard Leppert [Berkeley and Los Angeles and London: University of California Press, 2007], 186). For more on the spatial, temporal, and narrative borders of sound and their blurring see also Michel Chion, *Film, A Sound Art*, trans. Claudia Gorbman (New York: Columbia University Press, 2003), 247–261; David Neumeyer, "Diegetic/Nondiegetic: A Theoretical Model," *Music and the Moving Image* 2, no. 1 (Spring 2009): 26–39, https://www.jstor.org/stable/10.5406/musimoviimag.2.1.0026?seq=1#page_scan_tab_contents, and Jeff Smith, "Bridging the Gap: Reconsidering the Border Between Diegetic and Nondiegetic Music," *Music and the Moving Image* 2, no. 1 (Spring 2009): 1–25, https://www.jstor.org/stable/10.5406/musimoviimag.2.1.0001?seq=1#page_scan_tab_contents.
[64] Strickland, email message to author, January 23, 2010.

as ten-second samples for mobile phone ringtones (James Backhouse/Xylitol), and some are layered on top of each other, as in the night shot of Katalin lying in bed with her son followed by a zoom-in on the forest [00:16:26–00:17:04]. Even though it appears for the first time, the image of forest trees at night preceded by Katalin's whispering of "We're very near, my love. We're very near" and accompanied by a multitrack containing Pál Tóth's *Op. 70110*, Richard Stevens's *Mountain Tone*, and Nurse with Wound's *The Schmürz* is experienced as a nightmare vision, the embodiment of some inner turmoil, also unmistakably identified as the place from which her trauma originates.

Strickland emphasizes that the most important part of the process was the mixing stage, during which the materials he had prepared were combined and the soundscapes he envisioned were brought to life. His recollection of the process also provides a good argument for those who believe that despite all the advances in technology, "the human factor" is still the most critical one in delivering outstanding sound design:

> I have a rough cut from 2007 with pretty much the same sounds, but it needed that "shoe polish" of mixing the volume levels correctly and the stereo positioning. That's where György [Kovács] and Gábor [Erdélyi] were really essential.... It should be noted that we could only afford a 3.1 standard stereo mix. However, after György told me that all the films he did with Béla Tarr were mono, I was blown away. With a mono mix, they created so much space. We actually didn't need what the industry dictated—the 5.1 mix. What perhaps distinguished our sound from other films was the fact that we foregrounded sounds that are normally associated with the background, which alters one's sonic perspective. We learnt this from Robert Ashley's *Automatic Writing* and did this on some Sonic Catering recordings.[65]

The combination of pre-existing and originally composed pieces of *musique concrète*, carefully selected sound effects, and adjustments in sonic perspective creates the sonically vibrant presence of nature in *Katalin Varga*. At the same time, the musical content is often so tightly interwoven with the diegetic sound that it can be misconstrued for sound design, the overlapping of diegetic and nondiegetic realms echoing the ambiguity with which the film addresses the moral issues connected with its central subject of revenge. What is additionally intriguing about Strickland's approach to compilation scoring is that even his use of pre-existing recordings that are recognized as "music" carry a distinctive air of ambiguity, as I will demonstrate in the next section.

---

[65] Ibid.

The Aesthetics of Reticence and Music

It could be argued that the influences and ideas that shaped *Katalin Varga*'s exquisite soundscapes were channelled through two different aspects of Strickland's musical personality. The first is that of Strickland the avid listener, a connoisseur of all kinds of obscure artists and records, a fan of Sergei Paradjanov, Jordan Belson, Lynch's *Eraserhead*, and many others; the other aspect is that of an artist who is the "complete antithesis of the romantic notion of . . . the creator enforcing him or herself on nature and shaping it accordingly," a composer of *musique concrète* interested in an aleatoric exploration of natural acoustic phenomena and "the layering and juxtaposing of incongruous sounds."[66] The first aspect of Strickland's musical personality was dominant during the process of writing, when lyrical, nervous, and angry moods were summoned by listening to Scott Walker, Suicide, and The Cure, respectively, without influencing the film's musical content. A composer's instinct was required more in the process of combining the different layers of sound and in imagining the audiovisual juxtapositions that help create the film's unique mixture of suspense, anguish, and lyricism. One of the defining touches of his debut is provided by its main musical theme, "The Grave and Beautiful Name of Sadness," composed by Steven Stapleton of Nurse with Wound with Geoff Cox.[67] As Strickland explains:

> It was the extended choral, Gothic chill of the soundtrack . . . that put the eventual light on the page of my script, and guided me and the film's characters through the forests of Transylvania. It became apparent that not only would music be able to ghost-write my script, but also to shadow my protagonist's every move. The music became so central to the writing process that unless I had obtained permission to use it, there would have been no point in continuing.[68]

Strickland's decision to juxtapose images of rural, sunny landscapes with the unsettling and disconcertingly static electroacoustic theme has to be appreciated as a daring, almost risky gesture,[69] as it defies the conventional approach to

---

[66] Ibid.

[67] This theme was originally written for a documentary film by Stapleton's wife, Diana Rogerson, *Twisting the Black Threads of My Mental Marionettes.*

[68] Peter Strickland, "Epiphanies," *The Wire* 308 (October 2009): 106.

[69] Strickland's choice of the theme has provoked both positive and negative reactions. Critic David O'Connell noted that it is striking in a way that can be perceived as pretentious ("*Katalin Varga* @ The Melbourne International Film Festival," July 2009, accessed January 10, 2010, www.screenfanatic.com/katalin-varga-film-review/), while at a seminar organized by the Cork Film Festival in 2014, an Oscar-winning composer with an affinity for classical scoring proclaimed that the choice of Stapleton's and Cox's theme was completely unsuitable for the image in terms of its content, texture, and atmosphere.

scoring that requires music to respond to or illuminate certain aspects of a character or a scene in a flexible and unambiguous manner, and the more nuanced its responses are in harmonic, melodic, and rhythmic details, the more successful the score is deemed to be. Instead, the juxtaposition of the early images of Katalin travelling with her son through the stunning landscapes of the Carpathian Mountains with the track's chilling vocals is so unexpected and overwhelming that it brings to mind the audacity of the sound design in *Eraserhead*, where all expectations of image/sound synchronization are thwarted by the sound being treated as a protagonist with a life of its own. A similar example of music's functional autonomy was noted by Kevin Donnelly in relation to Popol Vuh's music for Werner Herzog's films,[70] which is interesting because Strickland says that the music from Herzog's *Nosferatu* is what he originally imagined as the score for his own film.[71] And like the sound in *Eraserhead* or Popol Vuh's film scores, the music in *Katalin Varga* is not prompted by particular situations or details in the story, with the exception of one scene where Katalin finds herself in the forest where she was raped; Stapleton and Cox's "Grave and Beautiful Name of Sadness" exists in the film's diegesis almost as an independent entity, a powerful force that, like Katalin's trauma, lies dormant and hidden until awakened by the protagonist's desire for revenge. It is the kind of music that does not exercise its kinetic potential but thrives on developing a sense of "presence"; it reaches for both the "vertical" and "horizontal" aspects of musical temporality, extending over the frames of the scene and even the plot itself. Its "out of time" quality finds its visual equivalent in the most memorable shot of the film—an image of Katalin and her son sitting on a cart, zoomed in on from behind. The first time this shot halts the narrative is early on, before Katalin's story is fully revealed, hinting at some overwhelming burden that hovers over her journey. Its second appearance is at the very end, the closing shot of the film that transcends the personal dimension of the story with its static, atemporal quality (Figure 3.4).

Strickland's refusal to exploit the affective power of music in scenes of great emotional intensity is reflected not only in the soundtrack, which utilizes the overlap between score and sound design, and in his daring choice of the main musical theme but also in the complete absence of scoring in some crucial scenes. This is particularly evident in the lake scene, in which Katalin, after finding her former assailant Antal, who doesn't recognize her, goes for a boat ride with him and his wife [00:50:17–00:56:40]. Katalin's long, captivating monologue in this scene not only reveals the graphic details of what happened to her but also gives us a glimpse of the emotional and spiritual damage inflicted on her (see Figure 3.5). At one point she

[70] Kevin Donnelly, "Angel of the Air: Popol Vuh's Music and Werner Herzog's Films," in *European Film Music*, ed. Miguel Mera and David Burnand (Farnham, Surrey: Ashgate, 2006), 116–130.
[71] Nick James, "The Sound of Silence," *Sight and Sound* 19 (November 2009): 35.

Figure 3.4. *Katalin Varga*: Katalin (Hilda Péter) with her son in the closing shot of the film.

Figures 3.5. *Katalin Varga*: Katalin telling the story of her plight.

even starts singing, recalling the folk song that Antal and his accomplice sang when they were leaving her after the crime. Her monologue is intercut with close-ups of Antal, who is obviously tortured by her words while at the same time trying not to react or show any emotion in front of his wife, who's unaware that her gentle, loving husband is the monster she is hearing about. Strangely enough, Katalin's recounting of how afterwards nature soothed her devastated body and soul through the appearance of forest animals and the cleansing rain is simultaneously comforting and disturbing. It is comforting because, owing to the serene beauty of the lake landscape, the rhythmic strokes of the oars, the rain that starts to fall at the end of Katalin's monologue, and Hilda Péter's entrancing performance, Katalin's horrific story begins to sound like the telling of a fairytale in which the heroine's suffering is transcended with the help of magical forces. It is at the same time disturbing because Katalin's monologue also suggests that her ordeal left wounds that did not heal, planting the seeds of desperation that would eventually turn her into a murderer. Additional weight is added to this scene by our knowledge that by this point Katalin has already committed a murder and is, to use Michael Brooke's words, "as morally compromised as anyone else."[72]

Apart from a few verses sung by Katalin in the lake scene, there is no other music in it, although this is exactly the type of scene that would normally receive a certain "musical emphasis." In fact, Strickland has mentioned on several occasions that he was urged a number of times to provide a musical soundtrack for it, confirming that the industry habitually responds to the challenges of music scoring with kneejerk reactions.[73] However, he deliberately chose to avoid the classic showdown between actor and score, preserving the full emotional impact of Hilda Péter's performance, as well as that of the setting.

While the decision not to score a scene of great emotional intensity generally represents the epitome of a soundtrack aesthetics that shuns any type of musical exploitation (as do many other scenes discussed in this chapter, which offer innovative scoring solutions for scenes of intense emotional content), this approach can sometimes be complemented with more conventional scoring methods. In Strickland's case, though, any solutions that might seem "ordinary" or banal are reframed by a context that prevents them from being perceived as such. Strickland's third feature, *The Duke of Burgundy* (2014), is an interesting case in point.[74] Here pre-existing electroacoustic music is used in a similar way to how it was employed in his previous two films, to provide soundscapes rich with atmosphere and interpretative possibilities.[75] This idiosyncratic compilation score is complemented with an original score written by Cat's Eyes, which emulates pop scores associated with the 1970s Euro-sleaze: it is diatonic, is harmonically

[72] Michael Brooke, "Katalin Varga," *Sight and Sound* 19 (November 2009): 69.
[73] See, for instance, James, "The Sound of Silence," 35.
[74] Between *Berberian Sound Studio* and *The Duke of Burgundy*, Strickland also codirected with Nick Fenton Björk's concert film *Björk: Biophilia Live* (2014).
[75] The ubiquitous Nurse with Wound is represented by a track from "Soliloquy for Lilith," while other memorable soundscapes in this film are provided by Flying Saucer Attack ("Three Seas") and the Irish improvisational artist Michael Prime, whose work escapes easy categorization, straddling the areas of music, sound art, and ecology. The soundtrack for *The Duke of Burgundy* also features a seven-inch record called "Entomological Acoustics" (2003) released by Strickland's own record label "Peripheral Conserve," which consists solely of field recordings of male and female mole crickets *Gryllotalpa gryllotalpa* and *Gryllotalpa vineae*.

simple, and deliberately emphasizes the cheesy aspect of those scores through a combination of soft harmonies layered with melodic lines sung by whispery female voices.

What enables reframing of the score here is the fact that *The Duke of Burgundy* follows the trajectory of Strickland's previous films by using a well-known genre as a starting point and then plays with it by unpeeling its tropes and twisting its conventions. In the same way *Berberian Sound Studio* is neither really horror nor *giallo* film, so *The Duke of Burgundy* is not an example of the soft-core Euro-erotica it cites as its inspiration, despite being in essence a story about the sadomasochistic relationship between two women. The film is nevertheless very sensual as it creates a tactile and lush sense of space—interior and exterior, aural and visual—that infuses every surface, sound, and colour with sensuality. The other twist on its not-very-respectable model-genre is that its conventions are employed to create a sensitive tale about a loving relationship challenged by the respective partners' conflicting needs.

In her doctoral thesis on the acoustic representation of sadomasochistic erotica in film, Anna-Elena Pääkkölä interprets the original score by Cat's Eyes as representative of kink-queer eroticism in the narrative, describing it as techno-neo-Baroque.[76] Pääkkölä argues that the score paraphrases the late Baroque era in its dance rhythms, structures, and the use of instruments such as oboe and harpsichord while "queering" it through the use of technology. Although, curiously, Pääkkölä never mentions the influence of soft-core erotica on the band's choices regarding harmonic language, instrumentation, and particularly the use of a female voice typical of the genre, she astutely notes that their employment of technology undermines any realistic reading of the scored scenes, maintaining "a distance to emotional depth that would otherwise be registered within the music," and encoding it "as erotic and fantastical rather than empathetic to the characters' emotional journeys."[77]

To that I would add that Strickland's narrative framing of the music often subverts its deliberate references to cheesy aspects of Euro-erotica scores apparent in simple melodic and harmonic language and the eroticized use of female vocals. An example of this is the scene in which the character known as "the Carpenter" (Fatma Mohamed) visits Cynthia (Sidse Babett Knudsen) and Evelyn (Chiara D'Anna) to take measures for a bed with a built-in coffin, which Evelyn wants for her birthday [00:40:00–00:42:17].[78] The scene makes a deliberate attempt to

---

[76] Anna-Elena Pääkkölä, "Sound Kinks: Sadomasochistic Erotica in Audiovisual Music Performances" (PhD diss., University of Turku, 2016), 78–101.

[77] Ibid., 82.

[78] This is the timing of the scene in the DVD release of *The Duke of Burgundy*, Artificial Eye, PAL, 2015.

capture the erotic tension between Evelyn and the Carpenter, which is suggested through the way they look at each other, the Carpenter's flirtatious play with a measuring tape, and Evelyn's palpable excitement. The scene is also funny, because Evelyn seems delighted about the prospect of sleeping in a coffin. The musical accompaniment in this scene is particularly suggestive of the 1970s genre known as Euro-sleaze, a sweet oboe solo accompanied by guitar and keyboard and vocalized by breathy female voices evoking its musical tropes. The subversive aspect of this scene—as well as of the whole film—is the fact that Strickland sets up his sadomasochistic lesbian protagonists and their habits as a "norm." First of all, they live in a village that seems to have only female occupants, which makes the idea of lesbian relationship the rule rather than an exception. From Evelyn's later exchange with the Carpenter it is also indicated that her sadomasochistic relationship with Cynthia is nothing out of the ordinary—in fact, Evelyn will be very disappointed to hear that her bed-coffin won't be ready for her birthday because the waiting list is so long. Strickland has mentioned in several interviews that he wanted to make sure his characters are not seen as outsiders and the extreme aspects of their sadomasochistic relationship are here mostly a tool used to emphasize the problem of the two partners having different needs and desires. At the same time, it is impossible not to see his choice as a challenge to our often overtly prudish and hypocritical attitude to sex and eroticism and to intolerance of homosexual relationships.

Instruments of Torture: *Berberian Sound Studio*

The blurring of the lines between score and sound design and between diegetic and nondiegetic that marks several key scenes in *Katalin Varga* constitutes the primary modus operandi in *Berberian Sound Studio*. This approach is dictated by the film's narrative in which the distinction between real and imagined is brought into question as the film's protagonist, Gilderoy, becomes consumed by the world of the *giallo* film he is working on. When Gilderoy first arrives in Italy from England, he seems intimidated by his surroundings and extremely uncomfortable about his job of providing sound effects for scenes of explicit brutality and sadistic violence, finding comfort only in recordings of a pastoral English countryside and in his mother's letters. As the air of black magic and satanic possession from the film he is working on, *The Equestrian Vortex*, begins to seep into his dreams and his waking life, we are made to question not only the nature of the later sequences in which Gilderoy appears uncharacteristically relaxed in his working environment and in his own skin, speaking Italian, but also the nature of what we have been led to believe is "reality." The breach of the boundaries between score and sound design is also the result of numerous pre-existing pieces of electroacoustic music and *musique concrète*, originally written music, and processed screams, singing, sighs, and whispers being interwoven into a story about film sound and its power "to confound and deceive."[79]

Both an homage and a critique of the *giallo* genre, *Berberian Sound Studio* thrives on contradictions and juxtapositions. The film's complex and tightly woven soundtrack was conceived in direct honour to the adventurous scores of *giallo* films informed by free jazz, prog-rock, and the influence of European modernism of the 1960s, but is nevertheless openly critical of the genre's exploitative and misogynistic tendencies. It celebrates analogue technology and the physicality of the process of making sound with magnetic tape with close-ups of mixing boards, dubbing charts, oscillators, filters, and oscilloscopes punctuating the film, but it was, unsurprisingly, shot and postproduced using digital technology. Finally, it puts into focus *giallo*'s own contradictions as a genre that marries "academia and trash"[80] by having its slasher stories scored by composers such as Bruno Maderna and Ennio Morricone (at the time a member of Gruppo di Improvvisazione Nuova Consonanza). Joining this list of contradictions is also the film's interest in the chasm between an on-screen illusion and the banalities and deceptions involved in its creation, "how something unspeakably horrific can be ridiculous once you take it to a foley stage."[81] While the dubious motives for protracted scenes of violence in *giallo* films are questioned by the conspicuous absence of their visual representation in *Berberian Sound Studio*, on-screen illusions are demystified by darkly humorous Foley sound sessions in which hacked watermelons, stabbed cabbages, and water sizzling in a heated pan provide visceral aural and visual substitutes for the atrocities committed in the film within a film, the leitmotif image of discarded vegetables rotting slowly in the studio hinting at the corrupting nature of the process.

Considering all its inherent contradictions, the different levels of ambiguity in the storyline, and the complex (and apparently split) personality of its protagonist, Gilderoy, Strickland's second film provides a typical example of an interrogative text that encourages the viewer to engage with its challenges. While supportive of the film's interrogative approach and painstakingly nuanced, the film's soundtrack could hardly be described as reticent—it is in fact quite lush, bursting with intertextual references and elaborately devised sonic delights. The attribute of "reticence" is more fitting when describing the film's narrative, which shuns visual depictions of violence and deliberately leaves some details in the story and about the character unexplained. Instead of reticence, the underlying

[79] Strickland quoted in Jason Wood, "The Art of Noise," *Sight and Sound* 22 (September 2012): 34.

[80] Strickland, "Special Features, Director's Commentary," *Berberian Sound Studio* DVD, Artificial Eye, PAL, 2012.

[81] Strickland quoted in Wood, "The Art of Noise," 32.

principle of this soundtrack is the same one that Strickland identified as the "code for entering the whole film"—musicality.[82]

One of the pieces that Strickland has singled out in his interviews as a particularly important inspiration for the creation of *Berberian Sound Studio* is Luciano Berio's *Visage* (1961). Written for his then-wife, virtuosic soprano Cathy Berberian, *Visage* is an extraordinary twenty-minute study of extended vocal techniques including inarticulate sounds, laughter, crying, and moaning. Instead of using actual excerpts from Berio's piece, however, Strickland asked a number of his composer friends to send him some treated screams, looking for recordings either more aggressive or more abstract than found in a typical horror.[83] These were provided by Andrew Liles, Colin Potter, and Steven Stapleton from Nurse with Wound, as well as by Jonathan Coleclough, Tim Kirby, and Clive Graham. The most haunting aspect of this soundtrack with its clear references to both *Visage* and the *giallo* taste for vocal effects is the seemingly ubiquitous presence of female voices whispering, singing, murmuring, and sighing, which punctuate the film with recurring persistency.[84] In addition, the film features performances by vocal improvisers Katalin Ladik (known in the 1970s as the Yugoslav Cathy Berberian) and Jean-Michel Van Schouwburg, who, appearing as themselves, provide the voices for the supernatural characters in *The Equestrian Vortex*, the film within the film.

Another obvious inspiration for this screenplay about engineering sounds for a horror film is the distinctive sonic makeup of Italian *giallo* soundtracks from the 1970s created by progressive rock bands like Goblin; composers Riz Ortolani, Fabio Frizzi, and early Morricone; and in particular Nicola Piovanni's *Footprints on the Moon* (*Le Orme*, 1975). These influences are channelled into the original score by British band Broadcast, who use organ, flute, and female voice as instruments often associated with *giallo* films and foreground melodic, harmonic, and instrumental juxtapositions typical of the same vocabulary—lyrical and aggressive, innocent and eerie, ecclesiastical and occult.

As in *Katalin Varga*, the most important musical influence came from Nurse with Wound recordings from the 1980s such as *Homotopy to Marie* (1982) and *The Sylvie and Babs Hi-Fi Companion* (1985). Nurse with Wound's eclectic style, which draws on the whole heritage of Western avant-garde, ambient, and industrial

---

[82] Strickland, "Special Features."

[83] Many screams were recorded by Eugenia Caruso, who plays the on-screen character Claudia/Monica. Strickland points out that the practice of one actor providing screams for different characters was typical in *giallo* films. He mentions the case of Suzy Kendall, the star of films such as *The Bird with the Crystal Plumage* (Dario Argento, 1970) and *Torso* (Sergio Martino, 1973), and who makes a guest appearance in *Berberian Sound Studio*, recording all the screams in *The Bird with the Crystal Plumage* (Wood, "The Art of Noise," 36).

[84] Some of the softer female sighs and whispers were produced by James Cargill from Broadcast, who pitched his voice up, multiplied it, and surrounded it with eerie echoes (Strickland, email to author, February 9, 2013).

music, as well as *musique concrète*, also left its trace on the film's narrative structure, which, as Strickland admits, "veers towards the abstract" in the finale.[85] Repetitions as a constitutive part of music are built into the film's structure on all levels, with an almost strophic reappearance of narrative motifs showing Gilderoy listening to recordings from home and reading his mother's letters, and rerecording screams and lines for the film within a film. These are complemented with visual leitmotifs of sound equipment, rotting vegetables, "silenzio" signs, and so forth. At the same time, even the thread of the plot in which Gilderoy's dreams and reality start to overlap, creating a parallel narrative streak in which he appears uncharacteristically confident and speaking Italian, has been credited with a musical influence. It is clear that these scenes are not part of the linear narrative development because they replicate certain situations from the beginning of the film, as if the protagonist got caught in a loop with a different dub. Most reviewers interpreted this narrative diversion as an indication of Gilderoy's descent into madness, reflected in the distortion and subsequent disintegration of images showing the engineer's face and its disappearance behind burning celluloid.[86] One also might notice that this "glitch" in the narrative mirrors Gilderoy's actual experience of postproduction work in which he rewinds, loops, and dubs only to seemingly become caught up in these processes himself.[87] In the director's commentary on the *Berberian Sound Studio* DVD, however, Strickland indicates that the original inspiration for this type of narrative subversion came from listening to music in which "it is a norm to have wildly incongruous sections" breaking the flow. This ambiguity of narrative is also mirrored in the symbolically dissolving boundaries between physical spaces done through editing techniques inspired by the work of Czechoslovakian director Juraj Herz and his film *The Cremator* (1969).[88] By creating seamless connections between different locations/scenes that place Gilderoy in the studio in one moment and then listening to his tapes from home in his living quarters in another, the film challenges our sense of spatial and physical boundaries. This is further emphasized by the pervasiveness of eerie music, screams, and whispers that surround Gilderoy like a mental fog and become increasingly denser as his confusion intensifies and his state of mind deteriorates.

Despite his both playful and critically charged pokes at the deceits involved in the filmmaking process, Strickland insists that all the sounds heard in the film can be traced to a diegetic source. He felt that, considering the ambiguity of the narrative context in which the film "eats its own tail," and the visual morphing

---

[85] Strickland, "Special Features."

[86] The idea of an "unstable," fluid reality/diegesis and the manipulation of the film track that reflects it visually is a tribute to Peter Tscherkassky's films, particularly his *Outer Space* (1999) (Strickland, "Special Features").

[87] I'm grateful to Randolph Jordan for this observation.

[88] Strickland, "Special Features."

of physical and sonic spaces, it was important to establish a certain anchor in
the film's diegetic realm by treating all sounds as diegetic.[89] Although some of
the disturbing, otherworldly, and chilling noises that surround the protagonist
might be occasionally amplified, giving the impression that they are nondiegetic,
all of them can be traced to the equipment in Gilderoy's sound studio and the
film within the film he is working on. Diegetic or not, the sounds belonging to
The Equestrian Vortex are often presented asynchronously, their pervasiveness
in Gilderoy's waking life and dreams inducing a sense of uneasiness and discomfort. Additionally, *The Equestrian Vortex* as a source of the diegetic soundtrack
is never seen on the screen, save its opening credits, and since these are the only
opening credits we see in Strickland's film, one starts to wonder if Gilderoy is
not indeed himself one of the characters in this imaginary film, caught in its
endless loops.

As in *Katalin Varga*, in *Berberian Sound Studio* a number of episodes were
built around existing pieces of electroacoustic music and *musique concrète*, including the scene in which Gilderoy creates the sound of a UFO using a light bulb
and what looks like a large toast rack, based on a piece by the Bohman Brothers;
a prolonged zoom on Silvia (Fatma Mohamed) screaming over an excerpt from
Nurse with Wound's "Glory Hole"; and two excerpts of the Sonic Catering Band
played along with diegetic sounds of boiling vegetables.[90] Interestingly, though,
particularly in the "Glory Hole" scene [00:58:00–00:59:10],[91] the effect of this
approach is somewhat different than in the "Ciconia" scene from *Katalin Varga*.

In this scene, Silvia, who plays one of the characters in *The Equestrian Vortex*,
comes to Gilderoy asking him to record her screaming. The "perfect," blood-
chilling scream is, of course, the Holy Grail of horror cinema as seen in Brian
de Palma's *Blow Out* (1980) and eloquently discussed by Chion in *The Voice in
Cinema*. "The *screaming point* in a cinematic narrative," says Chion, is "something that generally gushes forth from the mouth of a woman, which … must
fall at an appointed spot, explode at a precise moment … calculated to give
this point a maximum impact."[92] Chion insists that the screaming point is not
so much about the sound quality of the scream but rather its placement: it is
"a point of the unthinkable inside the thought, of the indeterminate inside the
spoken, of unpresentability inside representation."[93] This description resonates
well with Silvia's state of mind at the moment when she approaches Gilderoy.

[89] Ibid.
[90] Strickland, email message to author, February 9, 2013.
[91] This is the timing of the scene in the DVD release of *Berberian Sound Studio*, Artificial Eye,
PAL, 2012.
[92] Michel Chion, *The Voice in Cinema*, trans. Claudia Gorbman (New York: Columbia University
Press, 1999), 76–77.
[93] Ibid., 77.

Prior to that, her efforts to record Teresa's screams were derided by the film's producer Cosimo (Francesco Coraggio), who treats all the actresses with open contempt. When Gilderoy asks Silvia which reel he should record the scream for, she replies: "Forget the reel. I just need to scream." We also learn later that Silvia—like all the other women in the cast of *The Equestrian Vortex*—has been sexually harassed by the film's director Santini (Antonio Mancino), and although she will get her revenge by destroying all the recordings of Teresa's voice before leaving, in this scene she looks tired and defeated, her request obviously the result of suppressed anger and frustration. The "Glory Hole" scene thus becomes this film's "screaming point" where "speech is suddenly extinct, a black hole, the exit of being"[94] and also another example of genre subversion: instead of being exploited by the producers of *The Equestrian Vortex*, Silvia's scream remains an expression of an intimately desperate moment, witnessed only by Gilderoy (see Figure 3.6).[95]

Considered in the context of the earlier discussion about creating a "perceptual gap" by avoiding complete alignment between what is seen and what is heard, the "Glory Hole" scene can be interpreted in different ways. The actual Nurse with Wound piece starts with an uncharacteristically gentle melody sung by a female voice, which is gradually pushed into the background by screeching, yelping cries processed to the point of losing their human quality, producing quite a disturbing effect. The scream used in the film is taken from the closing moments of the piece beginning with what sounds like a woman taking a deep breath and then exploding into multiple consecutive screams and cries treated with echo and reverb. When paired with the image of Silvia screaming, though, the "limitlessness"[96] of the track's final scream becomes contained and its associative potential somewhat reduced to a very specific scream, bringing to mind Chion's argument about how the process of de-acousmatisation robs the previously hidden source of its powers of omnipotence, omniscience, and ubiquity.[97] Or, thinking in terms of Murch's theory of metaphoric sound and the benefits of the ambiguity rendered by it, one could say that giving a face and body to a musical scream reverses the process of establishing audiovisual ambiguity, which made the "Ciconia" scene from *Katalin Varga* so striking. It suggests that the semiotic ambivalence of pre-existing *musique concrète* is not guaranteed if the sonic content finds a "too suitable" visual match. However, despite the fact that the close audiovisual alignment seems to diminish the potential for a metaphoric

---

[94] Ibid., 79.
[95] I am grateful to Liz Greene for making this point in a Q&A session after my presentation at the *Cinesonica* conference at University of Ulster, Magee, February 15–17, 2013.
[96] Chion, *The Voice in Cinema*, 79.
[97] Chion, *Audio-Vision*, 130.

Figure 3.6. *Berberian Sound Studio*: Silvia (Fatma Mohamed) screaming in the recording booth—a visual reference to the first murder in Dario Argento's *Deep Red* (1975).

reading of Nurse with Wound's pre-existing track, this is not entirely true either. Reverberated, layered, and multiplied to chilling effect and married to the image of Silvia's face distorted by a scream disappearing into the black void as shown in Figure 3.6,[98] this one moment in the film gives voice to all the badly treated, harassed, and exploited women in the horror industry whose bodies have been slashed for entertainment and vocal chords used only for screaming.

Conclusion

All the strategies employed in Strickland's films that have been discussed here paint a picture of a personal aesthetic that not only resists the conventions of mainstream scoring but also manages to build a captivating audiovisual world in which music and sound design play important roles in establishing film as an interrogative text. Strickland's interrogations of sensitive topics such as physical and psychological trauma, the moral issues surrounding revenge, and the cinematic portrayal of violence in cinema, particularly towards women, are

[98] According to Strickland, the image of Silvia screaming with her palms pressed against the glass of a small recording booth is a visual reference to the first murder in *Deep Red* (Dario Argento, 1975) (Strickland, "Special Features").

aided by soundtracks that reflect the complexity of these topics in elaborate sound designs and intricate interactions between their different elements that undermine the divisions between pre-existing and originally composed scores; between music, sound, and noise; and between diegetic and nondiegetic. They intelligently and compellingly convey the most subtle aspects of the films' thematic undercurrents while simultaneously affirming that clear-cut characters, events, or their interpretations are not part of the films' or Strickland's view of the world. Informed by the director's musical experience and loaded with personal homages, soundtracks in Strickland's films prompt viewers to engage emotionally with the films without encouraging their passivity or supplanting their emotional reactions by recreating a parallel sonic narrative that duplicates what is presented on the screen.

Although Strickland's artistic principles have much in common with filmmakers who pursue the aesthetics of reticence through narrative and scoring methods, and his employment of pre-existing musical material qualifies his soundtracks as *auteur music*, his films do not easily fit into the mould of either practice. They present a new voice in European cinema that is adventurous and unique in its musical knowledge and interests. The imagination and refinement manifested in the employment of sound, music, and silence in his films position Strickland high among those directors who honour their audiences with evocative soundtracks designed to draw them deep into worlds with complex themes and characters without trying to ease their discomfort or patronize them through explicit scoring.

4

Musicalized Sound Design and the Erotics of Cinema

The previous chapter showed how the incorporation of pre-existing electroa-coustic music and *musique concrète* into a film's diegetic sound challenges the divisions between music, sound, and noise; between originally composed and pre-existing scores; and between diegetic and nondiegetic. This chapter further explores the musical qualities of these types of soundtrack and their relationship to forms of contemporary music such as *musique concrète* and soundscape com-positions, with the intention of illuminating how the methods of this practice foreground sensuous aspects of cinema. It also builds upon the discussion about aesthetic issues of the practice of blurring the line between score and sound de-sign initiated in the previous chapter in order to determine how they relate to questions of embodied spectatorship and the sensuousness of film form.

As I mentioned in the previous chapter, the work of Gus Van Sant was espe-cially instrumental in highlighting an approach that emphasized the materiality and musicality of sound in combination with a distinctive visual style. One of the crucial features of Van Sant's films from the beginning of the noughties is their sound design, which combines diegetic sound with pre-existing soundscape compositions and pieces of *musique concrète* by composers such as Hildegard Westerkamp and Francis White. In this chapter I want to focus on Van Sant's sonic methods that come from a less "premeditated" place—the director's fascination with quotidian details and actions, the *photogénie*[1] of cinematic movement, and the musicality of diegetic sounds, like those of walking, which underline purely sensuous aspects of the cinematic experience. The distinctive audiovisual style of Van Sant's Death Trilogy will be viewed in connection to Béla Tarr's methods typical of "ritualized" and "slow" cinema, which inspired Van Sant. A compar-ative study of Claire Denis's *Beau Travail* (1998) and Anna Rose Holmer's *The Fits* (2015) in the following section continues the thread of exploring the mu-sicality of diegetic sounds in the context in which the sensuousness of the film body is intertwined with a sensual depiction of a human body on screen. The

---

[1] *Photogénie* is the term used by French filmmaker Louis Deluc to describe the ability of the camera to make images and people appear intrinsically attractive, presenting the world from a per-spective different to our everyday perception of things.

Sound Design Is the New Score: Theory, Aesthetics, and Erotics of the Integrated Soundtrack. Danijela Kulezic-Wilson, Oxford University Press (2020). © Oxford University Press.
DOI: 10.1093/oso/ 9780190855314.001.0001

chapter concludes with a case study of Hou Hsiao-Hsien's *The Assassin* (2015), which offers a model of sensuousness startlingly different from the examples that precede it. Rather than being "grounded" in images and sounds that evoke the corporeality of everyday existence, the erotic charge of Hou Hsiao-Hsien's film is elusive and intangible, earned through a markedly rhythmic interplay of sonic and visual means, the result of a unique audiovisual alchemy.

These various methods of sonic and audiovisual integration will be viewed through the concept of the erotics of cinema, which draws on Vivian Sobchack's notion of film as a body, Laura Marks's work on sensory cinema, and the feminist concept of erotics as theorized by Susan Sontag and Audre Lorde in the 1960s and 1970s, respectively. I will particularly focus on how the use of sound encourages an intimate encounter with film that engages the listener intellectually, emotionally, and viscerally.

The Erotics of Cinema

Many of the examples of soundtrack musicalization discussed in this book foreground the materiality of cinema and its audiovisual sensuality. Recent phenomenological studies connect these tendencies with the issue of embodied spectatorship, as in the work by Vivian Sobchack, who states in her book *The Address of the Eye* that cinema "uses *modes of embodied existence* (seeing, hearing, physical, and reflective movement) as the vehicle, the 'stuff,' the substance of its language" and it "transposes, without completely transforming, those modes of being alive and consciously embodied in the world that count for each of us as *direct* experience."[2] Scholarly attention to the connection between the sensual appeal of cinema and embodied spectatorship not only gives due consideration to the experience of cinema through the senses but also, as Thomas Elsaesser and Malte Hagener argue, constitutes an approach that "cuts across formalist and realist theories" and "tries to close the gap between theories of authorship and reception."[3] While the notion of embodied spectatorship informs a great deal of the discussion that follows, I should say that what intrigues me even more in this context is the idea of film as a body. Thus, the word "sensuous" in this context has less to do with the exploration of embodied audiovisual spectatorship and more with the sensuousness of the medium itself—its sonic and visual textures, composition, movement, and flow. This is a matter of shifting the focus of the

---

[2] Vivian Sobchack, *The Address of the Eye: A Phenomenology of Film Experience* (Princeton, NJ: Princeton University Press, 1992), 4–5.

[3] Thomas Elsaesser and Malte Hagener, *Film Theory: An Introduction Through the Senses* (London and New York: Routledge, 2010), 11.

discussion rather than establishing a new one because both Sobchack and Laura Marks, whose book *Touch*[4] is another relevant source for this discussion, recognize the sensuous nature of film. However, instead of limiting my enquiry to the connection between the sensuousness of the medium and embodied experience, I am interested in how the sensuousness of the medium and embodied spectatorship inform aesthetic experience, or to be more precise, I'm interested in *the sensuousness of the aesthetic experience*.

Because of its history, aesthetics has generally been associated with intellectual activity and the philosophical evaluation of art. Admittedly, a fundamental aspect of this experience is indeed ineffable, to paraphrase Vladimir Jankélévitch,[5] but it nevertheless involves a certain type of pleasure that is partly the result of stimulation of the senses. The notion of "pleasure" in film spectatorship, however, is generally associated with the "invisible," illusionistic style and is entangled in an ideological minefield interspersed with issues of the male gaze, cultural appropriation, exploitation, and affective manipulation. Thus, I think it is worth reconsidering for a moment this notion in the context of the art experience.

There is a sense that the tension between a formal understanding of art versus a cultural one, and the shift from the former to the latter in the second half of the last century, not only undermined the concept of formal pleasure but also made it ideologically problematic. And yet, the very materiality of cinema and its sonic and visual textures, composition, rhythm, movement, and flow inevitably affect our experience of it. My choice of the word "sensuous" instead of "sensory" emphasizes an engagement with film that takes pleasure in the sensuousness of the form itself rather than "the pursuit of sensations" that is generally associated with advanced projection technology. In my mind film sensuousness captures the richness of an experience, which can be cerebral, embodied, and emotional at the same time, as the cinema experience often is. This notion of film sensuousness does not contradict the argument advocated by proponents of materialist theory such as Laura Marks, who herself recognizes the complexity and synesthetic nature of cinematic perception;[6] it is simply another step towards integrative perception and analysis that, following the backlash led by political awareness of critical and cultural theory against the idealist nature of aesthetics, wishes to retrieve the relevance of the aesthetic experience and view it as a form of "political" engagement with film.

[4] Laura Marks, *Touch: Sensuous Theory and Multisensory Media* (Minneapolis and London: University of Minnesota Press, 2002).
[5] Vladimir Jankélévitch, *La Musique et l'Ineffable* (Paris: Editions du Seuil, 1983).
[6] Marks, *Touch*, 13.

As Laura Marks argues in her compelling and highly personalized rumina-
tion on the ideological upheavals in the art world in the last chapter of her book
Touch, there are different ways of being political:

> A work that critiques popular culture reinforces its dependent relationship with
> popular culture. Its goal is political change at the level of language, which is col-
> lective but not deeply embodied. . . . By contrast, a work that is only about itself
> and the passion of creation offers a model of freedom from popular culture. Its
> goal is political change at the level of individual action—which is embodied
> but not collective. And of course in between these poles lay art that politicized
> personal, embodied experience. In short, the shift away from activist art to per-
> sonal art during the '90s can be seen as not a depoliticization but a shift in po-
> litical strategies.[7]

Marks's comment could be seen as an invitation to expand the pool of topics
and approaches that are seen as engaging with a wider cultural context and for
re-evaluating the cultural relevance of so-called navel-gazing art. Another perspective on this issue can be found in the discourse surrounding the world of
contemporary theatre and in the view of theatre theorist Hans-Thies Lehmann,
who proposes that "political engagement does not consist in the topics but in
the forms of perception."[8] Lehmann comments on the fact that our engagement
with political reality is influenced by the media, which persistently dramatizes
all events, creating the fantasy of its omnipotence and encouraging an illusion of
"being able to preside quite calmly over all realities . . . without being affected by
them oneself."[9] According to Lehmann, in the experience of reality mediated by
the media there is no relation between address and answer, which removes any
sense of responsibility from the audience. While theatre can't compete with the
superiority of media structures in terms of topicality, it can re-establish the connection between personal experience and perception through the *politics of perception* by putting at the centre the "*mutual implication of actors and spectators
in the theatrical production of images*."[10] Making the audience aware of that connection implicitly encourages them to contemplate their role in this relationship,
which, according to Lehmann, makes their experience not only aesthetic but also
ethico-political. Lehmann's argument indicates that the term "politics of perception" should not be understood in a purely phenomenological sense, not least
because his comments resonate in many ways with the discussion about how the

[7] Ibid., 199.
[8] Hans-Thies Lehmann, *Postdramatic Theatre*, trans. Karen Jürs-Munby (London and New York:
Routledge, 2006), 184.
[9] Ibid., 185.
[10] Ibid., 186 (emphasis in the original).

interrogative approach to narrative encourages audiences' active engagement with film. In fact, these comments invite us to consider how the aesthetic issues discussed in the previous chapter relate to the issues of embodied spectatorship and the sensuousness of film form. If we connect that to Marks's earlier comments about political and personal art, the question then follows: what could be a political strategy of art that focuses on personal, or rather, human issues that are not necessarily culturally specific, and what could be political about the scholarship that is interested in it? To suggest some possible answers I would like to look at the idea of the erotics of art, which was an important part of the feminist discourse in the 1960s and 1970s.

While thinking about the sensuousness of cinema and what it means to be "turned on" by it in intellectual, emotional, and maybe even spiritual terms, I thought of Susan Sontag's essay "Against Interpretation." In this essay Sontag posits that our compulsive habit to "violate" works of art by imposing upon them various interpretations "indicates a dissatisfaction (conscious or unconscious) with the work, a wish to replace it by something else."[11] This not only is a reflection of a belief that a work of art is primarily its content but also makes us oblivious to that which is "pure, untranslatable," and ripe with "sensuous immediacy."[12]

Sontag argues that hermeneutic approaches to art take the sensory experience of art "for granted" and explains that this is particularly problematic in the context of a culture that is based on excess and overproduction, resulting in a "steady loss of sharpness in our sensory experience."[13] Although Sontag's essay was written in 1964, her argument that the material plenitude and sheer crowdedness of modern life "conjoin to dull our sensory faculties" resonates even more strongly in our time when the average cinema experience revels in ever-more realistic CGI, 3D, and ear-bursting Dolby Sound. So, to recognize sensuality beyond the superficial onslaught facilitated by the use of digital technology and superior projection equipment, we must, as Sontag says, "recover our senses" and "learn to *see* more, to *hear* more, to *feel* more." "In place of a hermeneutics," says Sontag, "we need an erotics of art."[14]

But what is the erotics of art? For the answer I turned to another feminist text, Audre Lorde's essay "Uses of the Erotic," where she argues that the erotic is "that power which rises from our deepest and non-rational knowledge"[15] and a nurturer of understanding.[16] She reclaims the word "erotic" from patriarchal

[11] Susan Sontag, *Against Interpretation* (London: Vintage, 2001), 10.
[12] Ibid., 9.
[13] Ibid., 13.
[14] Ibid., 14.
[15] Audre Lorde, *Sister Outsider: Essays and Speeches* (Berkeley, CA: Crossing Press, 1984/2007), 53.
[16] Ibid., 53.

culture, which associates it specifically with corporeal love and pleasure—often confusing it with its opposite, the pornographic—to invoke instead its wider meaning as used in philosophy and psychology. Lorde does not specifically quote any philosophical or scholarly sources, but her interpretation of the Greek word *eros* as the personification of "creative power and harmony"[17] seems to recognize Plato's idealistic concept of *eros* as an aspiration and desire that can contribute to our understanding of truth and beauty. On the other hand, considering Lorde's feminist stance and her advocacy of intersectivity, her endorsement of the erotic might also have been inspired by Jung's qualification of *eros* as a feminine principle that, like the masculine *logos*, is looking for connection, interaction, and, ultimately, wholeness. After all, Lorde's understanding of the erotic emphasizes the power "which comes from sharing deeply any pursuit with another person"[18] to become a "lens through which we scrutinize all aspects of our existence."[19]

What gives a political slant to Lorde's understanding of the erotic is her criticism of the misrepresentation of the erotic as "the confused, the trivial, the psychotic, the plasticized sensation"[20] and its misuse by men against women. She cites pornography as an example of "direct denial of the power of the erotic," which "emphasizes sensation without feeling."[21] This is a point worth dwelling on because in the same way Lorde's understanding of the term "erotic" exceeds the domain of corporeal pleasure to include our attitude towards art, truth, and beauty, so her description of pornography can be seen as reflective of broader tendencies in our culture—cinema included—to stimulate the senses through spectacle devoid of substance, graphic violence, and representations of the body in distress. After all, it is not a coincidence that a subgenre of horror cinema fascinated with gore and violence is called "torture porn." Lorde's criticism of the suppression of the erotic as an internal power can also be read as a condemnation of a broader tendency in Western society to break up holistic concepts, create false dichotomies, and reduce powerful concepts to "trivial," "plasticized" versions of themselves (she also condemns the false dichotomy between the political and the spiritual).

Thus, taking into account both Sontag's and Lorde's thoughts about art and culture, I would argue that the idea of erotics as a form of experiencing art can be reclaimed through a sensual and intimate engagement with it that rejects the "trivial" version of sensuousness where sensory overload is mistaken for sensuality. The idea of erotics of cinema, however, should not be confused with film's subject matter but is rather the manner in which cinema approaches its

[17] Ibid., 55.
[18] Ibid., 56.
[19] Ibid., 57.
[20] Ibid., 54.
[21] Ibid.

subject and the relationship it establishes with the audioviewer. This also aligns with Marks's thoughts on the audience's erotic relationship with film. Calling on Sobchack's argument that cinema viewing is an exchange between two bodies— that of the viewer and that of the film—Marks takes it to the next stage, saying that "the oscillation between the two creates an erotic relationship"[22] since embodied perception is about "the viewer responding to the video as to another body and to the screen as another skin."[23] This statement not only emphasizes the spectator's sensuous engagement with film but also recognizes the medium's own sensuality.

Lawrence Kramer supports this sentiment when he declares that the cinematic body is "primarily or originarily erotic." Considering that the audience receives music as a direct address to sensation and affect, which is "the default mode of the reception of virtually all music—the music reveals that the cinematic body belongs to Eros."[24] Kramer is careful to point out that this does not mean that film music is erotic in the everyday sense of the term but rather that "the corporeality of the cinematic body is defined by the erotic potential of the marriage of music and gaze."[25] Although Kramer specifically refers to the use of classical music in cinema, the next section will show that there are no obvious reasons not to expand this argument to include sound in general.

The Erotics of Film Sound

I don't think it is in any way controversial to argue that one of film's quickest and most powerful routes to sensual intensity is through sound and music. Many experiments have proved that music has a direct effect on the body by affecting the autonomic nervous system, which results in accelerated heart and pulse rates, breathing becoming shallower, skin temperature rising, and the pattern of brain waves becoming less regular.[26] Apart from the corporeal effect on the audience, music also gives life to images themselves. As Lawrence Kramer points out:

> In order to flesh out the spectral image, the image must be joined to a vibratory depth, and to do that the cinematic image must be combined with music. The reason for this is less historical than it is phenomenological. The body *is* a

---

[22] Marks, *Touch*, 13.

[23] Ibid., 4.

[24] Lawrence Kramer, "Classical Music, Virtual Bodies, Narrative Film," in *The Oxford Handbook of Film Music Studies*, ed. David Neumeyer (Oxford and New York: Oxford University Press, 2014), 354.

[25] Ibid.

[26] Judith Becker, "Anthropological Perspectives on Music and Emotion," in *Music and Emotion: Theory and Research*, ed. Patrick N. Juslin and John A. Sloboda (Oxford: Oxford University Press, 2001), 142.

vibratory depth; its depth is where music vibrates; to add music to the primitive cinematic image is literally, not metaphorically but literally, to give the image a body.[27]

Despite the proven effectiveness and intensity of the impact sound has on the cinema spectator, this topic has traditionally been sidelined in film scholarship, so it is not particularly surprising that neither Sobchack nor Marks addresses the role of sound in a significant way, "important though it is," as Marks herself admits in her first book.[28] Nevertheless, a number of individual studies have begun to amend this oversight, including Ben Winters's exploration of corporeality and cinematic emotion, Lisa Coulthard's studies of haptic noise and sonic disgust, Miguel Mera's concept of 3D sound and the materiality of film music, and Caitriona Walsh's article about the corporeality of horror cinema.[29]

The sensuality of postclassical cinema and the role of sound in it are also addressed in Carol Vernallis's book *Unruly Media* and Anahid Kassabian's *Ubiquitous Listening*. In *Unruly Media* Vernallis describes the sensuality of postclassical cinema using the term "intensified audiovisual aesthetics." She notes that in this "mixing-board aesthetic" all parameters can become heightened, including lighting, gesture and performance, sets and costumes, colour, graphic typography, and sound.[30] More to the point, films based on intensified aesthetics synchronize the experience of the spectator with that of the film's body:

> Like music videos [these new films] express a human physicality that can unfold and expand in discovery, alongside the camera's and the music's trajectory. Camera, sound, and even CGI can each have their own way

[27] Kramer, "Classical Music," 353.

[28] Laura Marks, *The Skin of the Film: Intercultural Cinema, Embodiment, and the Senses* (Durham, NC, and London: Duke University Press, 2000), xv.

[29] Lisa Coulthard, "Dirty Sound: Haptic Noise in New Extremism," in *The Oxford Handbook of Sound and Image in Digital Media*, ed. Carol Vernallis, Amy Herzog, and John Richardson (Oxford and New York: Oxford University Press, 2013), 115–126. Lisa Coulthard, "Acoustic Disgust: Sound, Affect, and Cinematic Violence," in *The Palgrave Handbook of Sound Design and Music in Screen Media: Integrated Soundtracks*, ed. Liz Greene and Danijela Kulezic-Wilson (Basingstoke, Hampshire: Palgrave Macmillan, 2016), 183–193; Miguel Mera, "Towards 3-D Sound: Spatial Presence and the Space Vacuum," in *The Palgrave Handbook of Sound Design and Music in Screen Media: Integrated Soundtracks*, ed. Liz Greene and Danijela Kulezic-Wilson (Basingstoke, Hampshire: Palgrave Macmillan, 2016), 91–111; Miguel Mera, "Materializing Film Music," in *The Cambridge Companion to Film Music*, ed. Mervyn Cooke and Fiona Ford (Cambridge: Cambridge University Press, 2016), 157–172; Caitriona Walsh, "Obscene Sounds: Sex, Death, and the Body On-Screen," *Music and the Moving Image* 10, no. 3 (Fall 2017): 36–54, https://muse.jhu.edu/; Ben Winters, "Corporeality, Musical Heartbeats, and Cinematic Emotion," *Music, Sound and the Moving Image* 2, no. 1 (Spring 2008): 3–25.

[30] Carol Vernallis, *Unruly Media: YouTube, Music Video, and the New Digital Cinema* (Oxford and New York: Oxford University Press, 2013), 38.

of knowing the world, so we might call this new style pantheistic, or multi-perspectival-techno-embodied.[31]

As suggested by this quote, Vernallis also recognizes the musical logic behind the "ravishment of the senses"[32] that intensified audiovisual aesthetics strives for, singling out music video as the main influence on contemporary cinema's intensified audiovisual aesthetics and its musicality. Although I see film musicality as a much broader phenomenon historically and aesthetically, one that is not limited to postclassical cinema nor primarily indebted to music video,[33] I agree that the latter has undoubtedly contributed to its accelerated emergence in contemporary cinema. As Vernallis demonstrates in her case studies of *Moulin Rouge!* (2001) and *Eternal Sunshine of the Spotless Mind* (2004), examples of musicalization are usually achieved through the combination of narrative, visual, and sonic means that "increase [films'] sensual density" while maintaining the musicality of the flow.[34]

Like Vernallis, Kassabian also addresses the importance of sensory stimulation in contemporary culture by exploring the connection between affect and the senses. She argues that the move away from plot structure and character development towards "roller-coaster rides of hyper sound and vision" constitutes a whole new genre in contemporary cinema defined by "boom aesthetics" of sensory experience.[35] Both these scholars use case studies based on intense sensory stimulation involving elaborate sound and visual effects, advanced projection technology, and a general heightening of all parameters in tune with what Vernallis calls intensified audiovisual aesthetics. I argue, however, that although the appeal of contemporary cinema is often associated with enhanced sensory stimulation, the true erotic power of art is usually evoked through different, very measured means.

It would also be wise to remember that the sensuousness of cinema is not a consequence of the latest development in exhibition or postproduction technology. In his book *Film Music: A History*, in the chapter "A 'New Wave' of Film Music," James Wierzbicki quotes Gerald Must:

The new American cinema does not ask to be taken as reality but constantly announces that it is artificial. Rather than effacing the film's artfulness ... the

---

[31] Ibid., 41.
[32] Ibid., 76.
[33] See Kulezic-Wilson, *The Musicality of Narrative Film* (Basingstoke, Hampshire: Palgrave Macmillan, 2015).
[34] Vernallis, *Unruly Media*, 81.
[35] Anahid Kassabian, *Ubiquitous Listening: Affect, Attention and Distributed Subjectivity* (Berkeley: California University Press, 2013), xxx.

new directors throw in as many cinematic tricks as possible, which both inten-
sify the film's moods and remind the audience that it is watching a film.[36]

One of the consequences of this "deliberate artificiality," says Must, is "an emotional power in the visual assaults of the medium itself." The audience thus does
not just respond to "story and people but to the physical stimulation of eye and
ear for its own sake."[37]

Must's comments seem fit to describe a familiar strand of contemporary cinema concerned with sensory onslaught as described by Vernallis and
Kassabian, but what is interesting about his observations is that they were
written in the 1960s, commenting on the influence of the French New Wave on
New Hollywood cinema. If we compare these comments with those written in
response to developments in cinema since the beginning of the noughties, it
becomes clear how cyclical rather than linear trends in cinema are, since a similar
thing was observed in the previous chapter in relation to matters of aesthetics.
Our perceptions of the stylistic excesses of so-called postclassical cinema and the
focus on the sensory experience rather than the traditional features of narrative
such as plot structure and character development seem to be simply an upgraded
version of something that was witnessed in the 1960s, 1970s, and every decade
since. The main difference seems to be in the type of sensory impact facilitated by
the technology of the moment, whether we are talking about the Dolby system,
surround sound, digital editing, 3D vision, the use of digital audio workstations
(DAWs), and so forth. This is a good reminder that the sensory appeal of cinema
is not necessarily connected with technological developments in exhibition and
postproduction but is inherent to the medium itself. Chion makes a similar point
when he lists various examples of the sensuous use of sound in the pre-Dolby era,
observing that "Dolby simply permits films to multiply these sonic sensations
without necessarily confining them to particular sequences"[38] and that post-
Dolby cinema in fact "reconnects with the sensorial dimension that had taken
on great importance in the late silent era and early sound but was pushed aside
by classical film."[39] The case studies in the rest of this chapter further explore the
idea of audiovisual sensuousness that is not dependent on the fireworks of advanced cinema technology but is rather based on the principles of the aesthetics
of reticence. While the *photogénie* of the human body often plays a significant

[36] Gerald Must quoted in James Wierzbicki, *Film Music: A History* (London and New York:
Routledge, 2009), 201.
[37] Ibid.
[38] Michel Chion, *Film, A Sound Art*, trans. Claudia Gorbman (New York: Columbia University
Press, 2003), 128–129.
[39] Ibid., 133.

part in exploring the erotics of cinema, I will argue that even more crucial in this context is the treatment of the film body itself.

The Erotics of Audiovisual Musicality: Gus Van Sant and Béla Tarr

Gus Van Sant's films *Gerry, Elephant*, and *Last Days*—also known as his Death Trilogy—were released in quick succession between 2002 and 2005, followed in 2007 with the stylistically and thematically related *Paranoid Park*. After the director's stint with the mainstream in the late 1990s, which produced both surprising successes such as *Good Will Hunting* (1997) and highly publicized flops such as the *Psycho* remake (1998), the Death Trilogy films were hailed as Van Sant's return to his independent roots. But even in comparison to his early pivotal films, which assisted the rise of the New Queer cinema at the end of the 1980s and the beginning of the 1990s, the Death Trilogy pushed the boundaries of independent aesthetics into uncharted territories, exploring new paths towards "pure cinema." Far removed from the sensationalism of intensified audiovisual aesthetics and disregarding conventions of classical narration and narrative chronology, Van Sant's Death Trilogy focuses instead on formal issues of composition, rhythm, and movement, exploring the allure of temporal verticality and circularity, sonic and visual musicality, and what Randolph Jordan calls "reflective audioviewing."[40]

Some of the most fascinating scenes in these films show characters just walking. In *Gerry* and *Elephant*, these walks constitute the backbone of the audiovisual action and exploration. The paths of the *Elephant* characters—students in a high school whose lives are tragically curtailed in a mass shooting carried out by two of their schoolmates—are confined to the school grounds and corridors, recorded from close proximity by a stalking Steady-cam. In *Gerry*, two friends both called Gerry (played by Matt Damon and Casey Affleck) get lost in a desert looking for an elusive "Thing." They walk and walk, trying to navigate their way back to civilization by following animal tracks and climbing hills to scout. At the end they just stagger aimlessly, exhausted, dehydrated, and overwhelmed by the vastness of the desert. The image of the two figures lost in a big space, evocative of how Beckett describes his two characters in *Waiting for Godot*,[41] is emphasized

[40] Randolph Jordan, "The Ecology of Listening While Looking in the Cinema: Reflective Audioviewing in Gus Van Sant's *Elephant,*" *Organised Sound* 17, no. 3 (2012): 248–56, accessed October 8, 2017, https://doi.org/10.1017/S1355771811000458.

[41] Samuel Beckett quoted in James Knowlson, *Damned to Fame: The Life of Samuel Beckett* (New York: Simon & Schuster, 1997), 436.

by the film being shot in the majestic landscapes of the Death Valley desert in California.

In broadest terms, the forward-moving and tightly mediated content of mainstream cinema is in Van Sant's Death Trilogy replaced with an approach that creates the space/time for observation and contemplation, thus encouraging more active engagement. Only loosely based on real-life murders and deaths, including the Columbine High School killing and the suicide of Kurt Cobain in *Elephant* and *Last Days*, respectively, these films instead of plot or characters focus on the core features of cinematic form, the captivating quality of the cinematic time, the *photogénie* of cinematic movement, and the musicality of the films' visual and sonic rhythms. They foreground the sensuous aspects of the cinematic experience while also facilitating the space for reflexivity. As I mentioned earlier, the image/sound pairing in some of those scenes is akin to audiovisual *musique concrète* and the process during which the audioviewer becomes engrossed in the visual and sonic rhythms of the characters' lengthy treks can be compared to soundwalking, although it is not the films' protagonists who are soundwalking but rather the audience members, who are drawn slowly but insistently into the sounds and sensations of the films' diegetic universes.[42] Nevertheless, the soundwalking experiences in these two films diverge significantly, owing to the marked differences in their sound design. Randolph Jordan's reference to soundscape compositions and reflective audioviewing in relation to *Elephant* is a useful starting point for examining the impact of sound design in this film, while I'll use examples from *Gerry* to explore the sensuousness of audiovisual *musique concrète*.

Though the purpose of soundwalking, as conceived by members of the World Soundscape Project and R. Murray Schafer, is to focus on the sounds of the environment, this practice is by its nature more than just an auditory experience. It is not possible to move through the environment focusing on its sounds without also taking in its images, smells, and textures. Soundwalking is a multisensory experience in which the balance between watching and seeing, and between hearing and listening, is highly individualized, subject to both external conditions and personal affinities. The basic postulates of cinema aesthetics and technology, however, require that the audioviewer is served a product that is "standardized" in technical terms, including the aspect ratio of the image, the quality of the sound, and the balance between the two, which makes the sensory experience of watching a film fairly uniform, at least in ideal projection conditions. In addition, both the audiovisual and narrative contents of cinema

---

[42] Danijela Kulezic-Wilson, "Gus Van Sant's Soundwalks and Audio-visual *Musique concrète*," in *Music, Sound and Filmmakers: Sonic Style in Cinema*, ed. James Wierzbicki (New York: Routledge, 2012), 76–88.

are highly mediated. In mainstream cinema the hierarchical setup of a film's storytelling devices, including the soundtrack, revolves around the conventions of classical narrative that firmly guides the audioviewer's perception along a carefully planned route. In other words, conventional cinema provides very few opportunities for mindful attention to the environment and its sounds, which is an essential part of soundwalking. To this we should add that cinema and, even more, its scholarship have long sustained the accusations of a visual bias, mostly by film music and film sound scholars, which is still justified in many contexts and practices. So what is it about films such as Van Sant's Death Trilogy that creates the space for contemplation and individualized response that bring to the fore the sensual aspect of the audioviewing experience?

The title of Van Sant's *Elephant*, which is loosely based on a mass shooting that took place in Columbine High School in 1999, refers to the 1989 film of the same title by Alan Clarke. Set in Northern Ireland during the "Troubles," Clarke's film shows eighteen murders committed by nameless shooters who are silently followed by Steady-cam or in tracking shots on their way to shooting their victims. Van Sant's *Elephant* borrows the same formal approach, drawing attention to America's "elephant in the room" manifested in easy access to firearms and widespread gun violence. As in Clarke's *Elephant*, there is very little dialogue in the film as the narrative offers minimal information about the characters, focusing instead on quotidian details of their lives in the hours prior to the shooting and drawing the viewer into the rhythms of students' meandering walks through the school grounds and corridors. While the film's observational approach gives it almost a documentary feel, its illusion of realism is often subverted by the sound design, which frequently traverses the diegetic boundary, mixing diegetic sounds with pre-existing pieces of *musique concrète* and soundscape compositions by Hildegard Westerkamp and Francis White. Incorporated into the original sound design by Leslie Shatz, these pre-existing pieces challenge the expectations associated with the representation of diegesis, giving a quality of "estrangement" to everyday narrative spaces and an additional layer of ambiguity to stories without plots and characters destined to remain enigmatic.

Inspired by the principles of acoustic ecology from which the practices of soundwalking and soundscape composition originate, Randolph Jordan suggests contemplating Van Sant's *Elephant* and its organization of space through sound as a type of soundscape composition. It is worth remembering that the term "soundscape" is frequently used in the context of film music scholarship to refer to either the ambient sound of the scene or the soundtrack in its totality. Jordan, however, specifically refers to the type of electroacoustic compositional practice that invites acoustic exploration of space and the listener's engagement with it, arguing that thinking about film sound as a form of soundscape composition opens up new dimensions in our experience of the audiovisual construction of space in the film. Jordan draws on Katharine Norman's concept of *reflective listening* in soundscape compositions that prompts the listener "into active engagement with the soundscape being represented," arguing that reflective audioviewing can do the same in cinema.[43] He points out that Norman's concept of reflective listening uses Eisenstein's dialectic approach to montage as a model for explaining the tension between different listening modes that take place when the listener actively engages with a soundscape composition. It is worth emphasizing, however, that the dialecticism Norman refers to does not apply to Van Sant's visual style in the Death Trilogy, which is firmly rooted in the aesthetics of reticence and observational long takes. This dialecticism, as Jordan's illuminating analysis argues, is instead manifested in the tension between the image and its soundtrack, which combines "realist convention and free counterpoint." Focusing his analysis on two scenes that incorporate Hildegard Westerkamp's compositions "Doors of Perception" and "Beneath the Forest Floor" into the sound design, Jordan shows how "the specific points of synchronization work to ground Westerkamp's work within the space of the film, while the anomalies allow us to consider the nature of the space we see on screen and how the characters interact with this space."[44]

The dialectical tension between the image and the soundtrack that Jordan talks about is particularly apparent in the film's final tragic moments during which sounds from "Beneath the Forrest Floor," a composition that celebrates the peaceful and revitalizing spirit of nature, merge with diegetic sounds of a massacre. This provocative juxtaposition underlines the contrast between "a sense of balance and focus" transmitted by nature, which Westerkamp wanted to evoke in her piece, and the culture of alienation and violence that permeates all aspects of contemporary society.[45] The use of pre-existing soundscape and electroacoustic compositions in the first half of the film is less charged, however—these pieces are more difficult to identify as nondiegetic because they blend more seamlessly with diegetic sounds of the school environment. They are reflective of an approach that, by focusing on simple, quotidian details of a day in an ordinary American school, foregrounds sensuous aspects of the cinematic experience while also creating space for contemplation. As in a soundscape composition, which invites both the exploration of the acoustic space and the listener's engagement with it, the soundtrack in *Elephant* absorbs different types of musicality

---

[43] Jordan, "The Ecology of Listening," 248.

[44] Ibid., 255.

[45] In her programme note Hildegard Westerkamp says that "Beneath the Forest Floor" was created with the intention "to provide a space in time for the experience of [inner] peace" but also to "transmit a very real knowledge of what is lost if these forests disappear—not only the trees but also the inner strength they transmit to us, a sense of balance and focus, new energy and life. The inner forest, the forest in us." Quoted in *The Book of Music & Nature*, ed. David Rothenberg and Marta Ulvaeus (Middletown, CT: Wesleyan University Press, 2011), 239.

Figure 4.1. *Gerry*: The two Gerrys (Matt Damon and Casey Affleck) walking in the desert—a visual reference to a scene from Béla Tarr's *Werckmeister Harmonies* (see Figure 4.2).

while establishing the sound design as a core site of interrogation in a seemingly purely observational narrative.

The sound design in *Gerry* is less complex and less concerned with the tension between different audiovisual layers than in *Elephant*, and is more focused on the materiality of the sound/image relationship. Particularly in the first half of the film, the sound design reflects the bareness of the landscape. At the beginning, while the two friends are still close to the road, we hear distant traffic and planes flying overhead, but the dominant tone of their surroundings is silence intertwined with the sounds of walking, the wind, and occasional birdcalls. The turning point, exactly halfway through the film, is when the friends realize that their attempt to find water has been unsuccessful. Their relationship deteriorates, strained by exhaustion and creeping desperation, their amusing and relaxed banter dissolving into long silences. This point coincides with the sonically and visually most memorable scene in the film where the act of observation suddenly crystallizes into a distinctly sensuous and musical experience. Up to this moment, the walking scenes were mostly shot from a distance, in long and medium-long shots, with the volume of the sound correspondent to the framing. The turning-point shot captures the Gerrys' walk in close-up for the first time (as shown in Figure 4.1), showing their heads bobbing in close proximity in phase and out of phase [00:45:29–00:48:50].[46] The take is three minutes long, its duration emphasized even more by the repetitiveness of the action and the hypnotic rhythm it establishes. Matching the closeness of the shot, the volume is

---

[46] This is the timing of the DVD release of *Gerry*, Film Four, PAL, 2004.

noticeably increased, the sound of walking foregrounded into a loop of repetitive crunching punctuated by an occasional scrape of a boot and out-of-step drag. What makes this take so mesmerizing is the audiovisual counterpoint between the visual rhythm of heads bouncing and the sonic rhythm of stones crunching while the prolonged duration of the shot allows these rhythms to develop into a moment of visceral musicality that can be described as *audiovisual musique concrète*. By referencing a genre of music that harvests its sonic material from the environment, this term highlights the fact that the source of musicality in these scenes is a sort of *found* sound, a product of the simple action of walking rather than a stylized sound effect. At the same time, similar to *musique concrète* practice, the "found sound" in film is also inevitably manipulated in the process of postproduction, even if it was originally recorded on set. The term "audiovisual," on the other hand, refers to the fact that the musical effect of these scenes is complemented and augmented by the visual rhythm, intensifying the sensuous aspect of the experience.

Observing the process of walking during the prolonged takes in *Gerry* and *Elephant* highlights the ability of cinema to strike a balance between auditory and visual immersion, which is not possible in any other context. It exposes the relevance and interconnectedness of both senses in experiencing cinematic sensuousness, a phenomenon Chion described with the term "transsensorial perception."[47]

Van Sant's fascination with shots of people walking was famously inspired by watching Béla Tarr's films. Remembering his first encounter with Tarr's seven-hour-long *Sátántangó* (1994), Van Sant said:

> It was exactly what I needed to see at that exact moment in my life. It also summed up some things that I'd been thinking about for a long time and been influenced by but never put to use. The film was accomplishing those things, and a lot of that had to do with the timing of the story and how long he would take to describe certain actions that are simple yet the more you watch them the more they grow in their illumination.[48]

Commenting on the impact of *Sátántangó*'s distinctive pace, Van Sant refers not only to the film's extraordinary running time, which prevented its regular

---

[47] Chion explains "transsensorial" by using rhythm as an example of a film vocabulary element that is neither specifically auditory nor visual, but adds that transsensorial perception also applies to texture, material, and even language (*Audiovision: Sound on Screen*, trans. Claudia Gorbman [New York: Columbia University Press, 1994], 136–137).

[48] Ed Gonzales, "Gerrymandering: An Interview with Gus Van Sant," *Slant Magazine*, June 15, 2003, accessed August 12, 2017, http://www.slantmagazine.com/features/article/gerrymandering-an-interview-with-gus-van-sant/P2.

distribution in film theatres, but also to the length of individual takes. In those terms Tarr's films are typically representative of "slow cinema," exploring ideas of time, endurance, and decay through uninterrupted lengthy shots. But even in the company of directors such as Nuri Bilge Ceylan, Cristian Mungiu, Alexander Sokurov, or Abbas Kiarostami, the length of Tarr's shots, which often last somewhere between eight and eleven minutes, is considered unusual.[49] Tarr's films and Van Sant's Death Trilogy exemplify perfectly what Michel Chion calls "a ritualized temporal form" in which "the rhythmic recurrence of certain sounds ... generates an embryonic musical feeling."[50] Citing the examples of Jacques Tati's *PlayTime* (1967), Peter Yates's *Bullit* (1968), Kubrick's *2001: A Space Odyssey*, and Leone's *Once Upon a Time in the West* as typical of a "ritualized cinema," Chion argues that by having sequences that are extended far beyond their narrative necessity, these films become "a pure ritual in time" during which time becomes "as hard as cement," which effectively dismantles "the armature of musical scoring, voice-overs, and dialogue interwoven with images."[51] What is even more important in this context is that in ritualized cinema—whether we're talking about long scenes as Chion does or long shots as in Tarr's films— repetitive sound is allowed to last long enough to gain rhythmic and musical qualities. The distinctive audiovisual style of Tarr's films also draws attention to the materiality of cinema, and after *Sátántangó* pushed the boundaries of the duration of a static shot,[52] Tarr's following film, *Werckmeister Harmonies*, brought into focus the audiovisual hypnoticism of long takes showing people walking, which became known as the "Tarr-trudge."[53]

The previously described three-minute shot of the two Gerrys walking through the desert cites directly a scene from *Werckmeister Harmonies* showing the main character, János (Lars Rudolph), and his composer friend, György (Peter Fitz), walking down a street in an almost identically framed shot (see

---

[49] According to Béla Tarr himself, the seven-hour *Sátántangó* has around 150 shots, while *Werckmeister Harmonies* (2000) and Tarr's last film, *The Turin Horse* (2011), which both last 145 minutes, have 39 and 30 shots, respectively. Commenting on the distinctive pace of his films, Tarr acknowledged the influence of his editor (and spouse), Ágnes Hranitzky, explaining that he started to credit her as codirector since *Werckmeister Harmonies* because the decisions about editing were made during the shooting where her presence was essential: "She is always there and watches everything on the video monitor. She checks the rhythm of the scene, how two scenes will interact and things like that" (Eric Schlosser, "Interview with Béla Tarr: About *Werckmeister Harmonies* [Cannes 2000, Director's Fortnight]," *Bright Lights Film Journal*, October 1, 2000, https://brightlightsfilm. com/wp-content/cache/all/interview-bela-tarr-werckmeister-harmonies-cannes-2000-directors-fortnight/#.W4kTKbhG2Um).

[50] Chion, *Film, A Sound Art*, 112.

[51] Ibid., 113.

[52] Among the most memorable is a one-minute-long static shot of Estike's (Erika Bók) funeral in *Sátántangó*. The villagers gathered around her body are completely immobile so that the effect of the shot's prolonged duration feels like the narrative has been halted for a whole minute to show us a painting or a photograph.

[53] Michael Brooke, "The Weight of the World," *Sight and Sound* 19 (January 2009): 54.

Figure 4.2. *Werckmeister Harmonies*: György (Peter Fitz) and János (Lars Rudolph) walking down a street.

Figure 4.2) [01:05:17–01:07:10].[54] The rhythm of the scene in Tarr's film is uniform throughout because—unlike the two friends in *Gerry*—János and György hold a steady pace and always remain in step. Keeping with their synchronized walk, the rattle of the tiered metal food container carried by János always falls on the first or every other first beat of the duple rhythm of their walk.

Although the film's sound designer/editor, Gábor Erdélyi, says that most of the diegetic sounds in *Werckmeister Harmonies* were recorded on location, that certainly wasn't because the filmmakers were concerned with the notion of "authenticity."[55] On the contrary, from excessively long takes to the fact that most of the dialogue in Hungarian is visibly dubbed since all the main characters are played by German actors, *Werckmeister Harmonies* is typical of Tarr's tendency to challenge the convention of concealing artificiality in order to encourage critical or contemplative approaches to film. According to Erdélyi,[56] this is also the reason Tarr prefers to use the 4:3 image ratio and mono instead of 5.1 sound, supporting Larry Sider's point that 5.1 sound is generally associated with the aesthetics of immersive cinema, while mono sound stimulates more active engagement with

---

[54] This is the timing of the scene on the DVD release of *Werckmeister Harmonies*, Artificial Eye, PAL, 2003.
[55] Gábor Erdélyi, email message to author, January 26, 2011.
[56] Ibid.

the film.[57] Another detail that contributes to the musicalization of the sound design in Tarr's films is the use of background loops in long takes that feature repetitive diegetic sounds.

Explaining his modus operandi in Tarr's films, Erdélyi stated that he tends to mix two types of sounds in his designs: those that keep changing and for which he never uses samples (usually sounds of nature such as forests, wind, seashore) and sampled sounds associated with mechanization and urban living (traffic, city, machines).[58] In Tarr's famously long opening scenes this mixture of sampled and "changeable" sounds—the rattle of cable-car buckets in *Damnation* (1988), cows lowing at the beginning of *Sátántangó*, and the sound of waves and a distant storm in *The Man from London* (2007)—is usually combined with an electronically produced background that could be described as an electronic score but is, according to Erdélyi, provided by a sound designer.[59] Compared to Van Sant's strikingly elaborate soundscapes or the diversity of rhythmic patterns in the walking scene in *Gerry*, the uniform rhythmic patterns in Tarr's long takes and the use of looping in background sounds might seem monotonous, but one could argue that these patterns deliberately emphasize the artificiality of sound design, as well as its musicality. Most evocative of audiovisual *musique concrète* is the four-minute-long opening of *Damnation*, which shows coal buckets moving on cable wires, producing a repetitive rattling sound (see Figure 4.3). While there is nothing glaringly unrealistic about this scene, if one resists being drawn into the mesmerizing rhythm of the buckets travelling up and down the wires and focuses only on the sound, it becomes obvious that the rattling and scraping sounds that punctuate the background hum with metrically regular frequency are not tied to any particular on-screen movement and there are no obvious points of synchronization with the image. Even more notable is the fact that the sounds of machinery that start accompanying the rattling of buckets halfway through the scene are introduced at the point when the gradually widening frame reveals that the cable wires are being observed from inside a house by a man sitting at a window (see Figure 4.4). Realistically, the sound of machinery should become more distant when the point-of-view position moves to inside the house, while here the opposite happens. Loose synchronization of the diegetic sound and the unrealistic increase in its texture and volume halfway through the scene suggest that the musicality and materiality of

[57] Larry Sider, "Mono" (lecture presented at the Synch/Non-synch Symposium on Sound and Film, NUI Galway, February 19, 2014).

[58] Erdélyi, email message to author, January 27, 2011.

[59] Erdélyi, who was also sound designer in *Katalin Varga*, worked on three films with Béla Tarr (*Werckmeister Harmonies*, *The Man from London*, and *The Turin Horse*) as supervising sound editor. Answering my question about the electronically produced drone in the opening scene of *The Man from London*, he explained that he made it with his Kurzweil 2500 synthesizer and mixed it with the sound of wind and waves (email message to author, January 26, 2011).

Figures 4.3 and 4.4. *Damnation*: Cable wires observed by a man behind the window.

the sound design, as well as the psychological effect accompanying the revelation of a lonely figure behind a window, are of more importance in this context than the conventions of sound realism (see Figures 4.3 and 4.4).

The Erotics of Cinema and the Human Body: *Beau Travail* and *The Fits*

The principles of pure cinema and "ritualized form" in Van Sant's and Tarr's films encourage an embodied experience of film either by immersing the audioviewer into prolonged shots that highlight the passing of time or by stimulating various modes of audiovisual observation and listening. They also highlight experiential aspects of being in a body through on-screen actions, including scenes in which walking and the sound it produces are elevated to the significance of a main cinematic event. The human body, of course, is the alphabet of cinema language—studied in close-up or in action, it has proved to be an endlessly fascinating object of observation and desire, the root of the cinematic malady that Laura Mulvey termed "scopophilia." In Claire Denis's *Beau Travail* and Anna Rose Holmer's *The Fits*, which has likely been inspired by the formal discipline and sensuous elegance of Denis's film, the body and its repetitive movement in exercise—or dance—is both the subject and the raw material. The two films share many interesting points in their approach to narrative rhythm and audiovisual form: they deploy the language of physicality to comment on the rituals of exercise as a means of bonding and self-discovery, but they also harness images and sounds of physical action to augment the expressiveness and sensuousness of the film body.

Routine is at the centre of both narratives and provides a framework for establishing the main characters and their interests. In *Beau Travail*, the main character's, Galoup's (Denis Lavant), way of life based on self-discipline and ritual is brought into question when he becomes affected by the arrival of a new legionnaire, Sentain (Grégoire Colin). In *The Fits*, the routine of ten-year-old Toni's (Royalty Hightower) childhood life is broken once she joins a dance group, which becomes the catalyst for her feminine awakening.

In both films the score reflects some of the main narrative themes. In *Beau Travail* the masculine energy of the soldiers in the French Foreign Legion is embodied in the male choruses from Benjamin Britten's opera *Billy Budd*, which are contrasted with nondiegetic music from the discos the legionnaires frequent. In *The Fits*, the rite-of-passage story of a ten-year-old has an unusually austere score performed mostly on solo clarinet, but this too is juxtaposed with diegetic music coming from the dance halls where the girls rehearse. While these scores provide effective and memorable soundscapes, I want to focus here on the musicality of diegetic sounds and how their interaction with the score affects the sensuousness of the film body.

At the beginning of *The Fits*, Toni is introduced as a tomboy who goes to boxing training with her teenage brother Jermaine (Da'Sean Minor). At the cusp of her transformation into adolescence, she becomes drawn to the dancing group the Lionesses from the same community centre and abandons boxing to join them. As Toni starts participating in girlhood rituals of ear piercing and nail painting and swaps her boxing outfit for a sequined dance costume, the older girls in the group are, one by one, affected by mysterious, epileptic-like "fits." These fits gradually become a sort of rite of passage for the Lionesses. Toni, however, resists the idea that they have to "happen to everyone," as suggested by one of her younger friends, which alienates her from the rest of the group. The tension between the peer pressure to go through the communal rite of passage and Toni's deep sense of individuality culminates in the final scene in which Toni "performs" her "fit" in front of the stunned Lionesses as a highly personalized dance while levitating above the ground.

Director Anna Rose Holmer says that she wanted to make a story about the process of discovering one's identity and the awakening of femininity, which she views as separate from and preceding sexual awakening. She describes adolescence as "a dance of sorts, a choreography that we all learn."[60] The film subtly suggests that Toni's rehearsals with the dance group are as much about finding her place in the wider female community as about learning the Lionesses' routines. Commenting on the fact that the film is intensely physical and "built on the senses," Ginette Vincendeau suggests that, as a consequence, the exploration of girlhood and the joys of growing up female are only done through the body and that we are not given access to the characters' wishes, ambitions, or lives outside of the gym.[61] However, the film deploys the language of physicality with great eloquence, bringing insight—and sensuousness—to the processes of observation and physical action. Toni's training routines are unaccompanied, and the repetitive diegetic sounds of rope jumping, boxing, sweeping floors, and practicing "drill phrases" dominate the soundtrack. [62] There are many similar scenes in *Beau Travail* showing men on an obstacle course or just doing laundry, ironing, and preparing food. In his book *Transcendental Style in Film*, Paul Schrader comments on the role of everyday activities and routines in establishing what

---

[60] Kelli Weston, "Awakenings," *Sight and Sound* 27 (March 2017): 6.

[61] Ginette Vincendeau, "The Fits," *Sight and Sound* 27 (March 2017): 77–78.

[62] The film's sound designer/supervising sound editor, Chris Foster, and sound mixer, Gillian Arthur, started to discuss their approach even before the script was finished. They focused on obtaining as much direct sound as was possible and recorded all the dance rehearsals in stereo on location to minimize the use of Foley sound (Anna Rose Holmer, "DVD Extras: The Director's Commentary," *The Fits*, Lionsgate DVD, 2015).

Figure 4.5. *The Fits*: Toni (Royalty Hightower) practicing her routine on an overpass.

Byzantine scholars call *the surface-aesthetics* as an expression of religious discipline and a path to transcendence.[63] In cinema the surface aesthetics is manifested in the attention given to the quotidian minutiae of characters' lives and the details of their activities, which in both films draws the viewer into the rhythms of repetition, heightening their attention to detail, and to the sounds of the characters' surroundings.

Toni's version of the dance-form drill practiced by the Lionesses is rather "athletic" compared to the erotically charged dance moves of the older dancers and, especially at the beginning, it looks more like a warm-up for boxing than a dance. In that sense Toni's body language establishes her individuality, but it also signals that the change we are witnessing is more to do with the awakening of her femininity rather than her sexuality. One scene in particular is illustrative of the way the film subtly deals with this distinction, where Toni practices her dance routine on an overpass [00:30:50].[64] She begins by doing jumping jacks, the sound of her jumps almost drowned out by the noise of the traffic below. When she starts practicing the "drill phrases" of her routine, the diegetic sound of her jumps is replaced by a steady stream of sampled sounds organized in 4/4 patterns, which sound like a combination of clapping and stomping (see Figure 4.5). Towards the end of the scene the sampled sounds are complemented by a cello ostinato and then overlaid with a four-note clarinet phrase of ascending and descending semitones revolving around the note A.

---

[63] Paul Schrader, *Transcendental Style in Film: Ozu, Bresson, Dreyer* (Cambridge and New York: Da Capo Press, 1972), 61.

[64] In the Director's Commentary on DVD Extras Anna Rose Holmer says that, although she never shows Toni at home, she thought of the overpass as Toni's private space, her bedroom of sorts.

The score was composed by Danny Bensi and Saunder Jurriaans, who worked together on films such as Denis Villenueve's *Enemy* (2013) and Sean Durkin's *Martha, Marcy, May, Marlene* (2011). Their material is minimal, the main motif consisting of an ascending semitone performed in slow tempo by clarinet in high register. The composers say that they chose clarinet as the instrument to be associated with Toni because of its "breathy feel" since "the film is so much about the body." They created percussive effects by using nonmusical instruments—"a couple of baskets full of weird little trinkets and stuff"[65]—which, combined with sampled stomping, further blur the line between corporeality as one of the film's main themes and the materiality of the film body. The almost mechanical persistence of the soundtrack captures Toni's perseverance and obsessive dedication to her new drill. The musicalization of the diegetic sounds into sampled phrases is illustrative of the way Toni expresses herself—a combination of athleticism and determination. At the same time, it could be argued that the eventual addition of acoustic instruments to this mix evokes Toni's emerging sense of femininity.

An undoubtedly more sexualized representation of the human body that translates into a highly sensuous film form can be found in Claire Denis's masterpiece about emotional repression, *Beau Travail*. Known for her interrogative elliptical narratives and sensual audiovisual style, Denis has been described as a master of "cinema as an aching reverie of sweat and flesh."[66] None of her films fits this description more poignantly than *Beau Travail*, based on Herman Melville's *Billy Budd, Sailor (An Inside Narrative)*, a novella that also inspired Benjamin Britten's opera *Billy Budd*. Both opera and novella examine the issues of latent homosexuality, sensuality, jealousy, and repressed emotions. While the same themes are also explored in *Beau Travail*, the motivations of the main character, Galoup, and his affection for his superior, Captain Forrestier (Michel Subor), are ambiguous enough to allow the possibility that Galoup's jealous plotting against soldier Sentain could be as much about his craving for undivided parental affection and recognition from Forrestier as about his repressed desire for Sentain.

Regardless of the nature of those suppressed feelings, Denis's film convincingly captures the tension between the carefully controlled surface and the charge of the feelings simmering underneath it. This tension is also reflected in the contrast between the legionnaires' activities during the day and at night, and the forces of masculinity and femininity. As Heather Laing points out in her insightful analysis, the masculine and feminine domains are clearly divided in the film, the former being associated with daytime, outdoor exercise, self-discipline,

---

[65] Amber Wilkinson, "Noting the Difference: Composers Danny Bensi and Saunder Jurriaans Talk About *Christine, Frank & Lola* and *The Fits*," *Eye for Film*, accessed August 17, 2017, http://www.eyeforfilm.co.uk/feature/2016-03-01-saunder-jurriaans-and-danny-bensi-talk-about-christine-the-fits-frank-lola-feature-story-by-amber-wilkinson.

[66] Chris Drake, "Desire Is Violence," *Sight and Sound* 10 (July 2000): 16.

routine, and ritual, while the latter is associated with nighttime and a lack of control and order. In the soundtrack masculinity asserts itself in silence or is accompanied by Britten's male choruses, while the feminine takes over the nights filled with disco music that, as noted by Laing, "bursts onto the soundtrack at significantly greater volume than the surrounding scenes and cuts out all other diegetic sound," signalling the disruption of the order and control maintained during the day.[67]

The source of *Beau Travail*'s extraordinary sensuousness lies in the combination of mesmerizing editing rhythms, the captivating cinematography of Denis's regular collaborator Agnès Godard, and an inspired employment of sound and music. As Holmer uses the context of a dance community troupe and the metaphor of dance to explore the awakening of femininity, so Denis sets her story about masculinity, emotional repression, and desire in a French Foreign Legion camp and its daily routines. As in *The Fits*, an almost ritualistic approach to the daily tasks performed by the legionnaires under Galoup's watchful eye provides the scaffolding for the film's rhythmic macro-structure and the main framework for the exploration of the characters and their desires. And as Toni's steady training regime is disrupted by her desire to join the dancing group, so is Galoup's structured routine threatened by Sentain's arrival, stirring his jealousy, especially after Sentain's heroic act captures the attention of Captain Forrestier.

The images of legionnaires exercising under the blistering Djiboutian sun, washing their clothes, ironing, and preparing food provide the main building blocks of the film's enthralling macro-rhythm, punctuated by images of Galoup writing in his diary and the men's nighttime visits to the town and its disco. Galoup's voice-over, recalling the events that led to his demise, sets up another, sonic web of repetitions and patterns. Commenting on the process of achieving a "musical rhythm for editing," Denis reveals that the duration of the shots was not decided at the editing stage but even earlier, during the shooting ("When shooting I get goosebumps because of the passage of time and I have to trust that"),[68] similar to the working process of Béla Tarr and his codirector and editor, Ágnes Hranitzky.

The scenes most notably charged with audiovisual sensuality are those showing the men exercising in the desert, accompanied by male choruses from Britten's *Billy Budd*. The first group exercise we observe is accompanied by the chorus "Oh Heave, Oh Heave Away Heave" from Act One Scene One of the opera [00:04:08–00:06:31].[69] The deep richness of the voices underlines the sensuality

---

[67] Heather Laing, "'The Rhythm of the Night': Reframing Silence, Music and Masculinity," in *European Film Music*, ed. Miguel Mera and David Burnand (Furnham, Surrey: Ashgate, 2006), 167.
[68] Ibid., 18.
[69] This is the timing of the scene in the DVD release of *Beau Travail*, Artificial Eye, PAL, 1998.

of the image of male bodies spread out across the desert landscape, still and silent in their endurance. At first the gaze of the camera is downcast, revealing only the men's elongated shadows swaying. Then it gradually looks up to show the legionnaires standing with their arms upright, eyes closed, their naked torsos contrasted against the browns and greys of the ground and the blues of the sea and sky. As the first section of the chorus is repeated, we see the legionnaires on the boat, the camera studying each face in close-up, the two-colour palette of the previous scene replaced by the blue of the sea and the blue of the sky. The faces are striking—scarred, strong, and rough, studies of disciplined and impenetrable masculinity. As the timpani join the choir and the music swells, we are shown the last two faces on the boat—Sentain, unaware of Galoup's hostile attention, and Galoup, the only fully clothed person on the boat, his presence in the shot suddenly draining the blue of the sky in the background, leaving it a washed-out gray.

In the opera *Billy Budd* the male choruses are evocative of sea shanties— sailors' work songs that are sung to "coordinate effort and lighten labour aboard ships powered only by human muscles and the natural elements," their roaring choruses audible up to a mile away.[70] In Britten's opera sea shanties capture strong emotions of sensuality, fear, rage, and rebellion. In *Beau Travail* they are paired with images that symbolize strength, discipline, and endurance, pointing to the tension beneath the controlled surface. At the same time, the corporeal vigour of the music bestows a sonic layer of sensuousness upon the scenes of exercise, creating a memorable audiovisual marriage.

While the scenes accompanied by Britten's music constitute the sensual peaks of the film, there are many more that rely on diegetic sound only, as in *The Fits*. The lack of music in the scenes showing the legionnaires' daily exercises emphasizes another aspect of sensuousness—the actual blood-and-flesh corporeality of male bodies running, jumping, crawling, and climbing their way through an obstacle course, contrasting with scenes in which their presence is poeticized through music. The sounds of crunching, stomping, scraping, and heavy breathing foreground the materiality of the bodies on the screen but also the film body itself. Mirroring the routines of the legionnaire's life are the small daily jobs performed by Galoup on his own, in cloudy Marseille, awaiting his court martial after being discharged from the legion for attempting to get rid of Santain.

The scenes of training either show legionnaires going through an obstacle course one by one or show them exercising as a group (see Figures 4.6 and 4.7). Structured by the designed repetitiveness of the actions performed by a succession

---

[70] Roy Palmer, "Shanty," *Oxford Music Online*, accessed August 19, 2017, http://www. oxfordmusiconline.com/grovemusic/view/10.1093/gmo/9781561592630.001.0001/ omo-9781561592630-e-0000025583.

Figures 4.6 and 4.7. *Beau Travail*: Legionnaires working out in the desert.

or a group of uniformly dressed men, the body of Denis's film presents itself as a composition of contrasting colours and rhythmicized shapes and actions, a ballet of masculine discipline, strength, and sensuality. Some of the training scenes have discreet musical accompaniment, such as those in which Galoup's acousmatic singing or the somewhat ominous guitar slides in Eran Tzur's original score are mixed with diegetic sounds of the exercise. Many of them, though, are musical-ized by simply relying on repetitive actions and the diegetic sounds they produce, as in the exercise in which legionnaires stomp forwards and backwards in a circle around Galoup, their rhythmic stomping accentuated by shouts, or when they train for one-to-one battle by slamming into each other in a violent embrace, the clashing of their naked torsos accompanied by shouts and grunts.

This exhibition of masculinity and sensuality is complemented by the equally striking presence of Djibouti's landscape framed by Denis's long-term affection for Africa and the beauty of its land. As Pasquale Iannone observes, *Beau Travail* is the perfect manifestation of Denis's style: "body-as-landscape and landscape-as-body, a cinema of audiovisual intimacy that dissolves boundaries between objective and subjective reality."[71] And in the same way that the colours of the washed-out sand and the blues of the sky and the sea dominate the film's colour palette, so the sound of the sea dominates the soundscape not in volume but by its omnipresence.

Commenting on the sensuality of her audiovisual language and its significance in a cinematic context, Denis notes that "no other artform is as simultaneously trivial, vulgar and sublime" but that "real cinema is a way of transforming the technical and industrial material and making the sublime coincide with it."[72] I would argue that this cinematic alchemy is at work in both *The Fits* and *Beau Travail* on a number of different levels and that sound and music are a crucial part of it. In the same way that the surface aesthetics of the everyday discussed by Schrader was used by religious artists to reach out to the world "beyond," so do Holmer and Denis use trivial details of their protagonists' day-to-day activities to create a narrative framework that speaks about their lives and personalities. Both films deploy the language of physicality with eloquence and use our fascination with the human body in action to create rhythmical, sensuous film forms that also provide insight into the characters' suppressed desires and inhibitions, and their process of coming to terms with their individuality. And in the same way as our bodies surpass the limits of nonverbal communication through kinesics, so film uses its own body—image, sound, music, movement, and rhythm—to transform the technical and industrial into the sublime.

According to Denis, the key to enabling that transformation is sensuality: "Cinema cannot exist except through eroticism. The position of the spectator is like a kind of amorous passivity and hence is highly erotic."[73] Denis is careful to emphasize that her understanding of cinema eroticism is not about sex between the characters, but she mentions "the sexual charge that passes between the actors and the spectators."[74] While there is no reason to exclude

---

[71] Pasquale Iannone, "Beau Travail," *Sight and Sound* 24 (March 2014): 112.
[72] Drake, "Desire Is Violence," 17.
[73] Ibid.
[74] Ibid.

this type of audience response to cinema content, Denis's statement nevertheless complicates things if we interpret it as suggesting that the relationship between the *actors* and the audience is at the heart of the erotics of cinema. Thus, I should assert again that the notion of the erotics of cinema as explored in this chapter is not about eroticizing the body on screen and is certainly not limited to the visual; it is rather about the film in its totality and the sensuousness of both images and sounds and how they invite intimate engagement with the film, as *Beau Travail* does. In the case of Denis's film the sensuousness of the medium is indeed explored by focusing on the human body and its acoustic environment. But to demonstrate that the human body does not have to be the main source of or at the centre of cinema erotics, I will finish this chapter with an example that uses different methods for harnessing the sensuousness of the film body.

The Erotics of the Film Body: *The Assassin*

Released in 2015 to great critical acclaim,[75] Hou Hsiao-Hsien's *The Assassin* is yet another example of sensuous filmmaking that can be defined in opposition to so-called intensified audiovisual aesthetics. Instead of unleashing a sensory onslaught, *The Assassin*'s director exercises rigorous asceticism. Instead of a frantic pace, his film generates stillness. The only common thread between *The Assassin* and other films that foreground the sensory experience in some way is a loose approach to narrative conventions, which in this case translates to an open disregard for traditional plot and character development. *The Assassin* is Hou's first film in the *wuxia* genre, a martial arts movie that is traditionally set in the *jianghu*, "a mythic parallel universe with its own codes and laws of physics," in which quests and fights often have a philosophical or spiritual dimension.[76] Despite its *wuxia* story and setting, though, *The Assassin* does not offer much in the way of action, but it does conjure some *wuxia* conventions by endowing the characters with extraordinary skills and abilities and by referencing some of the genre's traditional stories and images.

The story is set in the time of the Tang Dynasty (c. 618–907 AD) and revolves around the character of Nie Yinniang (Shu Qi), a high-born child who is taken from her home to be trained as an assassin by her aunt, the Taoist nun Jiaxin (Sheu Fang-yi). After failing to complete her second assassination when she finds her target asleep with a child in his arms, Yinniang is punished by being sent to

[75] *The Assassin* won numerous accolades, including "Best Director" and "Best Soundtrack" at the sixty-eighth Cannes Film Festival and "Best Original Music" and "Best Sound" at the tenth Asian Film Awards.
[76] Tony Rayns, "Taipei Tang," *Sight and Sound* 26 (February 2016): 31.

kill Tian Ji'an (Chang Chen), the ruler of Weibo Province to whom she was once betrothed. From that point on, however, the story can be difficult to follow, especially for Western audiences unfamiliar with the original martial arts tale from the late ninth century, "Nie Yinniang" by Pei Xing, on which the film is loosely based. Not only are some characters and their relationships difficult to identify, but also the conclusions about the relationship between Yinniang and Princess Jiacheng (Fang-yi Sheu) suggested by the film are contradicted by explanations given by the director to the press.[77] Some fragments of the story only begin to make sense after watching the film more than once, as is often the case with films that favour sensuousness of style over narrative conventions. The fact is that the confusion surrounding the identity of certain characters could have been avoided by adding simple hints in the editing or dialogue, but Hou responded to those comments by saying that he was more interested in the type of message that can be conveyed through landscape, character, and details than the plot.[78] The director's disregard for narrative conventions has also been interpreted as a suitable approach to a film about an exile so that the viewer—like the protagonist, Yinniang—is "banished" to the "fringes of the experience," looking in from the outside.[79] As in films nurturing the aesthetics of reticence, it could be argued that a sense of mystery is part of the film's exquisite appeal because, despite confusing episodes and ambiguities in the plot, the film casts a lasting spell on the viewer owing to Hou's unique style.

Landscapes evocative of Chinese classical paintings constitute the film's main visual anchor. Hou Hsiao-Hsien stated that finding the right landscape was the crucial part of the process, after which he just "waited for things to happen," paying attention to changes of light and how "when the wind blows, things move in their own way."[80] This method of observation and patience applied to his work with the actors as well:

> If you sit an actor at the window and have him familiarise himself with the environment, well, then something happens. Some bright, splendid, overwhelming moment that we never expected. I call it unconscious acting. And it's the only way you can catch that precious moment.[81]

---

[77] In his article about *The Assassin*, Tony Rayns, who helped Hou with the English subtitles, quotes Hou saying that, unlike in the original tale, Yinniang is in the film version made Princess Jiacheng's daughter. The film suggests, however, that Princess Jiacheng didn't have any children and had adopted Tian Ji'an to make sure he remains the ruler of Weibo, which also means that Yinniang, who was betrothed to Tian Ji'an, cannot be her daughter (Rayns, "Tapei Tang," 30).

[78] Xan Brooks, "*The Assassin* Director: Why I Gave Plot the Chop," *The Guardian*, January 11, 2016, https://www.theguardian.com/film/2016/jan/11/hou-hsiao-hsien-the-assassin-martial-arts-movies.

[79] Roger Clarke, "The Assassin," *Sight and Sound* 26 (February 2016): 68.

[80] Hou Hsiao-Hsien, "DVD Extras: Behind the Scenes," *The Assassin*, Studiocanal DVD, 2015.

[81] Brooks, "*The Assassin* Director."

His audiovisual style is so controlled and meticulous that the smallest visual details such as a crane landing on the surface of a lake or the rustle of wind in trees register as visual and sonic accents in a landscape of stillness. In the words of Roger Clarke, Hou's film is like a "great sheet of jade-coloured water ruffled by the movement of a sword."[82]

The most fascinating thing about this film is its audiovisual rhythm—the interplay between visual and sonic elements, between movement and stillness, between sound and silence. Silence is not the opposite of sound, Zen teaches; rather, sound and music rise from silence or are framed by it. Likewise, movement rises from stillness and goes back to stillness. In *The Assassin*, stillness and silence are the raw material of the film from which everything else is created. The reason the narrative floats with a dream-like quality is partly due to the measured pace with which captivating images of landscapes and softly lit interiors progress on the screen. The sound design in these calm, observational takes is lightly textured but by no means simple, seamlessly intertwining diegetic sound and music with asynchronous speech and nondiegetic music. The fluent yet carefully syncopated rhythm of these audiovisual interplays is beautifully exemplified in the scene in which the images of Yinniang bathing and dressing on her return home after a long exile are interspersed with images of the late Princess Jiacheng playing the *guqin*, a traditional Chinese instrument, and then reciting an excerpt from the fifth-century classic poem "Qing luan wu jing" about the loneliness of a bird who only starts singing when it sees its reflection in the mirror [00:11:00–00:15:13].[83] Before we see the source of the music (a flashback), Jiacheng's playing is first heard over a shot of a group of tea traders riding through a field and then a shot of Yinniang having a bath. After the source of the music is revealed, another layer of syncopated audiovisual rhythm is added with the introduction of the first verse of the poem about the bird as a voice-over with an image of Jiacheng playing silently, while the final part of the poem is synchronized with an image of her speaking. This is followed by a shot of Yinniang getting dressed and then again of Jiacheng playing the *guqin*, but this time we don't hear the diegetic sound of her performance but rather the sustained flute notes from Lim Giong's original score (see Figures 4.8,4.9, and and 4.10). The only sonic constant throughout this scene is the sound of nature punctuated by distinctive bird calls that link the images from present and past, diegetic and nondiegetic musical sources, and asynchronous and synchronous speech.

This example and the use of music throughout this film bring to mind the earlier cited comments by Noël Burch about the "open" quality of non-Western music as heard in Mizoguchi's film *The Crucified Lovers*. Lim Giong's original

---

[82] Clarke, "The Assassin," 68.
[83] This is the timing of the scene in the DVD release of *The Assassin*, Studiocanal, PAL, 2015.

score is understated and subtle, shaped around the visual content and diegetic sound like a melodic line harmonizing with *musique concrète*. Its light texture is generally based on monodic flute lines playing sustained notes, or short phrases performed on *guqin*. The spaciousness of the score is drawn from long pauses between the phrases, allowing the music to interact seamlessly with sounds of

Figures 4.8, 4.9, and 4.10. *The Assassin*: Images of Yinniang (Shu Qi) bathing and dressing on her return home after a long exile interspersed with images of the late Princess Jiacheng (Fang-yi Sheu) playing the *guqin*.

Figures 4.8, 4.9, and 4.10. Continued

nature (which brings to mind the example from *The Rover* with Scelsi's music). And as the landscape evocative of Chinese classical paintings constitutes the foundation of the film's visual style and atmosphere, so sounds of nature dominate the sonic realm, providing a score of buzzing, chirping, squawking, and birds singing.

Another type of interaction between the visual and sonic elements with both structural and musical effects can be found in the opening scene in which Princess-Nun instructs Yinniang to kill a merchant who is about to pass by, saying "cut him as if he were a bird in flight." Before the killing happens we observe a line of horsemen advancing, their staccato shouts echoing through the landscape. The moment of attack punctures the diegetic flow with the action in slow motion wiped free from any diegetic sounds, followed by the sharp sound of a blade slashing through the silence. The most effective detail comes at the end: instead of falling immediately off the horse after the attack, the merchant remains on his mount for another few moments, carried into a gallop. When his body finally drops to the ground with a loud thump, the scene cadences with a shot of trees swaying and rustling in the wind. The scene combines stillness with moments of swift action; it observes time as it is passing through the shot but uses both temporal deviation in the form of slow motion and sound to puncture its flow. This type of rhythmic diversity in which a moment of action becomes an audiovisual accent is typical of martial arts films, but it is the cadence delivered in the final shot, the extended image of tree branches rustling in the wind, that makes the film's audiovisual phrasing so vividly sensual and musical. There is an incredible rhythmic and affective power in completing a dramatic audiovisual phrase with an extended shot of peaceful beauty that is comparable to the effect of a fermata in music. Hou harnesses this power carefully, deciding on the length of each shot with the sensitivity of a composer, as in the duel between Yinniang and a masked woman in the woods, which unfolds in a flurry of hits and slashes to conclude with two long-medium shots of each woman standing still; although there is no movement in these shots, apart from Yinniang's hair blowing in the wind, they still pulsate with the buzz of the fight that has just finished [01:07:15–01:09:22].

This example also gives an indication of the somewhat modified role of sound in *The Assassin* in comparison to traditional martial arts films. One of the main tools through which martial arts and action films signify connections between bodies on screen and create a connection with the body of the spectator is through sound. The sounds of punches, hits, and slashes are usually unrealistically exaggerated because, as Mack Hagood argues, "The fleeting nature of a punch ... requires a hard, staccato sound to fit it in time and to fix the punch in the spectator's memory."[84] In the more modern type of martial arts films, such as the previously discussed *House of Flying Daggers*, fight scenes provide an opportunity to create a highly musicalized sound design. Fights in *The Assassin* are particularly rare and also short in terms of genre expectations since, as Xan Brooks notes, instead of drawing on its conventions, Hou "twists the genre into abstract shapes." The fights are elegant and rhythmicized, punctuated with punching and swishing noises that sound more like percussion instruments piercing the stillness of the landscape than sonic imprints of body-on-body action trying to affect the audioviewers' visceral responses. Even the sound of drumming, which normally accompanies fight scenes, is here appropriated for atmospheric and musical purposes, being used in a number of scenes to connect different locations, unhurried but persistent, reflecting a sense of tension slowly building behind silky drapes.

Nevertheless, *The Assassin* does produce an unusual sense of bodily awareness, which is not the result of exploiting the corporeal features of the genre but rather of the delicacy of its audiovisual rhythm. I watched *The Assassin* in the cinema twice and both times, halfway through the film, I became aware of my body and of the fact that I was breathing slowly and evenly, as if I was in the middle of a meditation. My reaction was not a response to particular sounds or

[84] Mack Hagood, "Unpacking a Punch: Transduction and the Sound of Combat Foley in *Fight Club*," *Cinema Journal* 53, no. 4 (Summer 2014): 99.

their volume, or to images charged with intensity, but instead to the peculiar pace of this film's audiovisual content, which pulls the audioviewer—who is willing to submit to it—into its own rhythm. By drawing on the sensuousness embodied in the melodies and harmonies of the film's compositions, textures, and sounds, rhythm becomes the primary vehicle for creating the connection between the body of the audioviewer and that of the film. In this context the artistry of sound is not the result of an elaborate design that dazzles with its inventiveness or is foregrounded for dramaturgical or affective reasons; the purpose of sound is neither to support the image nor to oppose it in order to assert its independence. The focus instead is on forging a delicate interaction between sonic and visual elements to create a distinctly rhythmic audiovisual texture. "There is such delicacy and artistry in *The Assassin*," writes *The Guardian* critic Peter Bradshaw, "as if the film is spun from some exquisite, evanescent tissue of precious material."[85] This material is distinctly audiovisual, and the perfection of the sound design is manifested in its ability to match the delicacy of the visual elements and contribute to the film's evanescent glory.

Conclusion

As I have emphasized repeatedly throughout this chapter, the erotics of film form and the relationship between a film's body and that of the audioviewer is not directly related to the film's topics and certainly does not apply only to films that explore erotic relationships of some kind through the narrative. In some cases, as in *Beau Travail*, the sensuousness of film form is closely related to the sensual depiction of a human body on screen. But this is neither the rule nor the main source of film's sensuousness in general; this sensuousness is generated through different devices that emphasize the materiality of the medium and contribute to the creation of its sonic and visual textures, rhythm, and flow. The sensuousness of film form is not reliant on advanced use of technology or on intensified audiovisual aesthetics. Leaning on Sontag's and Lorde's discussions about the erotics of art and Marks's comments about the eroticism of the relationship between audioviewer and film, I have argued in this chapter that the sensuousness of film form is much more complex and sophisticated than an emphasis on excessive sensory stimulation facilitated by the use of digital technology or the aesthetics inspired by it.

[85] Peter Bradshaw, "*The Assassin* Review—Captivatingly Hypnotic, if Impenetrable, Wuxia Tale," *The Guardian*, January 21, 2016, https://www.theguardian.com/film/2016/jan/21/the-assassin-review-captivatingly-hypnotic-if-impenetrable-wuxia-tale.

To follow the metaphor of erotic liaison, in an industry where most films are made for "one-night stands," a long-term relationship between an audioviewer and a film is in many ways evocative of the relationship between two lovers. If there is a "spark" and one returns to the object of admiration and desire, the relationship becomes more intimate. As in a loving relationship, intimacy is won through investing time, patience, and genuine interest in the other: the more times we watch a film, the more equipped we become to understand its secrets and hidden depths. What might have been an initial attraction—certain aspects of the narrative, actors, the score, a sensuous audiovisual style—becomes just one element of the whole that is only revealed in an intimate relationship with someone (or, in this case, something). Also, let's not forget that the emphasis on the materiality of cinema—which should be credited for drawing attention to the issues of embodied spectatorship and reigniting the discussion about it—does not mean we should start ignoring the less palpable aspects of film's appeal and the way it communicates with and stimulates our intellect, stirs our concerns and desires, and fulfils our aesthetic craving. To push the original metaphor further: film is not only a body to which we respond as to another body, to paraphrase Marks. Film has also been theorized as a mind, a being, and a "life form" that negates the division between cognitive and sensory or between sight, sound, and other senses in our engagement with cinema.[86] As Elsaesser and Hagener say, paraphrasing Deleuze, "cinema is material and immaterial, a form of becoming rather than a mode of signification or meaning," a form of philosophy that "overcomes the Cartesian division between subject and object (*res cognitas* and *res extensa*) and the phenomenologist's assertion that consciousness is always the consciousness of something, and thus involves intentionality."[87] The crucial point here is the transformative effect of the exchange that takes place when we engage with a film on a profound level, which is comparable to the impact any relationship that we allow to change us might have, be that with a work of art or another human being.[88]

As this chapter has shown, there are a number of ways to establish the sensuousness of film form and to determine the role of sound in it. From conventional methods for providing realistic representations of everyday activities and focused observation of simple actions like walking, to looped tracks and innovative

[86] See Daniel Frampton, *Filmosophy* (London and New York: Wallflower Press, 2006); Elsaesser and Hagener, *Film Theory*.

[87] Elsaesser and Hagener, *Film Theory*, 158.

[88] Robert Sinnerbrink articulates the effect of this engagement persuasively when he says that the experience of film "invokes a mutual becoming, a dynamic, *transformative* relationship in which the *relata* in question are profoundly altered by their very engagement, opening them up to new relations with each other as well as with other things (as in any good relationship)" ("Re-enfranchising Film: Towards a Romantic Film-Philosophy," in *New Takes in Film-Philosophy*, ed. Havi Carel and Greg Tuck [Basingstoke, Hampshire: Palgrave Macmillan, 2011], 41, emphasis in the original).

soundscapes, sound is an essential aspect of our recognition of the erotics of film. As we have already seen in chapter 2 and will see over and over again, the use of repetition is one of the key tools in providing a context that allows and encourages us to perceive the musical qualities of sound design or the scene as a whole. Also one of the main compositional devices in music, repetition is employed with the explicit intention to emphasize the rhythmic qualities of certain actions and their inherent musicality. But, as shown in the last case study, the rhythm and phrasing of a scene does not always rely on repetition—either in soundtrack or on screen—but on a subtle interaction between sonic and visual elements attuned to the scene's inner rhythm. What seems to be the guiding principle in each context, however, is the recognition of the sensuousness of film form and the innovative ways in which sound can bring it to the fore.

5

The Musicalization of Speech and the Breakdown of the Film Soundtrack Hierarchy

The most compelling evidence of how much musical logic has affected recent changes in the conception and production of soundtracks is apparent in the approach to speech that foregrounds its musical qualities, challenging its essential denotative purpose and its dominant position in the soundtrack hierarchy. While past examples of what Chion calls "speech relativization"[1] were generally associated with nonmainstream cinema, a minor controversy following the release of Christopher Nolan's *Interstellar* in the autumn of 2014 indicates that the changes in this department have now reached even the heart of Hollywood.

According to a *Guardian* article published in the wake of the film's release, some viewers complained that at key moments the dialogue in *Interstellar* was unintelligible. The complaint received enough publicity to prompt one cinema in Rochester, New York, to post a notice confirming that its equipment was "in full working order," while a poster at the Cinemark Tinseltown read: "Christopher Nolan mixed the soundtrack with an emphasis on the music. This is how it is intended to sound."[2] Meanwhile, Nolan himself responded by admitting that his "impressionistic approach to sound" was maybe "unusual for a mainstream blockbuster" but was the "right approach for this experiential film":

> Many of the film-makers I've admired over the years have used sound in bold and adventurous ways. I don't agree with the idea that you can only achieve clarity through dialogue. Clarity of story, clarity of emotions—I try to achieve that in a very layered way using all the different things at my disposal—picture and sound.[3]

[1] Michel Chion, *Audio-Vision: Sound on Screen*, ed. and trans. Claudia Gorbman (New York: Columbia University Press, 1994), 178.
[2] Ben Child, "*Interstellar*'s Sound 'Right for an Experimental Film', Says Nolan," *The Guardian*, November 17, 2014, http://www.theguardian.com/film/2014/nov/17/interstellar-sound-christopher-nolan.
[3] Ibid.

Sound Design Is the New Score: Theory, Aesthetics, and Erotics of the Integrated Soundtrack. Danijela Kulezic-Wilson, Oxford University Press (2020). © Oxford University Press.
DOI: 10.1093/oso/ 9780190855314.001.0001

This anecdote highlights a couple of issues concerning the aesthetics and functional hierarchy of the contemporary cinema soundtrack that I intend to examine in this chapter. On one hand, it confirms audiences' habitual reliance on language and speech as the main sources of relevant narrative information obtained through sound. As Michel Chion pointed out, cinema is, like human listening, naturally voco- and verbocentric.[4] Attempts to relativize speech are rare because they not only undermine the ideological and aesthetic premises of classical narration but also—as this case confirms—are potentially disorienting, confusing, and even frustrating for audiences. While Nolan's "impressionistic" approach to sound is not explicitly reflective of the type of speech musicalization discussed in this chapter, his decision to challenge the norms and expectations regarding the dominance of speech in the mix and its intelligibility[5] brings to light the fact that these firmly established pillars of soundtrack hierarchy are slowly shifting to give space to new practices. Chion was, as usual, ahead of the curve when he wrote at the beginning of the 1990s in *Audio-Vision* that the "pursuit of sensations" and the improvement in Dolby technology gave more prominence to noise in cinema, "reintroducing an acute feeling of the materiality of things and beings." According to him, this was already a sign that "with the new place that noises occupy, speech is no longer central to films."[6] His pronouncement

---

[4] Chion, *Audio-Vision: Sound on Screen*, 5–6; *The Voice in Cinema*, trans. Claudia Gorbman (New York: Columbia University Press, 1999), 5.

[5] Nolan's film *The Dark Knight Rises* (2012) provoked similar complaints because the speech of Batman's nemesis Bane (Tom Hardy) sounded muffled since his face is covered with a mask. Apparently Nolan was asked by the producers to remix the prologue and he agreed to make minor changes but refused to "rework it." His response was the same as regarding *Interstellar*, arguing that "it is OK for a moviegoer not to understand what was said at times, as long as the overall idea was conveyed" (Borys Kit, "'The Dark Knight Rises' Faces Big Problem: Audiences Can't Understand Villain," *Hollywood Reporter*, December 20, 2011, https://www.hollywoodreporter.com/heat-vision/dark-knight-rises-christian-bale-batman-tom-hardy-bane-275489; see also Willa Paskin, "Dark Knight Rises to Be More Comprehensible," *Vulture*, January 3, 2012, https://www.vulture.com/2012/01/dark-knight-rises-to-be-more-comprehensible.html). Those who look favourably at Nolan's methods could contend that the muffled speech of Bane's character should be perceived as part of his identity since Bane is living with persistent physical pain. In *Interstellar*, however, the issue of speech intelligibility is more directly connected to the use of music as Zimmer's score is notably raised in the mix and dominates big stretches of the film. This "impressionistic mix," as Nolan calls it, will also become part of the soundtrack signature in his following film, *Dunkirk* (2017).

[6] Elaborating on the notion that speech is no longer central to cinema, Chion says that "Speech tends to be reinscribed in a global sensory continuum that envelops it, and that occupies both kinds of space, auditory and visual" (*Audio-Vision*, 155). In his later book *Film, A Sound Art*, he also mentions ritualized cinema, discussed in the previous chapter, as a place where dialogue and voice-over are "dismantled" to be interwoven with images (113). However, in the same book he seems to contradict his statement from *Audio-Vision* about the relativization of speech when he says: "the sound film sometimes claims—or seems to want to claim—to be able to relativize or reduce speech, make words into just another sound, an element of no particular consequence, which the spectator could take in just like any other sound in the film. It is remarkable that this enterprise fails and that every word spoken or half-spoken in a film becomes part of its very substance. Words are not soluble in the sea of cinema" (*Film, A Sound Art*, trans. Claudia Gorbman [New York: Columbia University Press, 2009], 355). I believe that the examples discussed in this chapter provide a convincing rebuttal of Chion's latter statement, supporting instead his earlier position presented in *Audio-Vision*.

might have heralded the breakdown of film soundtrack hierarchy a couple of decades too early, but it did identify two crucial protagonists in the changes to come: advancements in technology and the pursuit of the sensory aspect of the cinema experience, which have already been discussed in chapters 2 and 4. To these we should add music and the musical approach to film as other relevant factors that have contributed to the broader trend of challenging the structure of the classical soundtrack as discussed in previous chapters, promoting new modes of perception. Like audiovisual *musique concrète*, the musical approach to speech is yet another form of new practice that brings to the fore film's musical and sensuous qualities, encouraging an aesthetic engagement with film that is based on the combination of narrative and multisensory stimuli.

This chapter explores the main strategies involved in the musicalization of the spoken word by using examples from several recent films with strong musical underpinnings—Drake Doremus's *Breathe In* (2013), Harmony Korine's *Spring Breakers* (2012), and Shane Carruth's *Upstream Color* (2013). While none of these strategies—which include the use of verbal *chiaroscuro*, repetition, and asynchronous speech—is musical per se, this chapter will show how they become so when applied in a context governed by musical logic and in close interaction with the films' scores. All these films undermine the narrative sovereignty of the spoken word and endorse the interchangeability of speech and music, promoting modes of perception that transform our expectations of narrative film and emphasize its musical and sensuous qualities. The first section will provide the context for the ensuing analysis showing that even sporadic attempts to utilize the musical qualities of speech in the past generally related to directors' broader musical inclinations and their musical approach to film form.

Rhythmical and Affective Uses of Speech

In her case study of Stanley Kubrick's *Eyes Wide Shut* (1999), Claudia Gorbman dedicates one whole section to the opening scene accompanied by Shostakovich's Waltz No 2. from his *Jazz Suite*. Describing the "operatic" air that the music lends to the action on screen, Gorbman notes that its musicality extends even to the dialogue, which she compares to a "duet," saying: "The film's very first dialogue line coincides with the precise moment the second stanza begins; Tom Cruise may as well be singing his line."[7] To further emphasize her point, she presents a notated example of the waltz's opening bars with Cruise's line "Honey, have you seen my wallet?" inserted between the staves as typical of a score with vocal

---

[7] Claudia Gorbman, "Ears Wide Open: Kubrick's Music," in *Changing Tunes: The Use of Pre-existing Music in Film*, ed. Phil Powrie and Robynn Stilwell (Farnham, Surrey: Ashgate, 2006), 8.

parts. Gorbman's analysis stems from her wider argument about "auteur music" of *mélomanes* mentioned earlier. As is again confirmed by this example, the notion of "auteur music" maintains not only that the musical tastes and choices of directors like Kubrick are an important part of their sonic style but also that their musical inclinations often infiltrate their approach to form, editing, composition of certain scenes, and even use of dialogue. We have seen this time and again in previous case studies, but the fact that even speech is affected by this approach is possibly the most compelling evidence of how much recent changes in soundtrack practice have been influenced by a musical way of thinking. As this approach requires a closer collaboration between different departments in postproduction than is usual in mainstream productions, a musical employment of speech is more likely to be found in auteur projects and independent films, some of which have already been discussed in the previous chapters.

In Joe Wright's *Anna Karenina*, for instance, some scenes heighten the rhythmical and affective qualities of the spoken lines by using language as punctuation, as if taking over the duty of sound effects that have in turn been musicalized. Such use of speech turns on its head the relationship between dialogue and visual content in classical cinema. As Chion argues, classical cinema revolves around speech to the point that the action accompanying the speech is usually devised simply to accentuate certain remarks or the silence between them.[8] Taking a bite of food, swallowing a drink, lighting a cigarette, or stubbing it out in an ashtray— actions like these are not relevant to the plot but are there to give the audioviewer "time to meditate on what has just been said" or allow "what was said to sink in."[9] Chion even uses a musical comparison in this context to note that "while a character is talking or listening, we can choose to watch the plumes of smoke coming out of his mouth as poetic or musical extensions of the words that are spoken or heard."[10] Chion's observations apply to a number of scenes in *Anna Karenina* where choreographed gestures have a similar function, but the novelty here is that at other times it is words or sometimes even whole sentences that are tasked with punctuation. Short exclamations such as "I need your advice" and "It's so unfair!" appear as cadences to audiovisual phrases. Anna's most dramatic and revealing statements are clipped and delivered in succession to create an almost percussive quality. In a letter she sends to her estranged husband she says: "I beg you to come. I need your forgiveness. I am dying," and when she admits to him that she's having an affair with Vronsky, her words "I love him. I am his mistress. Do what you like to me" are accentuated at the end by a strong thump following the abrupt halt of the carriage she is travelling in.

---

[8]   Michel Chion, *Film, A Sound Art*, 74.
[9]   Ibid., 75.
[10] Ibid.

In Aronofsky's *Pi*, which shares the same musical underpinning of form as *Anna Karenina*, the protagonist's obsession with precision and patterns is expressed through rhythmical statements that pulsate through the narrative like the ticking of a metronome ("Personal statement"; "More evidence"; "Restate my assumptions"). In his later film *The Fountain* (2006), in which Hugh Jackman and Rachel Weisz play the main characters in three different storylines stretching over many centuries, the motif that connects all the character incarnations is the phrase "Finish it!" First whispered by the character of a dying woman to her husband, these words reverberate in the meta-diegetic spaces of all three men played by Jackman in temporally distant storylines. In both films words and sentences have been used—like sound effects in the previously discussed examples—both in a rhythmical manner and as punctuation. A similar approach can be found in *Run Lola Run* (Tom Tykwer, 1999), where the word "Die Tasche" is repeated ten times in succession to underline the moment in which Lola's (Franka Potente) boyfriend (Moritz Bleibtreu) realizes that he has made a potentially fatal mistake by leaving a bag full of money on the subway.

In Spike Lee's provocative exploration of race relationships in America, *Do the Right Thing* (1989), the language is colourful, funny, and musical but also dangerous. Treated as a weapon, it is sometimes used to ignite conflict, sometimes to deter it, like the brass knuckles with the words "love" and "hate" worn by one of the characters, Radio Rahim (Bill Nunn). The most memorable instance of language's injurious power is the "racial slur montage" in which different characters, looking directly at the camera, dispense a sustained list of ethnic insults aimed at various communities in their neighbourhood. Reflective of ethnic and racial divides in American society, the scene is nevertheless also funny because of the deliberately rhythmicized flow of the offensive chants evocative of rap battles. Counteracting the staccato insults are the announcements and comments of radio DJ Mister Señor Love Daddy (Samuel L. Jackson) based on repetitions and antimetabole. His extensive roll call of African American musicians recited over images of Brooklyn residents sizzling in the hottest day of the year sounds like an incantation of the powers of reason, imagination, and creativity.

All these examples emphasize rhythmical qualities of language and spoken words: sentences are either expanded to a rhythmicized roll call or are conversely short, sometimes even reduced to one word to provide them with a percussive quality; they are positioned at the end of scenes, acting as cadences to audio-visual phrases, or punctuate a film to create a sense of rhythmic form on the macro-scale. This approach is as indebted to the tradition of written poetry as to contemporary oral practices like rapping, as its affective impact relies on both rhythmic and metric features of language and its delivery.

In contrast to the percussive snappiness of the words and sentences in many of the aforementioned examples, in Jim Jarmusch's films the rhythmic and affective impact of language is realized on the level of the macro-form. Repetitions are more distant, positioned as structural accents that generate an affective quality cumulatively over the course of the film—a modern example of what Chion calls "ritualized cinema." The most striking example of this approach can be found in Jarmusch's film *The Limits of Control* (2009), which is built on continuous narrative, visual, and sonic repetitions so persistent and foregrounded that the scenes follow each other like stanzas in a strophic song. Repetition in language is set up as the primary device of storytelling at the very beginning, when the Lone Man (Isaach De Bankolé), who works as a hitman for what seems to be some kind of "existential police," meets the Creole (Alex Descas) and the Frenchman (Jean-François Stévenin) to receive instructions about his next job. The Creole's speech, which constitutes the nucleus of the text that will be repeated in different contexts throughout the film, is delivered in French and simultaneously translated by the Frenchman sentence by sentence into English. The main part of his speech ("He who thinks he's bigger than the rest must go to the cemetery. There he will see what life really is. It's a handful of dust") is repeated four more times in the film in Arabic and Spanish, including twice in a song that the Lone Man first hears performed live and then later in the car that takes him to his target.[11] After taking instruction from the Creole, the Lone Man travels through Spain meeting different people who each direct him towards the next stage of his journey. All his encounters begin with the question "You don't speak Spanish, right?" followed by another question—"Are you interested in … by any chance?," the object of the second question changing in each conversation (music, film, art, science, hallucinations). Even though these sentences spoken in a conversational tone do not have the same rhythmic qualities as the repeated phrases in Aronofsky's films, their continuous recurrences along with the segments of the Creole's speech echoed in later parts of the film establish a highly rhythmical form on the macro-level.

John Richardson also argues for recognizing the musical quality in different types of speech aestheticization, which include poetic speech, different types of delivery, technological manipulation, fetishization, and interaction of voices with environmental sounds or aestheticized nondiegetic sounds.[12] His in-depth analysis of Sally Potter's *Yes* (2004) illuminates a highly musical approach to soundtrack in which poetic dialogue written in Shakespearian iambic pentameter "does not work as an isolated element … but instead overflows from one

---

[11] Interestingly, the only sentence spoken by the Creole that is not translated by the Frenchman, or at any other point in the film when it is heard or seen written in Spanish, seems to be the main motto of the organization for which the Lone Man works: *La vida no vale nada* (Life is worthless).

[12] John Richardson, "Between Speech, Music, and Sound: The Voice, Flow, and the Aestheticizing Impulse in Audiovisual Media," in *The Oxford Handbook of Sound and Image in Western Art*, ed. Yael Kaduri (Oxford and New York: Oxford University Press, 2016), 479–501.

element of the multiplanar soundtrack to the next, both synchronously and dia-chronically, in a form of audiovisual phrasing in which each part is recognized as an element within a constantly changing larger assemblage."[13]

Richardson observes that one of the reasons Potter manages to sustain the mu-sicality of the audiovisual flow is because there is little distinction between the characters' inner and external voices and other sounds of the diegetic world.[14] This approach has been developed into a type of mannerism by Terrence Malick in his films *The Thin Red Line* (1998), *The Tree of Life* (2011), *To the Wonder* (2012), and *Knight of Cups* (2015). Conceived as journeys through protagonists' inner land-scapes led by their ruminations and filled with memories, Malick's films unfold in fragments of constantly moving images in which diegetic sound effects and speech are often layered with nondiegetic music and pensive voice-overs. Although these poetic voice-overs are generally intelligible, they are usually delivered in a sub-dued or whispered manner, interweaved with the score or diegetic speech as if the meaning of the words is of less importance than the timbre of the voice and its affective quality. In Wim Wenders's *Wings of Desire* (1987), where the thoughts of Berliners are overheard by city's angels Damiel (Bruno Gunz) and Cassiel (Otto Sander) as a constant stream of inner monologues, the denotative purpose of lan-guage is downplayed even more. These voice-overs are less notable for their meaning than for their sonic continuity, stepping into the role usually provided by music. In the famous library scene [0:15:41–0:20:00][15] the latent musicality of the voice-overs is even transformed into an actual musical cue, the murmur of inner thoughts and reading becoming the sound of a mixed choir.

Daniel Falck[16] compares the use of speech in *The Thin Red Line* to what Chion calls "emanation speech": speech that "becomes a sort of emanation of the char-acters, not essential for understanding significant action or meaning."[17] The rarest among the three modes of speech that Chion recognizes in film—the other two being theatrical and textual speech—emanation speech is not always fully heard or understood and is not "intimately tied to the heart of ... the narrative action."[18] Its modes of appearance might vary but they all defy the verbocentric nature of cinema by *relativizing* speech, inscribing it in a "visual, rhythmic, ges-tural, and sensory totality where it would not have to be the central and deter-mining element."[19] The use of emanation speech is even more pronounced in

[13] John Richardson, *An Eye for Music: Popular Music and the Audiovisual Surreal* (Oxford and New York: Oxford University Press, 2012), 137.

[14] Ibid., 141.

[15] This is the timing of the scene in the DVD release of *Wings of Desire*, Axiom Films, 1987.

[16] Referenced in Anahid Kassabian, *Ubiquitous Listening: Affect, Attention, and Distributed Subjectivity* (Berkeley, Los Angeles, and London: University of California, 2013), 34.

[17] Chion, *Audio-Vision*, 222.

[18] Ibid., 177.

[19] Ibid., 178.

Malick's later films such as *The Tree of Life* and *Knight of Cups*, which strive to
move, as Kent Jones argues, "away from human specificity and toward humanity
as one vast organism."[20] In that sense it could be argued that this type of speech
not only is emanation of a character but also can be emanation of a particular
state of mind, or indeed, a collective consciousness.

What is particularly interesting in this context is Chion's observation that
the decentering of speech, as one of the most subtle ways of its relativization,
allows new possibilities for integrating it into the audiovisual context. If different
aspects of visual content such as acting, movement, framing, and editing are "not
centred around speech," then the possibilities of their mutual fusion are much
greater and more fluid.[21] The case studies in the following sections will demonstrate how far the taste for decentralized use of speech has evolved in recent years,
undermining the narrative sovereignty of the spoken word and endorsing the interchangeability of speech and music. They will also illuminate the influence of
musical logic in the presentation of speech, which does not necessarily defy the
rule of intelligibility as in *Interstellar* but is rather directed towards bestowing a
musical quality on certain scenes or even the whole film.

Musicalization of the Soundtrack and "Verbal chiaroscuro": *Breathe In*

In all the films that are examined in this chapter, music plays a number of different roles beyond its conventional functions. In *Breathe In*, a story about a
middle-age high school teacher who falls for a much younger foreign exchange
student staying in his house, music is from the beginning established as the primary means of communication in both narrative and narrating terms. The two
main characters are both musicians: Keith Reynolds (Guy Pearce), a former rock
musician tired of his teaching job with the ambition of becoming a chair cel-
list in a symphony orchestra, and Sophie Williams (Felicity Jones), a precocious
music student whose passionate and virtuosic musicianship stirs deep-seated
desires in Keith. In addition to diegetic performances of music by Chopin and
Schumann, the film is submerged in Dustin O'Halloran's warm, atmospheric
score, which is given the same attention as the dialogue, sometimes simmering
in the background like the characters' suppressed desires, sometimes dominat-
ing the sonic field.

Language, on the other hand, is approached with less reverence than is typical
of narrative film and is treated almost with distrust. According to the director,

[20] Kent Jones, "Signs and Wonders," *Sight and Sound* 26 (June 2016): 44.
[21] Chion, *Audio-Vision*, 182.

the actors were encouraged to improvise their lines around certain plot points and those scenes were then rigorously workshopped until they had been "distilled into the essence of the mood/emotion. The goal [was] to say as little as possible."[22] Most of the time spoken words are intelligible, but they are usually combined with music in such a way that their denotative importance becomes less significant than the characters' body language, glances, and silences.

This ongoing dialogue between speech and music is established at the very beginning. The opening credits on a black screen are at first accompanied only by gentle arpeggios in piano; before the blackness is replaced by the first image, a tranquil melody in middle register is introduced, followed by sounds of chatter that are soon identified as coming from Keith and his family. The musical intro and a slight delay in matching the voices with their visual source not only allow us to become attuned to the film's tone with our hearing first but also encourage us to perceive the voices as part of the music. The first shot is interior, showing a big window looking out at a garden in which Keith poses for a family photo with his wife and daughter, their figures reduced to a single corner of a symmetrically framed shot, their voices equally indistinct. Although the next shot moves outside to the garden, showing the characters in wide and then medium shots, their chatter does not become more distinct nor does the volume of their speech significantly change, even though our point of view/hearing does. If anything, the music becomes slightly more prominent, enveloping the chatter of the characters.

The effect produced by this approach is best described by Chion's expression *verbal chiaroscuro*,[23] which refers to the type of speech relativization where "we can understand what is said at one moment and at another understand less, or even nothing at all."[24] This approach is not necessarily unusual in the context of scenes whose purpose is to paint the everyday atmosphere of family life—chatting at the dinner table, visiting friends—as opposed to the use of speech that conveys information relevant to the plot. Chion employs this term to describe situations in Max Ophuls's films where characters move around a lot as they speak, producing noises that occasionally obscure their speech.[25] This example also brings to mind the films of Robert Altman in which an improvisatory style of acting conveys everyday situations where people interrupt each other, speak at the same time, shout over the noise of traffic, and so on. In that sense, verbal

---

[22] Drake Doremus, "Special Features: Interview with Drake Doremus," *Breathe In* DVD, Curzon Film World, 2013.

[23] *Chiaroscuro* is a term used in painting that refers to the use of strong contrast between light and dark or the "quality of being veiled or partly in shadow" (Merriam-Webster Dictionary online). Chion here refers to the latter meaning.

[24] Chion, *Audio-Vision*, 178.

[25] Ibid., 182.

Figure 5.1. *Breathe In*: Keith (Guy Pearce) and Sophie (Felicity Jones) at the river.

chiaroscuro is not an inherently musical device but a type of speech decentralization that, as explained earlier, allows a more fluid interaction between image and sound on one hand, and between different elements of the soundtrack on the other. In the context of Doremus's film, however, this fluidity is notably utilized to facilitate an approach to the soundtrack dominated by musical logic.

Among the most memorable scenes that demonstrate this approach is the one in which Keith and Sophie meet at the river after realizing that their feelings for each other are mutual [01:02:11–01:05:50].[26] They talk about escaping the constraints of their lives and what it means to be free, but instead of the conventional framing usually applied in dialogue scenes, the protagonists here are often shot from a distance or from behind while they are speaking, or the camera rests on the face of the person not speaking, on details of the couple touching each other, holding hands, Keith playing with Sophie's hair, and so on (see Figure 5.1). The only moment that employs a variation on shot–reverse shot editing in dialogue and synchronous sound is when Sophie asks Keith what makes him happy and he replies that there is only one thing at the moment that makes him happy, his unfinished sentence the closest their conversation gets to acknowledging their feelings verbally. After that point their speech becomes even more fragmented and is again mostly presented asynchronously, their whispered words (Sophie: "What do you think?" and Keith's "I want you to steal me away") barely audible and only comprehensible after multiple viewings. Music, however, is present throughout the scene, the sounds of piano and string quartet enveloping the characters, filling the spaces between their words, and replacing their words completely towards the end of the scene.

---

[26] This is the timing of the scene in the DVD release of *Breathe In*, Curzon Film World, PAL, 2013.

The process of mixing is, obviously, crucial here in striking a well-judged balance between music and spoken word that ensures the audibility of both. What really enables this type of aesthetics, however, is the director's working style, which involves the composer in every stage of the filmmaking process and considers music "as the fifth character of the ensemble of characters."[27] That both Keith and Sophie are musicians is an important detail because the way they respond to each other's musical performances is crucial to the plot development. It could be argued that Keith starts thinking about Sophie only after hearing her highly accomplished performance of Chopin's Ballad No. 2 in F, op. 38 in class. The other turning point is when Sophie, after revealing that her reluctance to perform is connected with the fact that her uncle who taught her piano recently died, decides to play for Keith. The soft, yearning melody Sophie plays (O'Halloran's "Opus 20") communicates her feelings more eloquently than she could do with words and Keith responds by touching her for the first time. The choice of style, texture, and instrumentation in the original score is also relevant here as it enables an easy sonic interaction between music and spoken words. O'Halloran's score in the tradition of Romantic piano literature spins a web-like texture, its gentle arpeggios and delicate melodies revolving around the middle register, like the characters' voices. The result is a soundtrack in which the familiar hierarchy between its elements is replaced by a more fluid relationship in which music and speech alternately come in and out of focus, an approach that supports the film's visual emphasis on *mise-en-scène* and the protagonists' nonverbal communication conveyed through close-ups of their faces, touching hands, and stolen glances.

The attention given to music in the soundtrack, its narrative significance, and the way it gently interacts with the characters and their spoken words create an audiovisual field that invites the audience to loosen its vococentrist stance and accept language as an element no more relevant to the story than music or *mise-en-scène*. In that sense, Doremus's film supports Nolan's assertion that clarity of dialogue is not essential for achieving "clarity of story and emotions." That *Breathe In* is more effective in this approach than *Interstellar* is partly due to the fact that it is much easier for the audience to accept an "impressionistic" mix of dialogue and music in a context that deals with basic human emotions and where there are no plot twists involving a journey through time and different dimensions, as in Nolan's film. Instances of successful verbal *chiaroscuro* are still relatively rare, though; in most cases the musicalization of speech relies on other devices, including the use of repetition, rhythmic editing, and asynchronous sound, examples of which will be examined in the following sections.

---

[27] Doremus, "Special Features."

Repetition and Asynchronous Sound: *Spring Breakers*

Despite the general perception that narrative forms based on linear storytelling avoid repetition and focus instead on establishing forward, goal-oriented movement, all forms that aim for some kind of rhythm in their structure, including film, employ repetition to create patterns, "rhyming effects,"[28] and networks of associations.[29] As one of the essential compositional devices, repetition is also integral to most musical scores, not least those in the classical Hollywood tradition with their elaborate networks of leitmotifs and themes.

The situation with repetition in speech in a narrative context is somewhat different though. Repetition in dialogue, for instance, not only clashes with the goal of making the narration as fast and forward moving as possible but also poses a threat to the carefully constructed illusion of the "invisibility" of means cultivated by classical cinema. Nevertheless, as Cormac Dean illustrates with numerous examples from film and TV, repeated and redundant speech in film is not that rare, and once past its informative function it can then be affective, comical, idiosyncratic, or playful.[30] Or, as my earlier discussion about *The Limits of Control* demonstrates, repetitions in speech can be part of a broader strategy to create a rhythmic macro-form. To this should be added that repetition is often utilized for the purpose of creating a musical effect, as can be heard in Harmony Korine's *Spring Breakers*, where it is usually paired with an asynchronous use of speech.

Spring Breakers is the story of four childhood friends, Faith (Selena Gomez), Candy (Vanessa Hudgens), Brit (Ashley Benson), and Cotty (Rachel Korine), whose spring break in Florida takes a violent turn after they get involved with local rapper and drug dealer Alien (James Franco). Inspired by contradictions in a youth culture in which "sexualised and violent imagery" is juxtaposed with "childlike pop-culture indicators, the fluorescent bathing suits and Hello Kitty bags,"[31] Korine's film walks a fine line between exploitation and a critical take on the excesses of youth culture. Simon Reynolds compares the film's phantasmagorical and hyperbolical representation of spring break and the girls' descent into crime and murder to Bakhtin's definition of carnival as "an event in which all rules, inhibitions and regulations which determine the course of everyday life are

[28] Raymond Bellour, "Segmenting/Analysing," in *Genre: The Musical*, ed. Rick Altman (London, Boston, and Henley: Routledge and Kegan Paul, 1981), 103.

[29] Annabel J. Cohen, "Music Cognition and the Cognitive Psychology of Film Structure," *Canadian Psychology* 43, no. 4 (2002): 227.

[30] Cormac Deane, "Redundancy and Information in Explanatory Voice-Ins and Voice-Offs," in *The Palgrave Handbook of Sound Design and Music in Screen Media: Integrated Soundtracks*, ed. Liz Greene and Danijela Kulezic-Wilson (Basingstoke, Hampshire: Palgrave Macmillan, 2016), 361–375.

[31] Korine quoted in Amy Taubin, "Cultural Mash-up," *Sight and Sound* 23 (May 2013): 29.

suspended," adding: "the world is turned upside down in a potlatch of pleasure, profanity and insubordination."[32] Although very different from Doremus's film in terms of narrative style and content, Korine's film is nevertheless, like *Breathe In*, also deeply steeped in music, combining Cliff Martinez's mellow, deep-pulsating techno evocative of his score for Steven Soderbergh's *Traffic* (2000) with more aggressive, penetrating tracks by Skrillex. The film's musical spirit is not confined to the score, though, but permeates the whole film, affecting editing patterns, the use of sound effects, and speech.

Although the film's general narrative arc is linear, a very small part of it is presented through the conventional means of continuity editing and synchronized speech. The story is mostly told through montage sequences immersed in music and bathed in day-glo colours, showing the girls in their everyday habitat at the beginning—sitting in class, smoking, taking drugs, driving in a car—and later partying, getting arrested, making out with Alien, and so on. These sequences are assembled nonchronologically, many of them using already seen shots just in a different order. According to the director, this structure, which "recirculates" micro-scenes, was inspired by loop-based and trance-like electronic music, which is also the basis of Martinez's original score soundtrack.[33] Its ambient textures and soft harmonies provide the montage sequences with a sense of continuous flow, creating a "floaty," dreamy feel and a suitable background for music-like repetitions of spoken words.

The theme of violence dominates the narrative, both visually and aurally. Allusions to guns permeate the story from the beginning, with characters using squirt guns or miming the gestures of firing guns. The sounds of cocking a gun and actual gun shots are employed throughout the film as punctuation marks between scenes, becoming more frequent as the story moves towards its violent ending. They sonically contaminate the film's core to the point that even "innocent" Foley sounds like Faith's friends opening the shutters in her room when they come to wake her up [00:09:20][34] or flicking a lighter [00:11:45] are given a harsh, metallic quality, evocative of the sound of a cocking gun. In one of the later scenes the same sound is synchronized with the gesture of Alien miming taking a photo—a foreboding substitute for the sound of a camera shutter [0:49:43]. Not long after the girls meet Alien, this pervasive sound finally becomes synchronized with its actual source—real guns being cocked.

One of the crucial devices aiding the repetitions, "loopy" editing, and score to supply a "dreamy" feel to the film is a fairly consistent asynchronous use of language. As Mary Ann Doane pointed out, matching audio and visual perception

[32] Simon Reynolds, "You Only Live Once," *Sight and Sound* 23 (May 2013): 28.
[33] Taubin, "Cultural Mash-up," 29.
[34] This is the timing of the scene in the DVD release of *Spring Breakers*, Universal, PAL, 2013.

Figure 5.2. *Spring Breakers*: Alien (James Franco) intimidates Faith (Selena Gomez).

is at the heart of cinematic illusion, even more so, Kevin Donnelly adds, than the illusion of continuity.[35] The point of synchronization is what "holds everything together," "the crucial lynchpin in the process of retaining a sensible, often comforting discourse from a collapse into disturbing meaninglessness and chaotic psychological and material disorder," says Donnelly.[36] The fact that words in *Spring Breakers* are often divorced from their visual source undermines our usual expectations of realistic representation of characters and events. This somewhat "detaching" impact of asynchronous speech and nonchronological editing becomes particularly obvious when compared to one of the rare moments in which dialogue is presented synchronously, the scene in which Alien tries to persuade Faith not to return home [00:44:16–00:47:20]. Bar one editing intervention that interrupts this scene with an image of Faith surrounded by her friends, crying, and pleading that they all return home, the exchange between Alien and Faith is mostly presented synchronously and in real time. As a consequence, Alien's predatory body language and Faith's fear and discomfort come across as more real and unsettling than the later scenes of violence (see Figure 5.2).

The asynchronous image/sound editing also facilitates the use of repetition in speech. The first explicit appearance of repetition coincides with the initial turning point in the narrative, when Candy, Brit, and Cotty decide to rob a diner with toy guns to get cash for their spring break trip. Their lines "Just pretend it's

[35] See Mary Ann Doane, "Ideology and the Practice of Sound Editing and Mixing," in *Film Sound: Theory and Practice*, ed. Elisabeth Weis and John Belton (New York: Columbia University Press), 54–62; "The Voice in the Cinema: The Articulation of Body and Space," in *Film Sound: Theory and Practice*, ed. Elisabeth Weis and John Belton (New York: Columbia University Press, 1985), 162–176; Kevin Donnelly, *Occult Aesthetics: Synchronization in Sound Film* (Oxford and New York: Oxford University Press), 202.

[36] Donnelly, *Occult Aesthetics*, 8.

a fucking video game," "Act like you're in a movie, or something," "You can't be scared of shit, you have to be hard," and similar, are initially paired with images of the girls talking themselves into carrying out the robbery, interspersed with images of them taking drugs [00:13:13–00:13:45]. These lines are then repeated verbatim asynchronously over shots of the road, details of the car in motion, and the girls standing in the rain [00:13:52–00:14:14].

After Faith and later Cotty depart Florida to go home, leaving Brit and Candy with Alien, the story edges further towards fantasy, encouraging the impression that the characters are indeed becoming part of a video game; the connection between image and speech becomes even looser, and words are more subject to repetition. Alien's speech patterns are particularly musicalized, including the often cited scene in which he lists his possessions, punctuating his monologue with the boastful "Look at my shit!" His monologues are sung like nursery rhymes ("Four little chickies ... ," "Four little girls ... ") while his sing-song repetitions of the film's title ("spring breaaak, spring breaaak, spring break fo-rever") punctuate the second half of the film like chants. According to Korine, these repetitions stem from his original idea of conceiving the film as a "liquid" narrative with "things that would repeat like mantras or choruses in pop songs."[37]

The extensive repetitions are applied not only to monologues and fragments of dialogue but also to actual dialogue exchanges, as in the montage sequences showing the characters kissing, having sex, and playing with guns. A few lines of dialogue (Alien: "So you wanna do this or what?" Brit: "You're scared, aren't you?" Candy: "Scaredy Pants." Candy: "Are you scared?" Alien: "I'm real scared.") are first heard at 01:14:00 following a montage sequence of Alien, Candy, and Brit making love in a pool after Cotty's departure. Following the film's familiar editing pattern, the scene is then interrupted by the insertion of a montage sequence showing previously seen images of the girls partying, here accompanied by Alien reciting his "Four little girls ..." rhyme. As the rhyme finishes with him chanting "spring breaak, spring breaak, spring break fo-rever," we are transported back to the scene in the pool and the lines "Y'all wanna do this or what?," "You're scared, aren't you," "Scaredy pants," and "I'm a big ol' fuckin' scaredy pants" are repeated three more times consecutively, punctuated by lazy, erotic laughter.

Repetitions of spoken lines also resonate on the level of the macro-form, combined with a traditional use of asynchronous speech to expose the underlying contradictions in the characters or even their hypocrisy.[38] In *Spring Breakers* this

[37] Korine quoted in Taubin, "Cultural Mash-up," 29.

[38] A memorable example is the iconic baptism scene in *The Godfather* (Francis Ford Coppola, 1974) in which Michael Corleone's (Al Pacino) vows to accept God and denounce the devil are paired with images of his opponents being slaughtered on his orders; or more recently, in *Killing Them Softly* (Andrew Dominik, 2012), speeches by George W. Bush, Barack Obama, and other politicians commenting on the American financial crisis on the eve of the 2008 presidential election are juxtaposed with a story about small-time crooks trying to get away with a big robbery.

type of juxtaposition is first heard in the scene in which Faith's phone message to her grandmother is matched with images of wild partying ("This place is special. I'm starting to think this is the most spiritual place I've been.... I think we found ourselves here.... I can't believe how many new friends we made ...") [00:18:20–00:19:35]. Her words are echoed at the very end by Candy, accompanying the scene in which she and Brit take out all Big Arch's people during the final (and particularly unrealistic) shoot-out: "I think we found ourselves here.... We saw some beautiful things here.... I know we made friends that will last us a lifetime...."

Apart from this formal closure using repetition and asynchrony to hammer home its message about unsettling aspects of youth culture, in all other cases repetitions are redundant from the narrative point of view. Instead of being used for a denotative or even connotative function, language is employed here for its rhyming and rhythmic properties. Its asynchronous use is an important part of this because by divorcing the spoken word from its source, the film-maker draws our attention to its purely sonic aspects, emphasizing its musical qualities. We find a similar situation in *Breathe In*: even though the musical approach to language in this film does not rely on repetition, the most musical instances of verbal *chiaroscuro* in it all involve asynchrony, as if its free-floating deployment divorced from the image "liberates" the language from its visual anchor and allows the filmmaker to use it in a more musical way, almost as a score.

The musicalization of language in *Spring Breakers* is a significant departure from the conventions of classical narrative that still dominate mainstream cinema. Considering Korine's penchant for the controversial, innovative, and downright subversive, as demonstrated in his previous films such as *Gummo* (1997), *Julien Donkey-Boy* (1999), and *Trash Humpers* (2009), his use of nonconventional strategies in *Spring Breakers* is not a surprise. However, despite the film's provocative content and representation of female characters about which critics couldn't agree if it was sexist and exploitative or feminist, Korine's film also features audience-friendly names such as James Franco and Disney princesses Selena Gomez and Vanessa Hudgens. While it could be argued that the film's infiltration of the mainstream and box-office success indicate audiences' increasing tolerance of strategies typical of nonmainstream cinema, one should not forget that in the case of *Spring Breakers* this tolerance was greatly facilitated by the film's musical "feel" and audiovisual style, which its target audience raised on MTV would have been accustomed to.

The final film I intend to discuss uses all the devices addressed so far—nonchronological editing, asynchronous use of speech, verbal and visual repetition, verbal *chiaroscuro*, and musicalized sound effects. Although they are incorporated into a unique narrative style that cannot be easily compared or categorized, I will argue in the next section that its innovative features are, as in the previous two case studies, informed by a distinctly musical logic.

The Musically Conceived Soundtrack and Editing: *Upstream Color*

Shane Carruth's *Upstream Color*, like his first feature *Primer* (2004), breaks some new ground by seemingly operating from a space not accountable to any narrative conventions and, as Jonathan Romney says, "may even mark the emergence of a new strain of narrative film language … which requires us to engage with [Carruth's] singular mind-set, on his terms."[39] In that sense, the breakdown of soundtrack hierarchy discussed in this chapter goes hand in hand with the breakdown of storytelling and editing conventions, resulting in an immersive but also in many ways enigmatic story with a strong musical undercurrent. Carruth's DIY approach, also applied in his debut, includes writing, directing, acting, producing, coediting, and cinematography. The fact that he also composed the score for the film—while still working on the script—indicates the extent to which music was from the beginning considered an integral part of the film's expressive language. Even more interesting in this context is Carruth's comment that he was "hoping people would watch this film repeatedly, as they might listen to a favourite album,"[40] which suggests the existence of a more comprehensive idea of musicality extending beyond the score, as in the previously discussed films. This approach, which foregrounds the sensuous aspect of cinema, seems inseparable, or possibly stems, from Carruth's distinctive storytelling methods, which do not shy away from the bizarre and confusing.

The narrative of the film is organized in three distinct sections, each representing a particular part of the journey experienced by the protagonist Kris (Amy Seimetz) either externally or internally. The first part shows Kris being kidnapped by the Thief (Thiago Martins) and contaminated with a worm that keeps her in a trance-like state during which she is made to perform a number of meaningless tasks, including copying Thoreau's *Walden*. After signing over all her possessions to the Thief, Kris wakes up with the worm crawling under her skin and is dewormed by the Sampler (Andrew Sensenig), who transfers the parasite into a pig that maintains a physical and/or metaphorical connection to Kris. Kris later meets and falls in love with Jeff (Shane Carruth), who, we later discover, has been a victim of the same ordeal. The last third sees Kris searching for the cause of her trauma. After tracking down and killing the Sampler and finding

[39] Jonathan Romney, "Enigma Variations," *Sight and Sound* 23 (September 2013): 51.
[40] Carruth quoted in Romney, "Enigma Variations," 52.

evidence of his collaboration with the Thief, Kris contacts all the previous vic-tims and together they take over the maintenance of the pigs that they became connected to in the process of deworming.

Carruth makes it clear that the third section is not a "classical" resolution of the plot and should not be taken at face value because it is "nothing but sub-text."[41] He says that the plot is veiled for a reason as the film "is really trying to change the form that it exists in. . . . It's trying to adopt the language that we've come to understand—and then, proving that it understands that language, it's trying to push it as far as it will go."[42] As a consequence, the two main themes of the film—being influenced by unknown forces and the invisible connection between people who share a similar trauma—are conveyed through audiovisual devices that actively destabilize the audience's passive position. Their purpose is to conjure a sense of the protagonists' brokenness and the connection between them, rather than simplify our understanding of the plot. In addition, hardly any information that could be considered vital is communicated through lan-guage. The outer parts of the film barely feature any speech at all, while elsewhere some lines, like Kris reciting passages from *Walden*, are employed as much for "musical" as for narrative effect, reminding us of the protagonists' deep-buried trauma.

One of the most eloquent tools in Carruth's unconventional approach to storytelling is editing, for which he shares the credit with fellow indie director David Lowery (*Ain't Them Bodies Saints*, 2013; *A Ghost Story*, 2017). On the one hand, editing is responsible for confusing the timelines of a number of events involving the protagonists or for mixing their storylines with those of people who don't seem to have any relevance to their story; on the other hand, it empha-sizes the link between the two main characters and the Sampler and his pigs. Editing also undercuts the significance of speech across the film. When we hear conversations, they are fragmented and often appear as asynchronous, matched with temporally displaced visual segments of the characters not speaking. As in *Breathe In*, we're encouraged to focus on body language or *mise-en-scène* rather than trying to discern every spoken word. For instance, the sequence depict-ing Kris and Jeff repeatedly meeting on a train does not contain any speech at all. However, a handful of shots showing Jeff stealing looks at Kris indicate the passing of time and Jeff's increasing interest in and attraction to her.

Repetition is embedded in every aspect of the nonchronological ellipses that dominate many sequences, creating syncopated audiovisual rhymes. This ap-proach is particularly obvious in the montage sequence in which Kris and Jeff

---

[41] Shane Carruth, "New Directors/New Films Q&A: *Upstream Color*, Shane Carruth," Film Society of Lincoln Center, April 6, 2013, https://www.youtube.com/watch?v=5cjq_Lb2F2I.

[42] Carruth quoted in Romney, "Enigma Variations," 51.

argue over the ownership of their memories, whose similarities suggest that they were implanted during the characters' kidnappings [00:59:05–01:02:02].[43] Here, both the passing of time and the recurrence of the characters' argument is conveyed through the repetition of images that become visual refrains: Kris and Jeff lying on the floor, walking, and watching birds flying above trees; Kris putting her make-up on; the couple touching each other. Their conversations are also fragmented and rhythmicized through repetition, but are presented "in syncopation" with the visual repetitions. For instance, the opening lines—Jeff saying, "we should go on a trip"; Kris asking, "where should we go?"; and him responding, "somewhere bright"—are at first heard in sync with the image of the couple lying on the floor. The following few shots accompanied only by music symbolize the "honeymoon" phase of their relationship, the couple kissing or holding hands. The rest of the dialogue consists of snippets of their conversations about different childhood memories, some of them heard in sync with their source—Kris and Jeff in different interior and exterior locations—and some of them appearing as voice-overs over images of the protagonists not speaking. A shift in mood, pointing towards the dark mystery behind the uncanny overlap in their memories, is marked by a repetition of the same dialogue heard at the beginning of the sequence starting with Jeff saying, "we should go on a trip," but this time played asynchronously over the shot of him and Kris moving into their own place. The rest of the conversation, which increasingly sounds like an argument, is created from nonchronologically assembled snippets of similar conversations in which Kris accuses Jeff of taking her childhood memories and making them his own. The only repeated sentence that is always matched with similar images is "They could be starlings." Uttered by Jeff and then repeated by Kris, this sentence is paired with an image of the couple looking at birds (see Figures 5.3 and 5.4). This audiovisual "sample" is repeated twice more, the call-and-response exchange between the couple emphasizing the underlying strength of their connection and anchoring the scene in a more positive light.

Mary Ann Doane argues that the use of asynchronous speech threatens to expose "the material heterogeneity of cinema" by drawing our attention to the space beyond what is represented by the image and the hidden artifice.[44] She adds, though (paraphrasing Pascal Bonitzer), that narrative film exploits this marginal anxiety "by incorporating its disturbing effects within the dramatic framework."[45] This utilization of asynchrony is typical of *Upstream Color*: the spatio-temporal fragmentation and the scarcity of sync points reflect a sense of

---

[43] This is the timing of the scene in the DVD release of *Upstream Color*, New Video, PAL, 2013.

[44] "The use of the voice-off always entails a risk—that of exposing the material heterogeneity of the cinema. Synchronous sound masks the problem and this at least partially explains its dominance" (Doane, "The Voice in the Cinema," 167).

[45] Ibid.

Figures 5.3 and 5.4. *Upstream Color*: "They could be starlings."

displacement in the characters and a lack of grounded identity. This is particularly apparent in the middle third of the film, which presents the characters
trying to understand their place in the world: "Kris and Jeff are dealing and react-
ing to things that they don't understand.... [T]he characters are being affected at
a distance in the way that they can't speak to, so all cinema tools are being used to
convey that subjective experience."[46]

Matching the characters' loss of a stable sense of self and their place in the
world is the loss of a privileged and centralized point of view or point of audition: viewers are thrown into an audiovisual space without clear temporal or
spatial coordinates; one day merges into another, which could be a week or a
month later; some events happen in two places at once! Temporal displacement
of the image and dialogue here is evocative of Carruth's use of sound in his debut
Primer, where it appears as the result of several overlapping temporalities and

[46] Carruth, "New Directors/New Films."

an unknown number of protagonists' doppelgangers produced by time travel.[47] In *Upstream Color* time/space bending is reserved for the idea that the protagonists' lives are affected from a distance by the Sampler, but also for Kris and Jeff in the scene where they are shown lying in bed and also in the middle of the pig farm, which emphasizes the connection between the pigs and the main characters. Significantly, the spatio-temporal overlap in the scene in which Kris kills the Sampler, which happens simultaneously in an empty apartment and at the pig farm, is one of the clues suggesting that this "killing" should be understood in metaphorical terms, possibly as Kris's breakthrough in facing and confronting the source of her brokenness, anxiety, and paranoia.

It should be noted, though, that despite this flexibility in the representation of the unity of time and space and the extensive use of nonchronological ellipses that reinforces the idea of living with a shattered sense of identity, the film maintains fluency in purely sensuous terms. This is mostly thanks to Carruth's score, which, with its soft ambient colours and sustained chords, provides a feeling of continuous flow. Its unobtrusive but reassuring presence brings to mind the idea of running water, which is one of the key narrative motifs. For one thing, it is implied in the title, which is related to Conrad's *Heart of Darkness* and the idea of "going upriver to solve the problem in some way."[48] The film is also punctuated with images of the stream into which the Sampler throws piglets or pages of his score, repeated shots of the taps in Jeff's and Kris' apartments, and the leitmotif of Kris diving into a swimming pool to collect stones. It is appropriate, then, that the main association produced by the presence of the prolonged electronic sounds that feature in most of the scenes without dialogue is that of being submerged: events and spoken words lying under the layer of sustained chords in the same way the characters' memories and sense of identity are buried deep in the subconscious following the drug-induced trauma and loss of memory.

While the score is embedded in the film's foundations but remains unobtrusive, and speech is often relativized through fragmentation, sound effects have a prominent narrative role, sound being the Sampler's main means of communication with the kidnapping victims. When Kris wakes up from her trance-like state with the worm crawling under her skin, the Sampler summons her to the site for deworming by broadcasting a repetitive whooshing sound from speakers face-down on the ground, creating vibrations in the soil [00:19:30]. Another striking montage sequence [00:36:00–00:39:12] shows the Sampler recording outdoor sounds and composing. His recordings of water gurgling, bricks falling,

---

[47]   For a detailed analysis of the sound in *Primer* see Nessa Johnston, "Beneath Sci-fi Sound: *Primer*, Science Fiction Sound Design, and American Independent Cinema," *Alphaville: Journal of Film and Screen Media* 3 (Summer 2012), accessed on January 17, 2013, http://www.alphavillejournal.com/Issue%203/HTML/ArticleJohnston.html.

[48]   Carruth quoted in Romney, "Enigma Variations," 52.

stones sliding down an iron pipe, and similar, merge with sounds that Kris and Jeff make at home and at work—photocopier buzzing, bathroom tap running, sewing machine humming—and then fuse again with the Sampler's recordings, eloquently pointing to the communication between the three of them.

In one sense this scene acts as an exposure of cinematic means of construction, a reflexive glimpse into usually hidden processes of production. Like the theme of filmmaking in David Lynch's films, recording sound in *Upstream Color* can be seen as a symbol of the multilayered nature of reality. Even more important, it is a look "behind the scenes" of Kris's and Jeff's lives and how they are influenced by the Sampler's actions. It articulately illuminates some of the main themes of the film, the questions of what we are made of, what determines our behaviour, and the sense of who we are. In the context of the narrative, the Sampler's role, actions, and relationship to all the characters can be interpreted as a metaphor for subconscious "programming"—all the familial, social, and cultural influences that we are exposed to from an early age. On another level, presenting the Sampler as a composer and sound artist whose actions affect the protagonists' lives symbolically portrays him as a Creator and simultaneously establishes sound making and musicality as the film's primary creative principles. The noises of scraping, whooshing, masonry falling, and water gurgling all activate aesthetic pleasure the way listening to music does, except that these sounds also involve visual stimuli and are contextualized narratively. The dominance of sound and its amplified materiality in these scenes stimulates both sensory and affective responses to the soundtrack and the sensuous aspects of the film, the director luring us into his world like the Sampler with his speakers sending vibrations deep into the ground.

Conclusion

The privileged position of speech and dialogue in the soundtrack has been one of the constants of the cinema tradition, rarely challenged outside the confines of modernist and experimental cinema. In that sense we can draw some parallels between the strategies applied in the three films discussed here and the modernist experiments with form and soundtrack conducted by Alain Resnais and Jean-Luc-Godard in the 1960s, for instance, but we will also find significant differences between them. One might be particularly tempted to compare the editing rhymes of *Upstream Color* to the looped conversational patterns in *Last Year in Marienbad* (Alain Resnais, 1961), not least because both films address processes of the mind through cinematic devices (even though Carruth admitted in one interview that he had never heard of Resnais).[49] The sense of deliberate

---

[49]   Ibid., 53.

artifice that permeates Resnais's film, however, or Godard's Brechtian decon-structions of classical form[50] differ significantly from Carruth's attempt to create an engaging story with a strong emphasis on the tactile and sensuous aspects of cinema.

At the same time, all the examined films are permeated with a musical logic that goes beyond the soundtrack alone, affecting different aspects of film form. Korine's idea of a "liquid narrative" inspired by electronic music can be applied to Carruth's film as well, both films employing nonchronological editing rhythmi-cized through repetitions to convey a sense of "morphing" and the protagonists' distance from reality. In each film the actual music is not only crucial for supply-ing the flow of continuity to the jagged narrative but also elevated to the role of an actual character, to paraphrase Doremus. Both *Breathe In* and *Upstream Color* feature protagonists who are musicians, while Carruth's film is even scored by the director himself. And in each film music provides a suitable background or is a partner for the musical use of words, lending itself to the musical use of language.

Each example also demonstrates that the asynchronous use of language is a crucial part of its musicalization. On one hand it encourages us to focus on the sonic properties of the spoken word; on the other, it facilities the emancipation of speech from the constraints of narrative causality. Divorced from the image, speech is then able to establish its own flow, becoming yet another line in the sonic counterpoint of the soundtrack in which there are no previously assigned roles and no pre-established hierarchy.

All three films emphasize sensuous aspects of cinema, sometimes even at the expense of comprehensible storytelling and intelligibility of speech. *Upstream Color* in particular, like *The Assassin*, is one of those films that demands more than one viewing to satisfy one's intellectual desire to grasp the principles of its storytelling, but even on first encounter it does not fail to provide a sense of aes-thetic fulfilment through the combination of intellectual, emotional, and sen-sory stimulation that foregrounds the sensuous aspect of the medium itself and its sonic and visual textures, composition, movement, and flow.

Although this book focuses on elucidating the significance of aural stimuli in accentuating the musical qualities of film soundtrack, it is worth remembering that what activates the aesthetic dimension of film's sensuousness is the *combi-nation* of the tightly interwoven strands of music, speech, and sound effects *with* narrative and visual elements. Each of the examined films suspends the classical rules of narration to different degrees, foregrounding music and the language

---

[50] See Annette Davison, *Hollywood Theory, Non-Hollywood Practice: Cinema Soundtracks in the 1980s and 1990s* (Farnham, Surrey: Ashgate, 2004); Allan Williams, "Godard's Use of Sound," in *Film Sound: Theory and Practice*, ed. Elisabeth Weis and John Belton (New York: Columbia University Press), 332–345.

of *mise-en-scène* and, in two cases, nonchronological editing rather than relying on dialogue or continuity editing to tell their stories. All three films also stimulate what Marks calls "haptic visuality"[51] not only by highlighting the narrative and visual importance of tactile actions such as musical performances, erotic encounters, or, as in *Upstream Color*, repeated images of hands touching surfaces or the protagonists touching each other[52] but also through other visual and sonic means, whether the assault of day-glo colours in *Spring Breakers* or the whooshes and rumbles emanating from big speakers, pipes, and machines in *Upstream Color*. Owing to these combined stimuli and the musical logic behind many of the decisions determining the films' structures and flow, all three possess a quality that allows repeated viewings in a manner similar to that Carruth alluded to when he compared recurring encounters with his film to listening to one's favourite album.

---

[51] See Laura Marks, *The Skin of the Film: Intercultural Cinema, Embodiment, and the Senses* (Durham, NC, and London: Duke University Press, 2000).
[52] According to Carruth, the visual language of tactility in his film is related to the theme of the characters trying to understand their place in the world: "hands searching and fingertips touching surfaces is the only way you can know where you are" (Carruth, "New Directors/New Films").

6

Concluding Thoughts

As has been pointed out frequently in recent years, after a long history of being "unheard," music in film has become one of its main selling points (metaphorically and literally), luring audiences with lush orchestral sound, electronic beats, and songs that rule the charts. Especially since the introduction of compilation scores and popular music to cinema, film music has not only proved that it has market value but also been embraced by a new generation of directors determined to make their musical choices relevant and "heard." In fact, it could now be argued that it is sound design that these days tends to be unacknowledged, overlooked, or misunderstood, obscured by disagreements about its purpose, its methods of production, and even its very existence. This book argues not only that sound design is a crucial aspect of an integrated soundtrack but also that in the context of recent trends associated with it, the roles of score and sound design have been transformed to the point of being interchangeable, subverting their traditional statuses and functions. By addressing the history, theory, aesthetics, and erotics of the integrated soundtrack that erases the line between score and sound design, I hope I have provided greater insight into the changes affecting contemporary film soundtrack; their effects on the narrative, sensuous, and affective aspects of film; and the significance of a musical way of thinking in instigating new approaches to the soundtrack.

Considering all the arguments and examples presented in the book, it is clear that some of the main themes binding the discussions about the musical approach to the soundtrack and blurring the line between score and sound design are integration, inclusion, the erasure of boundaries, and the toppling of hierarchies. Driven by musical sensibility and supported by various advancements in technology, different manifestations of the practice bent on undermining the boundaries between soundtrack elements and their prescribed functions carry the spirit of egalitarianism and adventurousness. But behind this language evocative of some utopian filmland, there is also a strong current of disruption: of previously established borders and hierarchical relationships, of the lines between diegetic and nondiegetic, acoustic and electronic, score and sound design, music and sound effects, speech and music, and so on.

Commenting on the nature of crossing the border between diegetic and non-diegetic, Robynn Stilwell argues that the phrase "fantastical gap" is particularly apt for describing this liminal space because it encapsulates "both its magic and

Sound Design Is the New Score: Theory, Aesthetics, and Erotics of the Integrated Soundtrack. Danijela Kulezic-Wilson, Oxford University Press (2020). © Oxford University Press.
DOI: 10.1093/oso/ 9780190855314.001.0001

its danger, the sense of unreality that always obtains as we leap from one solid edge toward another at some unknown distance and some uncertain stability—and sometimes we're in the air before we know we've left the ground."[1] Stilwell's words convincingly capture the complexity and unpredictability associated with boundary crossing to enter any liminal space between two well-defined realms, not only that between diegetic and nondiegetic—the mixture of excitement, adventurousness, and uncertainty associated with exploring something that cannot be fully known. She also notes that such a liminal space is associated with ambiguity, transgression, destabilization, and even rather violent action when she says that "there seems to be little possibility of moving from one [realm] to the other without piercing the skin that explodes the two 'universes.'"[2] This language is not out of place in the discussion about crossing the boundary between score and sound design either. Although it is probably more appropriate to talk about "fusion" rather than "explosion," the consequences of the changes taking place in the film industry and soundtrack production are certainly far-reaching.

As I argued in relation to the aesthetics of reticence, once the melodic-oriented score is replaced with one that is not necessarily perceived by everyone as music, this inevitably affects the perception of the film's narrative world. If the semiotic guidance and emotional support traditionally provided by the score are missing, there is more space left for the "terror of uncertain signs" and the ensuing discomfort. And yet, the ambiguity of a soundscape created by blurring the line between score and sound design is at the heart of the aesthetics that values the power of reticence and "sensory incompleteness," trusting the intelligence of the audience and its appetite for stories that reflect the complexities of life more accurately than those in which all questions are resolved by the end credits.

Take, for example, some earlier-discussed scenes such as the one from *You Were Never Really Here* where Joe finds Nina after she has murdered her abductor, and that from *Katalin Varga* where Antal finds his dead wife. These scenes feature soundtracks that are intentionally ambiguous not only on the level of sonic content that eschews any musical material of a traditional kind but also because they feature nondiegetic scores that are employed as diegetic sound. In both cases the soundtrack straddles the shores of the fantastical gap quite deliberately, reflecting the deeply troubling content of scenes where either characters, situations, or both are also complex and ambiguous. These are exactly the

---

[1] Robynn J. Stilwell, "The Fantastical Gap Between Diegetic and Nondiegetic," in *Beyond the Soundtrack: Representing Music in Cinema*, ed. Daniel Goldmark, Lawrence Kramer, and Richard Leppert (Berkeley, Los Angeles, and London: University of California Press, 2007), 187.
[2] Ibid., 186.

types of scenes where traditional functions of the score offering some kind of comment in the form of dramatic emphasis or comfort by empathizing with the victims might be expected and welcomed by the audioviewer. From the film-makers' point of view, however, this solution would be dishonest, as there is nothing about either of these scenes that could offer true resolution or comfort. Instead, ambiguous and intensely sensuous sound that is both music and sound design, both diegetic and nondiegetic, insists that we have to take the truth of these scenes undiluted and unresolved, accepting our own ambiguous feelings about them.

The affinity for blurring the line between sound design and film music com-position is increasingly viewed, even in popular media, as part of the "inevi-table evolution of the art form."[3] However, over the course of this book I have shown that what we tend to see as the evolution of film soundtrack practice is generally punctuated by the cyclical nature of the trends affecting its histor-ical progress. On a basic level, the present trend can be seen simply as a matter of developing a taste for a musical language that draws on the whole world of sound rather than being limited to pitch-oriented scores, the taste defined by our moment, its musical and cultural climate, and the available technology. After all, a sonically driven language has been part of contemporary music for almost a century now, so it is not surprising that film scoring is finally catching up with it. However, other aspects of practices described in this book, in-cluding the musical approach to soundtrack, aesthetic trends such as the aes-thetics of reticence, and fascination with the materiality, texture, and hapticity of sound, all have precedents of some kind in the past.[4] What this book shows is that these moments of disruption, rebellion, adventurousness, and hunger for change typical of this particular moment are substantially influenced by music of all genres.

In this book I have also touched upon the political dimension of an art that is seemingly more concerned with issues of aesthetics and formal aspects of "pure cinema" than openly engaging with current political, social, or cultural debates. Bearing in mind Laura Marks's comments about political change at the level of individual action, "which is embodied but not collective," as well as Hans-Thies Lehmann's argument that political engagement does not consist in the topics but in the forms of perception, I would argue that the films and practices addressed in this book can be viewed as political in a number of ways, as their engagement

[3] Kristopher Tapley, "'Arrival,' 'Jackie' Composers Push Boundaries of Music and Sound Design," *Variety*, October 19, 2016, https://variety.com/2016/artisans/production/music-sound-arrival-jackie-1201892755/.
[4] Michel Chion's *Film, A Sound Art* and James Wierzbicki's *Film Music: A History* are particularly useful in getting a sense of the cyclical nature of these trends as they both cite many early examples of the practices discussed in this book.

is not reflected only in the films' content. But to start with topics, a number of the case studies discussed here deal, in fact, with highly topical issues of gender politics, violence against women, violence in media and in general, and issues of trauma, identity, and powerlessness, although their approach to these themes is not only subtle but also often ambiguous to the point of allowing completely opposite interpretations. While I have heard some scholars describe the representation of gender politics in *Katalin Varga* and *Berberian Sound Studio* as "problematic," I find it insightful, empathetic, and unequivocally critical of violence against women. While Gus Van Sant's *Elephant* has been criticized for being "irresponsible" because of its noncommittal, observational approach to one of America's most infamous contemporary tragedies, I find its subtle comments about a society that has lost its way, sewn into audiovisual juxtapositions and a highly aestheticized form, resonant and timely. *Spring Breakers* might seem equally "irresponsible" in its hedonistic, intensely musicalized representation of violence, but I would argue that its asynchronous use of language and nightmarish hue of day-glo colours speak quite eloquently about the contradictions and challenges of contemporary youth culture. Deliberately provocative and politically or socially engaged topics notwithstanding, what I also think is political about the approaches to the soundtrack discussed in this book is their open resistance to rules of convention and audience expectation; resistance to "safe" approaches and unambiguous messages; a refusal to bend to the laws of the box office and the courage to experiment even if that means failing to garner undivided praise; and the courage to be confusing and misunderstood, hoping that if someone is compelled to experience a film more than once, as he or she would do with music—as suggested by Shane Carruth—even the most obscure message will get through.

Another important aspect of the methods described in this book and the way they are applied in the case studies is sensuousness. The sensory aspect of the cinema experience is an increasingly popular topic in both film and film music studies, explored either from a phenomenological point of view or in connection to the impact of technology on film production and exhibition. Drawing on the existing research in this area, including the idea of the erotics of art popular among feminist writers in the 1970s, I have tried to shift the focus of attention from phenomenologically based enquiry to examining the sensuousness of the film form itself, the erotics of the film body, and the role of sound in nurturing the sensuousness of the aesthetic experience. It is indisputable that the use of Dolby stereo and digital surround technology were prominent factors in changing the overall sensory experience of film in the last four decades by increasing the frequency and dynamic range of sound, using spatialized sound effects, and using higher precision and clarity in rendering sonic details. However, despite Chion's argument that the highly defined sounds and contrasts provided by

Dolby technology discouraged any attempts at creating a "unified soundtrack," we have seen that the affinity for erasing the sonic and functional boundaries between different elements of the soundtrack have remained active, generating a new sensory dimension of the cinematic experience. The foregrounding of the materiality of sound and the "haptic dirtiness" of music; the emphasis on timbre rather than melody; using technology to blur the line between acoustic and electronic, and between sound and noise—these are some of the techniques that define the practice and that have proved effective in releasing film's erotic potential through sound. This approach activates the seductive power of the film soundtrack without confusing sensuousness with sensory excess, encouraging a multifaceted engagement with it that can be experienced aesthetically, physically, and intellectually.

Finally, it is worth looking again at the claim that the modes of integrated soundtrack examined in this book are inspired by music or informed by musical logic. In many cases the evidence is readily available, noted in the statements of directors, editors, composers, and sound designers such as Darren Aronofsky, Shane Carruth, Johnnie Burn, Jóhann Jóhannsson, Harmony Korine, Walter Murch, Peter Strickland, and Edgar Wright—to mention only some—who volunteered information about genres, compositions, and popular songs that inspired them and often found their way into their soundtracks. But one does not need a written statement to understand how crucial a musical sensibility is in the process of incorporating sound effects into the silences of a Scelsi piece so that they sound like part of the composition, as Sam Petty did in *The Rover*; or in equalizing ambient sounds to make sure they are "in tune" with musical cues, as Johnnie Burn did in *Under the Skin*; or in editing sound effects in such a way that they can be transposed into notation as a metrically regular rhythm or absorbed into the score as was done in films of Aronofsky, Richard Ayoade, Béla Tarr, Edgar Wright, Joe Wright, and others. Whether sound effects are produced by musical equipment or software, as has been done since synthesizers were first introduced into films, or electroacoustic pieces of music are placed on a soundtrack to blend with or *become* diegetic sound, the musical nature of that act should not be overlooked. That the meanings of the words "music" and "musicality" are so much broader and more inclusive than a century ago has certainly played an important part in the evolution of this practice and the way we interpret it. But that is partly the point of my argument and an important feature of this practice: the fact that a musical approach to the soundtrack is not limited to those who are named as "composers" in the credits because they create scores that are heard as music (whether they are notated or electronically produced) and can be sold as soundtrack albums; it is part of the process of anyone involved in the creation of a soundtrack who approaches it with a musical sensibility. Whether their ear is attuned to popular music or *musique concrète* is irrelevant; the important thing is that their decisions have been informed by their musical tastes, experiences, and sensibilities. The overarching result of the democratization, collaboration, and integration of sound postproduction is an exciting, erotic, stimulating soundtrack, and if we are attentive to its sounds, we can hear its music.

Bibliography

Adorno, Theodor, and Hanns Eisler. *Composing for the Films*. London and Atlantic Highlands: Athlone Press, 1947/1994.

Altman, Rick. "The Evolution of Sound Technology." In *Film Sound: Theory and Practice*, edited by Elisabeth Weis and John Belton, 44–53. New York: Columbia University Press, 1985.

Altman, Rick. "Moving Lips: Cinema as Ventriloquism." *Yale French Studies*, no. 60, Cinema/Sound (1980): 67–79.

Anderson, Gillian B. "The Shock of the Old: The Restoration, Reconstruction, or Creation of 'Mute'-Film Accompaniments." In *The Routledge Companion to Screen Music and Sound*, edited by Miguel Mera, Ronald Sadoff, and Ben Winters, 201–212. London and New York: Routledge, 2017.

Anderson, John. "The Many Worlds of Darren Aronofsky." *DGA Quarterly*, Fall 2013. https://www.dga.org/craft/dgaq/all-articles/1304-fall-2013/darren-aronofsky.aspx.

Aronofsky, Darren. *π: Screenplay & The Guerilla Diaries*. London: Faber & Faber, 1998.

Barthes, Roland. *S/Z*. Translated by Richard Miller, preface by Richard Howard. Oxford: Blackwell Publishing, 1974/2002.

Beck, Jay. "Acoustic Auteurs and Transnational Cinema." In *The Oxford Handbook of Sound and Image in Digital Media*, edited by Carol Vernallis, Amy Herzog, and John Richardson, 732–751. Oxford and New York: Oxford University Press, 2013.

Beck, Jay. "The Sounds of 'Silence': Dolby Stereo, Sound Design and *The Silence of the Lambs*." In *Lowering the Boom: Critical Studies in Film Sound*, edited by Jay Beck and Tony Grayeda, 68–83. Urbana and Chicago: University of Illinois Press, 2008.

Becker, Judith. "Anthropological Perspectives on Music and Emotion." In *Music and Emotion: Theory and Research*, edited by Patrick N. Juslin and John A. Sloboda, 135–160. Oxford: Oxford University Press, 2001.

Bellour, Raymond. "Segmenting/Analysing." In *Genre: The Musical*, edited by Rick Altman, 102–133. London, Boston, and Henley: Routledge and Kegan Paul, 1981.

Belsey, Catherine. *Critical Practice*. 2nd ed. London and New York: Routledge, 1980/2002.

Binns, Alexander. "'Sounding Japanese': Traditions of Music in Japanese Cinema." In *The Routledge Companion to Screen Music and Sound*, edited by Miguel Mera, Ronald Sadoff, and Ben Winters, 428–439. London and New York: Routledge, 2017.

Bordwell, David. *Narration in the Fiction Film*. London and New York: Routledge, 1985.

Bresson, Robert. "Notes on Sound." In *Film Sound: Theory and Practice*, edited by Elisabeth Weis and John Belton, 149. New York: Columbia University Press, 1985.

Brooke, Michael. "The Weight of the World." *Sight and Sound* 19 (January 2009): 54–55.

Brooks, Xan, "*The Assassin* Director: Why I Gave Plot the Chop," *The Guardian*, January 11, 2016. https://www.theguardian.com/film/2016/jan/11/hou-hsiao-hsien-the-assassin-martial-arts-movies.

Brophy, Philip. *100 Modern Soundtracks*. London: British Film Institute, 2004.

Brown, Royal S. *Overtones and Undertones: Reading Film Music*. Berkeley: California University Press, 1994.

Sound Design Is the New Score: Theory, Aesthetics, and Erotics of the Integrated Soundtrack. Danijela Kulezic-Wilson, Oxford University Press (2020). © Oxford University Press.
DOI: 10.1093/oso/ 9780190855314.001.0001

Buhler, James. "Analytical and Interpretative Approaches to Film Music (II): Analysing Interactions of Music and Film." In *Film Music: Critical Approaches*, edited by K. J. Donnelly, 39–61. Edinburgh: Edinburgh University Press, 2001.

Buhler, James, David Neumeyer, and Rob Deemer. *Hearing the Movies: Music and Sound in Film History*. Oxford and New York: Oxford University Press, 2010.

Burch, Noël. *Theory of Film Practice*. Princeton, NJ: Princeton University Press, 1981.

Carruth, Shane. "New Directors/New Films Q&A: *Upstream Color*, Shane Carruth." Filmed at the Film Society of Lincoln Center, April 6, 2013. https://www.youtube.com/watch?v=5cjq_Lb2F2I.

Casanelles, Sergi. "Mixing as a Hyperorchestration Tool." In *The Palgrave Handbook of Sound Design and Music in Screen Media: Integrated Soundtrack*, edited by Liz Greene and Danijela Kulezic-Wilson, 57–72. Basingstoke, Hampshire: Palgrave Macmillan, 2016.

Child, Ben. "*Interstellar*'s Sound 'Right for an Experimental Film', Says Nolan." *The Guardian*, November 17, 2014. http://www.theguardian.com/film/2014/nov/17/interstellar-sound-christopher-nolan.

Chion, Michel. *Audio-vision: Sound on Screen*. Edited and translated by Claudia Gorbman. New York: Columbia University Press, 1994.

Chion, Michel. *Film, A Sound Art*. Translated by Claudia Gorbman. New York: Columbia University Press, 2003.

Chion, Michel. *The Voice in Cinema*. Translated by Claudia Gorbman. New York: Columbia University Press, 1999.

Ciment, Michel. "I Seek Not Description but Vision: Robert Bresson on *L'Argent*." In *Robert Bresson*, edited by James Quandt, 499–511. Bloomington: Indiana University Press, 2011.

Clarke, Roger. "The Assassin." *Sight and Sound* 26 (February 2016): 68.

Cohen, Annabel J. "Music Cognition and the Cognitive Psychology of Film Structure." *Canadian Psychology* 43, no. 4 (2009): 215–232.

Collis, Clark. "How Director Edgar Wright Steered *Baby Driver* to Global Success." *Entertainment*, December 4, 2017. http://ew.com/movies/2017/12/04/edgar-wright-baby-driver-success-sequel-spacey/.

Constantini, Gustavo. "Walter Murch Interviewed by Gustavo Constantini." *New Soundtrack* 3, no. 1 (2010): 33–46.

Coulthard, Lisa. "Acoustic Disgust: Sound, Affect, and Cinematic Violence." In *The Palgrave Handbook of Sound Design and Music in Screen Media: Integrated Soundtracks*, edited by Liz Greene and Danijela Kulezic-Wilson, 183–193. Basingstoke, Hampshire: Palgrave Macmillan, 2016.

Coulthard, Lisa. "Dirty Sound: Haptic Noise in New Extremism." In *The Oxford Handbook of Sound and Image in Digital Media*, edited by Carol Vernallis, Amy Herzog, and John Richardson, 115–126. Oxford and New York: Oxford University Press, 2013.

Coulthard, Lisa. "From a Whisper to a Scream: Music in the Films of Michael Haneke." *Music and the Moving Image* 5, no. 3 (Fall 2012): 1–10. Accessed January 17, 2013, doi:10.5406/musimoviimag.5.3.i.

Davison, Annette. *Hollywood Theory, Non-Hollywood Practice: Cinema Soundtracks in the 1980s and 1990s*. Farnham, Surrey: Ashgate, 2004.

Davison, Annette, and Nicholas Reyland. "The Janus Project: Cristobal Tapia de Veer's *Utopia*, Anempathetic Empathy and the Radicalization of Convention." In *The Palgrave Handbook of Sound Design and Music in Screen Media: Integrated Soundtracks*, edited by

Liz Greene and Danijela Kulezic-Wilson, 305–319. Basingstoke, Hampshire: Palgrave Macmillan, 2016.

Deane, Cormac. "Redundancy and Information in Explanatory Voice-Ins and Voice-Offs." In *The Palgrave Handbook of Sound Design and Music in Screen Media: Integrated Soundtracks*, edited by Liz Greene and Danijela Kulezic-Wilson, 361–375. Basingstoke, Hampshire: Palgrave Macmillan, 2016.

Demers, Joanna. *Listening Through the Noise: The Aesthetics of Experimental Electronic Music*. Oxford and New York: Oxford University Press, 2010.

Dienstfrey, Eric. "The Myth of the Speakers: A Critical Reexamination of Dolby History." *Film History* 28, no. 1 (2016): 167–193. doi:10.2979/filmhistory.28.1.06.

Doane, Mary Ann. "Ideology and the Practice of Sound Editing and Mixing." In *Film Sound: Theory and Practice*, edited by Elisabeth Weis and John Belton, 54–62. New York: Columbia University Press, 1985.

Doane, Mary Ann. "The Voice in the Cinema: The Articulation of Body and Space." In *Film Sound: Theory and Practice*, edited by Elisabeth Weis and John Belton, 162–176. New York: Columbia University Press, 1985.

Donnelly, K. J. "Extending Film Aesthetics: Audio Beyond Visuals." In *The Oxford Handbook of New Audiovisual Aesthetics*, edited by John Richardson, Claudia Gorbman, and Carol Vernallis, 357–371. Oxford and New York: Oxford University Press, 2014.

Donnelly, Kevin J. "Angel of the Air: Popol Vuh's Music and Werner Herzog's Films." In *European Film Music*, edited by Miguel Mera and David Burnand, 116–130. Farnham, Surrey: Ashgate, 2006.

Donnelly, Kevin J. *Occult Aesthetics: Synchronization in Sound Film*. Oxford and New York: Oxford University Press, 2013.

Donnelly, Kevin J. *The Spectre of Sound: Music in Film and Television*. London: BFI Publishing, 2005.

Doremus, Drake. "Special Features: Interview with Drake Doremus." *Breathe In*. Curzon Film World, 2013. DVD.

Drake, Chris. "Desire Is Violence." *Sight and Sound* 10 (July 2000): 16–18.

Eisenstein, S. M., V. I. Pudovkin, and G. V. Alexandrov. "A Statement." In *Film Sound: Theory and Practice*, edited by Elisabeth Weis and John Belton, 83–85. New York: Columbia University Press.

Elsaesser, Thomas, and Malte Hagener. *Film Theory: An Introduction Through the Senses*. London and New York: Routledge, 2010.

Fischer, Lucy. "Enthusiasm: From Kino-Eye to Radio-Eye." In *Film Sound: Theory and Practice*, edited by Elisabeth Weis and John Belton, 247–264. New York: Columbia University Press, 1985.

Flinn, Caryl. *Strains of Utopia: Gender, Nostalgia and Hollywood Film Music* Princeton, NJ: Princeton University Press, 1992.

Frampton, Daniel. *Filmosophy*. London and New York: Wallflower Press, 2006.

Gorbman, Claudia. "Auteur Music." In *Beyond the Soundtrack: Representing Music in Cinema*, edited by Daniel Goladmark, Lawrence Kramer, and Richard Leppert, 149–162. Berkeley, Los Angeles, and London: University of California Press, 2007.

Gorbman, Claudia. "Ears Wide Open: Kubrick's Music." In *Changing Tunes: The Use of Pre-existing Music in Film*, edited by Phil Powrie and Robynn Stilwell, 3–18. Farnham, Surrey: Ashgate, 2006.

Gorbman, Claudia. "Music and Character." Keynote Lecture presented at the Fourth Music and Media Study Group Conference, Universita di Torino, June 28–29, 2012.

Gorbman, Claudia. *Unheard Melodies: Narrative Film Music.* London: BFI Publishing and Bloomington: Indiana University Press, 1987.

Greene, Liz. "Ambiguity: Walter Murch and the Metaphoric Use of Sound in *The Godfather, The Conversation* and *Apocalypse Now.*" *Film and Film Culture* 3 (2004): 107–113.

Greene, Liz, and Danijela Kulezic-Wilson. "Introduction." In *The Palgrave Handbook of Sound Design and Music in Screen Media: Integrated Soundtracks,* edited by Liz Greene and Danijela Kulezic-Wilson, 1–13. Basingstoke, Hampshire: Palgrave Macmillan, 2016.

Hagood, Mack. "Unpacking a Punch: Transduction and the Sound of Combat Foley in *Fight Club.*" *Cinema Journal* 53, no. 4 (Summer 2014): 98–120.

Haneke, Michael. "71 Fragments of a Chronology of Chance: Notes to the Film." In *After Postmodernism: Austrian Literature and Film in Transition,* edited by Willy Riemer, 171–175. Riverside, CA: Ariadne, 2000.

Hegarty, Paul. *Noise/Music: A History.* New York, London, New Delhi, and Sydney: Bloomsbury, 2007.

Hertzberg, Ludvig, ed. *Jim Jarmusch: Interviews.* Jackson: University Press of Mississippi, 2001.

Hodgkinson, Tim. "An Interview with Pierre Schaeffer." In *The Book of Music and Nature,* edited by David Rothenberg and Marta Ulvaeus, 34–44. Middletown, CT: Wesleyan University Press, 2001.

Holmer, Anna Rose. "DVD Extras: The Director's Commentary." *The Fits.* Lionsgate, 2015. DVD.

Hou, Hsiao-Hsien. "DVD Extras: Behind the Scenes." *The Assassin.* Studiocanal, 2015. DVD.

Hough, John. "Under the Skin of Film Sound—An Interview with Johnnie Burn." In *The Palgrave Handbook of Sound Design and Music in Screen Media: Integrated Soundtracks,* edited by Liz Greene and Danijela Kulezic-Wilson, 377–384. Basingstoke, Hampshire: Palgrave Macmillan, 2016.

Hubbert, Julie. "'Whatever Happened to Great Movie Music?': Cinema Vérité and Hollywood Film Music of the Early 1970s." *American Music* 21, no. 2 (Summer 2003): 180–213.

Iannone, Pasquale. "Beau Travail." *Sight and Sound* 24 (March 2014): 112.

Ihde, Don. *Listening and Voice: A Phenomenology of Sound.* New York: State University of New York, 2007.

Jaffe, Ira. *Slow Movies: Countering the Cinema of Action.* London and New York: Wallflower Press, 2014.

James, Nick. "The Sound of Silence." *Sight and Sound* 19 (November 2009): 32–35.

Jankélévitch, Vladimir. *La Musique et l'Ineffable.* Paris: Editions du Seuil, 1983.

Johnston, Nessa. "Beneath Sci-fi Sound: *Primer,* Science Fiction Sound Design, and American Independent Cinema." *Alphaville: Journal of Film and Screen Media* 3 (Summer 2012). http://www.alphavillejournal.com/Issue%203/HTML/ArticleJohnston.html.

Jones, Kent. "Signs and Wonders." *Sight and Sound* 26 (June 2016): 44–46.

Jordan, Randolph. "Acoustical Properties: Practicing Contested Spaces in the Films of Philippe Grandrieux." In *The Oxford Handbook of Image and Sound in Western Art,* edited by Yeal Kaduri, 289–314. Oxford and New York: Oxford University Press, 2016.

Jordan, Randolph. "The Ecology of Listening While Looking in the Cinema: Reflective Audioviewing in Gus Van Sant's *Elephant.*" *Organised Sound* 17, no. 3 (Special

Issue, Sound, Listening and Place II) (2012): 248–256. https://doi.org/10.1017/S1355771811000458.

Jordan, Randolph. "The Work of Hildegard Westerkamp in the Films of Gus Van Sant: An Interview with the Soundscape Composer (and Some Added Thoughts of My Own)." *Offscreen* 11, 8–9 (2007). http://offscreen.com/view/jordan_westerkamp.

Kalinak, Kathryn. *Setting the Score: Narrative Film Music.* Madison: University of Wisconsin Press, 1992.

Kassabian, Anahid. "The Sound of a New Film Form." In *Popular Music and Film*, edited by Ian Inglis, 91–101. London and New York: Wallflower, 2003.

Kassabian, Anahid. *Ubiquitous Listening: Affect, Attention, and Distributed Subjectivity.* Berkeley, Los Angeles, and London: California University Press, 2013.

Kit, Borys. "'The Dark Knight Rises' Faces Big Problem: Audiences Can't Understand Villain." *Hollywood Reporter*, December 20, 2011. https://www.hollywoodreporter.com/heat-vision/dark-knight-rises-christian-bale-batman-tom-hardy-bane-275489.

Knausgård, Karl Ove. *A Man in Love: My Struggle: Book 2.* Translated by Don Bartlett. London: Harvill Secker, 2013. Kindle.

Knowlson, James. *Damned to Fame: The Life of Samuel Beckett.* New York: Simon & Schuster, 1997.

Kramer, Lawrence. "Classical Music, Virtual Bodies, Narrative Film." In *The Oxford Handbook of Film Music Studies*, edited by David Neumeyer, 351–365. Oxford and New York: Oxford University Press.

Kulezic-Wilson, Danijela. "After Excess—Abstinence: Notes on a New Trend in Music Scoring (and Its Absence) in Film and TV." Paper presented at the Film Music Conference, University of Leeds, November 6–9, 2009.

Kulezic-Wilson, Danijela. "Gus Van Sant's Soundwalks and Audio-visual Musique concrète." In *Music, Sound and Filmmakers: Sonic Style in Cinema*, edited by James Wierzbicki, 76–88. London and New York: Routledge, 2012.

Kulezic-Wilson, Danijela. "The Music of Film Silence." *Music and the Moving Image* 2, no. 3 (Fall 2009): 1–10. https://www.jstor.org/stable/10.5406/musimoviimag.2.3.0001?seq=1#page_scan_tab_contents.

Kulezic-Wilson, Danijela. "The Musicality of Film and Jim Jarmusch's *Dead Man*." *Film and Film Culture* 4 (2007): 8–20.

Kulezic-Wilson, Danijela. *The Musicality of Narrative Film.* Basingstoke, Hampshire: Palgrave Macmillan, 2015.

Kulezic-Wilson, Danijela. "Sound Design and Its Interactions with Music: Changing Historical Perspectives." In *The Routledge Companion to Screen Music and Sound*, edited by Miguel Mera, Ronald Sadoff, and Ben Winters, 127–138. London and New York: Routledge, 2017.

Kulezic-Wilson, Danijela. "Sound Design Is the New Score." *Music, Sound and the Moving Image* 2, no. 2 (2008): 127–131.

Kulezic-Wilson, Danijela. "Soundscapes of Trauma and the Silence of Revenge in Peter Strickland's *Katalin Varga*." *New Soundtrack* 1, no. 1 (2010): 57–71.

Laing, Heather. "'The Rhythm of the Night': Reframing Silence, Music and Masculinity." In *European Film Music*, edited by Miguel Mera and David Burnand, 163–177. Farnham, Surrey: Ashgate, 2006.

Langford, Barry. *Post-classical Hollywood: Film Industry, Style and Ideology Since 1945.* Edinburgh: Edinburgh University Press, 2010.

Lehmann, Hans-Thies. *Postdramatic Theatre*. Translated by Karen Jürs-Munby. London and New York: Routledge, 2006.

Lorde, Audre. *Sister Outsider: Essays and Speeches*. Berkeley, CA: Crossing Press, 1984.

Lynch, David. "Action and Reaction." In *Soundscape: The School of Sound Lectures 1998–2001*, edited by Larry Sider, Diane Freeman, and Jerry Sider, 49–53. London and New York: Wallflower Press.

Mancini, Mark. "The Sound Designer." In *Film Sound: Theory and Practice*, edited by Elisabeth Weis and John Belton, 361–368. New York: Columbia University Press, 1985.

Marks, Laura. *The Skin of the Film: Intercultural Cinema, Embodiment, and the Senses*. Durham, NC, and London: Duke University Press, 2000.

Marks, Laura. *Touch: Sensuous Theory and Multisensory Media*. Minneapolis and London: University of Minnesota Press, 2002.

McGavin, Patrick Z. "Q&A: Cristin Mungiu." *StopSmiling Online*, February 26, 2008. Accessed November 2, 2015. http://stopsmilingonline.com/story_detail.php?id=985,

McGuire, Colin. "Music and Martial Arts: Intertextuality in the Sounds of Diasporic Chinese Kung Fu." Paper presented at the FUAIM Research Seminar, Department of Music, University College Cork, November 23, 2017.

Mera, Miguel. "Materializing Film Music." In *The Cambridge Companion to Film Music*, edited by Mervyn Cooke and Fiona Ford, 157–172. Cambridge: Cambridge University Press, 2016.

Mera, Miguel. "Towards 3-D Sound: Spatial Presence and the Space Vacuum." In *The Palgrave Handbook of Sound Design and Music in Screen Media: Integrated Soundtracks*, edited by Liz Greene and Danijela Kulezic-Wilson, 91–111. Basingstoke, Hampshire: Palgrave Macmillan, 2016.

Mera, Miguel, and David Burnand. "Introduction." In *European Film Music*, edited by. Miguel Mera and David Burnand, 1–12. Farnham, Surrey: Ashgate, 2006.

Murch, Walter. *In the Blink of an Eye: A Perspective on Film Editing*. 2nd ed. Los Angeles: Silman-James Press, 2001.

Murch, Walter. "Sound Design: The Dancing Shadow." In *Projections 4: Film-makers on Film-making*, edited by John Boorman, Tom Luddy, David Thompson, and Walter Donohue, 237–251. London and Boston: Faber and Faber, 1995.

Murray, Noel. "'I Love Winds': David Lynch on the Sound of 'Twin Peaks.'" *New York Times*, August 17, 2017. https://www.nytimes.com/2017/08/17/arts/television/david-lynch-twin-peaks-interview.html?_r=0.

Nancy, Jean-Luc. *Listening*. Translated by Charlotte Mandell. New York: Fordham University Press, 2007.

Neumeyer, David. "Diegetic/Nondiegetic: A Theoretical Model." *Music and the Moving Image* 2, no. 1 (Spring 2009): 26–39. https://www.jstor.org/stable/10.5406/musimoviimag.2.1.0026?seq=1#page_scan_tab_contents.

Neumeyer, David. *Meaning and Interpretation of Music in Cinema*. Bloomington and Indianapolis: Indiana University Press, 2015.

O'Connell, David. "*Katalin Varga* @ the Melbourne International Film Festival." *Screen Fanatic*. August 2009. Accessed January 15, 2010. http://www.screenfanatic.com/katalin-varga-film-review/.

O'Falt, Chris. "'Mother!': Why Darren Aronofsky and Jóhann Jóhannsson Scrapped the Original Score for a More Expressive Soundscape." *IndieWire*, September 9, 2017. http://www.indiewire.com/2017/09/mother-score-eliminated-johann-johannsson-darren-aronofsky-sound-design-1201874404/.

Ondaatje, Michael. *The Conversations: Walter Murch and the Art of Editing Film.* New York: Alfred A. Knopf, 2002.

Pääkkölä, Anna-Elena. "Sound Kinks: Sadomasochistic Erotica in Audiovisual Music Performances." PhD diss., University of Turku, 2016.

Paskin, Willa. "Dark Knight Rises to Be More Comprehensible." *Vulture*, January 3, 2012. https://www.vulture.com/2012/01/dark-knight-rises-to-be-more-comprehensible.html

Plaat, Jay. "The Rhythm of the Void: On the Rhythm of Any-Space-Whatever in Bresson, Tarkovsky and Winterbottom." Master's thesis, Radboud University Nijmegen, 2015–2016.

Rayns, Tony. "Taipei Tang." *Sight and Sound* 26 (February 2016): 29–32.

Reyland, Nicholas. "Corporate Classicism and the Metaphysical Style: Affects, Effects, and Contexts of Two Recent Trends in Screen Scoring." *Music, Sound and the Moving Image* 9, no. 2 (Autumn 2015): 115–130. doi:10.3828/msmi.2015.8.

Reynolds, Simon. "You Only Live Once." *Sight and Sound* 23 (May 2013): 26–31.

Richardson, John. "Between Speech, Music, and Sound: The Voice, Flow, and the Aestheticizing Impulse in Audiovisual Media." In *The Oxford Handbook of Sound and Image in Western Art*, edited by Yael Kaduri, 479–501. Oxford and New York: Oxford University Press, 2016.

Richardson, John. *An Eye for Music: Popular Music and the Audiovisual Surreal.* Oxford and New York: Oxford University Press, 2012.

Romney, Jonathan. "Enigma Variations." *Sight and Sound* 23 (September 2013): 50–53.

Rose, Tricia. *Black Noise: Rap Music and Black Culture in Contemporary America.* Hanover, NH: Wesleyan University Press, 1994.

Sadoff, Ronald H. "Scoring for Film and Video Games: Collaborative Practices and Digital Post-production." In *The Oxford Handbook of Sound and Image in Digital Media*, edited by Carol Vernallis, Amy Herzog, and John Richardson, 663–681. Oxford and New York: Oxford University Press, 2013.

Salt, Berry. "Film Style and Technology in the Thirties: Sound." In *Film Sound: Theory and Practice*, edited by Elisabeth Weis and John Belton, 37–43. New York: Columbia University Press, 1985.

Schlosser, Eric. "Interview with Béla Tarr: About *Werckmeister Harmonies* (Cannes 2000, Director's Fortnight)." *Bright Lights Film Journal*, October 1, 2000. https://bright-lightsfilm.com/wp-content/cache/all/interview-bela-tarr-werckmeister-harmonies-cannes-2000-directors-fortnight/#.W4kTKbhG2Um.

Schrader, Paul. *Transcendental Style in Film: Ozu, Bresson, Dreyer.* Cambridge and New York: Da Capo Press, 1972.

Schreger, Charles. "Altman, Dolby, and the Second Sound Revolution." In *Film Sound: Theory and Practice*, edited by Elisabeth Weis and John Belton, 348–355. New York: Columbia University Press, 1985.

Sergi, Gianluca. "Organizing Sound: Labour Organizations and Power Struggles That Helped Define Music and Sound in Hollywood." In *The Palgrave Handbook of Sound Design and Music in Screen Media: Integrated Soundtracks*, edited by Liz Greene and Danijela Kulezic-Wilson, 43–56. Basingstoke, Hampshire: Palgrave Macmillan, 2016.

Sider, Larry. "Mono." Paper presented at the Synch/Non-synch Symposium on Sound and Film. NUI Galway, February 19, 2014.

Sinnerbrink, Robert. "Re-enfranchising Film: Towards a Romantic Film-Philosophy." In *New Takes in Film-Philosophy*, edited by Havi Carel and Greg Tuck, 25–47. Basingstoke, Hampshire: Palgrave Macmillan, 2011.

Smith, Jeff. "Bridging the Gap: Reconsidering the Border Between Diegetic and Nondiegetic Music." *Music and the Moving Image* 2, no. 1 (Spring 2009): 1–25. https://www.jstor.org/stable/10.5406/musimoviimag.2.1.0001?seq=1#page_scan_tab_contents.

Smith, Jeff. "The Sound of Intensified Continuity." In *The Oxford Handbook of New Audiovisual Aesthetics*, edited by John Richardson, Claudia Gorbman, and Carol Vernallis, 331–356. Oxford and New York: Oxford University Press, 2013.

Smith, Jeff. *The Sounds of Commerce: Marketing Popular Film Music*. New York: Columbia University Press, 1998.

Sobchack, Vivien. *The Address of the Eye: A Phenomenology of Film Experience*. Princeton, NJ: Princeton University Press, 1992.

Sontag, Susan. *Against Interpretation*. London: Vintage, 2001.

Spicer, Daniel. "Cross Platform: Sound in Other Media." *The Wire* 343 (September 2012): 18.

Spring, Katherine. "From Analogue to Digital: Synthesizers and Discourses of Film Sound in the 1980s." In *The Palgrave Handbook of Sound Design and Music in Screen Media: Integrated Soundtracks*, edited by Liz Greene and Danijela Kulezic-Wilson, 273–288. Basingstoke, Hampshire: Palgrave Macmillan, 2016.

Stilwell, Robynn J. "The Fantastical Gap Between Diegetic and Nondiegetic." In *Beyond the Soundtrack: Representing Music in Cinema*, edited by Daniel Goldmark, Lawrence Kramer, and Richard Leppert, 184–202. Berkeley, Los Angeles, and London: University of California Press, 2007.

Strickland, Peter. "Bear Necessities." Blog. Accessed November 12, 2009. http://peter-strickland.blogspot.com.

Strickland, Peter. "Epiphanies." *The Wire* 308 (October 2009): 106.

Strickland, Peter. "Special Features, Director's Commentary." *Berberian Sound Studio*. Artificial Eye, 2012. DVD.

Strickland, Peter. "Special Features, Director's Commentary." *The Duke of Burgundy*. Artificial Eye, 2015. DVD.

Tapley, Kristopher. "'Arrival,' 'Jackie' Composers Push Boundaries of Music and Sound Design." *Variety*, October 19, 2016. https://variety.com/2016/artisans/production/music-sound-arrival-jackie-1201892755/.

Tarkovsky, Andrei. *Sculpting in Time: Reflections on the Cinema*. London: Bodley Head, 1986.

Taubin, Amy. "Cultural Mash-up." *Sight and Sound* 23 (May 2013): 29.

Thanouli, Eleftheria. *Postclassical Cinema: An International Poetics of Film Narration*. London and New York: Wallflower Press, 2009.

Theberge, Paul. *Any Sound You Can Imagine: Making Music/Consuming Technology*. Hanover and London: Wesleyan University Press, 1997.

Thom, Randy. "Designing a Movie for Sound." In *Soundscape: The School of Sound Lectures 1998–2001*, edited by Larry Sider, Diane Freeman, and Jerry Sider, 121–137. London and New York: Wallflower Press, 2003.

Vernallis, Carol. *Unruly Media: You Tube, Music Video, and the New Digital Cinema*. Oxford and New York: Oxford University Press, 2013.

Vincendeau, Ginette. "The Fits." *Sight and Sound* 27 (March 2017): 77–78.

Walker, Elsie. *Hearing Haneke: The Sound Tracks of a Radical Auteur*. Oxford and New York: Oxford University Press, 2018.

Walker, Elsie. "Hearing the Silences (as Well as the Music) in Michael Haneke's Films." *Music and the Moving Image* 3, no. 3 (Fall 2010): 15–30. doi:10.5406/musimoviimag.5.3.i.

Walker, Elsie. *Understanding Sound Tracks Through Film Theory.* Oxford and New York: Oxford University Press, 2015.

Walsh, Caitríona. "Obscene Sounds: Sex, Death, and the Body On-Screen." *Music and the Moving Image* 10, no. 3 (Fall 2017): 36–54. Accessed July 18, 2018. https://muse.jhu.edu/.

Weis, Elisabeth. "The Evolution of Hitchcock's Aural Style and Sound in *The Birds*." In *Film Sound: Theory and Practice*, edited by Elisabeth Weis and John Belton, 298–311. New York: Columbia University Press, 1985.

Weston, Kelli. "Awakenings." *Sight and Sound* 27 (March 2017): 6.

Whittington, William. *Sound Design & Science Fiction.* Austin: University of Texas Press, 2007.

Wierzbicki, James. *Film Music: A History.* London and New York: Routledge, 2009.

Wierzbicki, James. "Sound as Music in the Films of Terrence Malick." In *The Cinema of Terrence Malick: Poetic Visions of America*, edited by Hannah Patterson, 110–122. New York: Columbia University Press, 2003.

Wierzbicki, James. "Sound Effects/Sound Affects: 'Meaningful' Noise in the Cinema." In *The Palgrave Handbook of Sound Design and Music in Screen Media: Integrated Soundtracks*, edited by Liz Greene and Danijela Kulezic-Wilson, 153–168. Basingstoke, Hampshire: Palgrave Macmillan, 2016.

Wilkinson, Amber. "Noting the difference: Composers Danny Bensi and Saunder Jurriaans Talk About *Christine, Frank & Lola* and *The Fits*." *Eye for Film*, 2016. Accessed on August 17, 2017. https://www.eyeforfilm.co.uk/feature/2016-03-01-saunder-jurriaans-and-danny-bensi-talk-about-christine-the-fits-frank-lola-feature-story-by-amber-wilkinson.

Williams, Alan. "Godard's Use of Sound." In *Film Sound: Theory and Practice*, edited by Elisabeth Weis and John Belton, 332–345. New York: Columbia University Press, 1985.

Winters, Ben. "Corporeality, Musical Heartbeats, and Cinematic Emotion." *Music, Sound and the Moving Image* 2, no. 1 (Spring 2008): 3–25.

Wood, Jason. "The Art of Noise." *Sight and Sound* 22 (September 2012): 32–36.

Wright, Benjamin. "Sculptural Dissonance: Hans Zimmer and the Composer as Engineer." *Sounding Out!*, July 10, 2014. https://soundstudiesblog.com/author/wrightonfilm/.

Wright, Benjamin. "What Do We Hear? The Pluralism of Sound Design in Hollywood Sound Production." *New Soundtrack* 3, no. 2 (2013): 137–157. doi:10.3366/sound.2013.0043.

Index

Sound Design Is the New Score: Theory, Aesthetics, and Erotics of the Integrated Soundtrack. Danijela Kulezic-Wilson, Oxford University Press (2020). © Oxford University Press.
DOI: 10.1093/oso/ 9780190855314.001.0001